SCOTTISH
ROYAL PALACES

The Architecture of the Royal Residences during the Late
Medieval and Early Renaissance Periods

JOHN G. DUNBAR

TUCKWELL PRESS

HISTORIC SCOTLAND

First published in Great Britain in 1999 by
Tuckwell Press Ltd
The Mill House
Phantassie
East Linton
East Lothian EH40 3DG
Scotland

Typeset and originated by Carnegie Publishing, Lancaster
Printed and bound by GraphyCems, Spain

The title page decoration is one of the Stirling Heads,
a series of carved oak medallions (*c.*1540) from the ceiling
of the King's Presence Chamber in the palace at
Stirling Castle (see fig. 5.12).

RCAHMS

CONTENTS

PREFACE

THE EARLIEST WRITER to chart the history of the royal residences appears to have been the Rev. John Jamieson, best known for his Scottish dictionary, who collaborated with the artist William Brown to publish, in 1830, a handsomely illustrated work entitled *Select Views of the Royal Palaces of Scotland*. Jamieson's approach was largely anecdotal, with much emphasis on historical highlights, and it was left to Helen Douglas-Irvine to produce, in her *Royal Palaces of Scotland* (1911), a succinct, but wide-ranging, account of the development of the royal residences from the twelfth century to the reign of Queen Victoria. Her work was grounded upon primary documentary sources and, although overtaken by the advance of knowledge in many areas, can still be read with profit today. Meanwhile, the publication of MacGibbon and Ross's *Castellated and Domestic Architecture of Scotland* in 1887–92 had provided a firm base for the architectural analysis of the surviving castles and palaces and since that time numerous studies of individual residences have appeared, some as entries in the Royal Commission on the Ancient and Historical Monuments of Scotland's county Inventories, others as guide books and monographs issued by Historic Scotland and its predecessor bodies, or as articles in historical and archaeological journals. During the last two decades or so the flow of such material has greatly increased as the royal houses have become more intensively investigated and researched, better presented and more widely visited.

This book is an amplified version of the six Rhind lectures delivered in Edinburgh in March 1998 at the invitation of the Society of Antiquaries of Scotland. It focuses on the royal castles and palaces of the fifteenth and sixteenth centuries and in particular on the building activities of James IV (1488–1513) and James V (1513–42) at their principal residences of Linlithgow, Falkland, Stirling, Holyroodhouse and Edinburgh Castle. Because the Scottish royal houses became largely redundant soon after the departure of king and court to Whitehall in 1603, these early palaces, with the notable exception of Holyroodhouse, were never replaced or renewed. In consequence Scotland possesses a surprisingly large number of royal residences of late medieval and early Renaissance date, many of them structures of great architectural interest.

The arrangement of the book stems directly from the format of the lectures. The first three chapters examine the architectural development of the individual castles and palaces, taking account both of documentary sources and of the evidence presented by the buildings themselves. Chapters 4, 5 and 6 discuss the component parts of the residence, including hall, chapel, chamber, wardrobe, lodgings and ancillary buildings. The layout, planning, decoration and fittings of these elements are described and an attempt is made to show how they functioned when the king and his household were in residence. A final chapter, much of it not delivered in lecture form, outlines the financial and administrative organisation of the royal works and looks at the roles of the principal officials and tradesmen responsible for the construction and maintenance of the king's houses.

I am grateful to the President and Council of the Society of Antiquaries of Scotland for their invitation to give the Rhind Lectures and to the Society's Director, Mrs Fionna Ashmore, for smoothing my path during what turned out to be a highly enjoyable, if rather busy, weekend. During the preparation of the lectures and their subsequent adaptation to book form I have received a great deal of help from friends and former colleagues and would like, in particular, to acknowledge my debt to Dr Richard Fawcett and Dr Athol Murray, both of whom read substantial portions of the text and made many valuable suggestions, and also to Dr Andrea Thomas, who allowed me to use certain material from her forthcoming book on the court of James V. Others to whom I am especially grateful are Dr David Breeze, Miss Marilyn Brown, Mr Neil Cameron, Dr Ian Campbell, Mr Dennis Gallagher, Mr Neil Hynd, Professor Charles McKean, Dr Aonghus MacKechnie, Mr Iain MacIvor, Mr Roger Mercer, Mr E. J. Priestley, Dr Denys Pringle, Dr Grant Simpson and Mr Geoffrey Stell. Both Historic Scotland and the Royal Commission on the Ancient and Historical Monuments of Scotland have given generous assistance towards the provision of illustrations and Historic Scotland has also made a most welcome grant towards publication costs. The line drawings are by Miss Jane Siddall. Tuckwell Press has been unfailingly helpful and I am particularly grateful to Dr John and Val Tuckwell and Professor Sandy Fenton for their friendly support. My greatest gratitude, however, must be for the tolerance and understanding shown over the years by my wife, Elizabeth, who, like an early reviewer of *1066 and All That*, 'looks forward keenly to the appearance of the author's last work'.

ILLUSTRATIONS

Chapter 3

Chapter 4

Chapter 5

Chapter 6

Colour Photographs

RCAHMS = Royal Commission on the Ancient and Historical Monuments of Scotland.

INTRODUCTION

During the period under discussion in this book the available complement of royal residences changed constantly as the crown acquired new properties or alienated existing ones. When James I returned from captivity in England in 1424 he found the crown lands greatly depleted, with little but the Stewart patrimony in Bute, Ayrshire and Cowal to supplement the prime holdings in the Forth Valley, with their major residences at Edinburgh, Stirling and Linlithgow. Almost at once, however, the forfeiture of the Albany Stewarts brought the earldoms of Fife and Menteith into the possession of the king, and of the two key castles thus acquired, Falkland became one of the most favoured palaces of James IV and James V, while Doune remained with the crown until the end of the sixteenth century. James I also annexed the earldom of Mar, with its castles of Kildrummy and Kindrochit, while the forfeiture of the Earl of Atholl in 1437 added the lands of Methven, with its notable castle of the same name, and the forfeiture of the Black Douglases in 1455 brought a further crop of castles and houses, including Threave, Darnaway and Newark in the Forest of Ettrick. During the reigns of James III and James IV the extensive lands of the lordship of the Isles and the Boyd lordship of Kilmarnock also fell to the crown, while James V brought the royal estates to their greatest extent ever by swallowing the Red Douglas earldom of Angus and the lordship of Glamis (Murray 1975; *ER*, vi, pp. lxxii–cxlvi).

Only a handful of the numerous properties thus inherited or acquired ever ranked as major royal residences. A few, like the Border castles of Berwick and Roxburgh, remained for long periods in English occupation or, like Urquhart, were seized back from the crown by those who regarded themselves as their rightful owners. Others, like Dunoon and Rothesay, were placed in the hands of hereditary constables who eventually came to enjoy full rights of ownership. Others again, like Robert I's splendid manor of Cardross or James I's little known palace in Leith, were allowed to fall into decay or, like the castles of Dundonald and Darnaway, were in the course of time granted by the king to supporters or dependants (Douglas-Irvine 1911, 1–47).

Some properties were favoured because they provided opportunities for

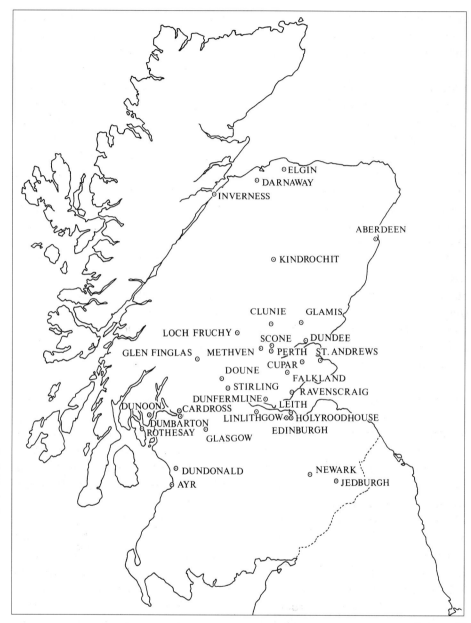

Map showing locations of the principal royal residences during the later Middle Ages.

hunting and these tended to be occupied mainly on a seasonal basis. Such were the hunting lodges erected by James II in the forests of Glenfinglas and Strathbraan in the central highlands, although most of the permanent residences also provided facilities for sport and recreation. When staying in the larger towns the king would probably be accommodated either in one of the older royal castles or in a purpose-built lodging. When James II visited Inverness in 1460 he was housed within the castle, but at Aberdeen he stayed in his own lodging in the burgh, whose facilities appear to have included a tennis court (p. 205). At Elgin in 1458 he lodged not in the castle, but in one of the cathedral manses, where a kitchen was built for his use, while in Ayr he was accommodated in a house belonging to a certain Margaret Mure (*ER*, vi, 391, 483–484). In Perth there was a royal lodging in the Dominican friary, which stood close to the site of the earlier royal castle, and it was here that James I was assassinated in 1437 (Duncan 1974, 40–41; Simpson and Stevenson 1982, 31–32). The lodging was evidently still in use a century later for in 1532 James V ordered the building to be repaired and provided with a new portal (*MW*, i, 111). Other religious houses, especially those that were royal foundations, had for long been accustomed to provide hospitality for the king and his household and two of these, Dunfermline and Holyrood, eventually became independent royal palaces. At St Andrews, where James V was a frequent visitor during the latter part of his reign, the king is said to have been accommodated in the archbishop's castle, but he also refurbished the nearby priory guest-house, known as the New Inns (*hospitium novum*), for the reception of Mary of Guise in 1538 (Fleming 1924, 53–57; Millar 1895, i, 297). The (rebuilt) gateway of this lodging still survives and bears the royal arms, together with those of its original builder, Prior John Hepburn (1482–1522).

Of the three dozen or so properties that might be described as regular royal residences at this period, only about half survive and almost all of these have been altered to a greater or lesser extent by reconstruction or decay. In seeking to identify the chief characteristics of the royal houses, therefore, I have concentrated on those for which the most evidence is available, namely the great castles and palaces of Fife and the Forth Valley between the beginning of James I's effective rule in 1424 and the death of James V in 1542. I have also taken account of earlier work at one or two castles, such as Edinburgh and Doune, where this throws light on later developments, and have included brief accounts of a number of the lesser houses, including the castles of Rothesay, Newark and Ravenscraig. Space does not permit consideration of all the smaller or more remotely situated residences, which are in general less well documented and less well preserved. I have therefore made only passing reference to these and the same is true of those properties, such as the castles of Jedburgh, Dumbarton and Glamis, which now contain little or no identifiable work of the period, or no work that can be associated with royal occupation. As the title indicates, the focus of this book is the domestic and residential functions of the royal houses and castles and I have not attempted to deal with the many other aspects of the subject.

1.1 Linlithgow Palace. View from the south-east showing east range, north-east (kitchen) tower and footings of bulwark.

Chapter 1

THE PALACES OF
LINLITHGOW AND FALKLAND

Linlithgow Palace

JAMES I'S NEW PALACE

The existing palace is built on the site of an earlier royal residence which first comes on record *c.*1300 (RCAHMS 1929, 219–231; MacWilliam 1978, 291–301; Pringle 1989; Cross 1994, 417–427). It occupies a promontory lying immediately to the north of the parish church of St Michael and bounded on two sides by the waters of Linlithgow Loch. Although Edward I did his best to turn this earlier residence into a castle, it seems to have been primarily domestic in character, being referred to in the documents as the king's house or manor (*ER*, iii, 463, 614). In the same year that James I returned from captivity in England (1424), there was a disastrous fire at Linlithgow which, according to Walter Bower (1987–98, 8, 242–243), consumed the town, the palace and the nave of the adjacent church. The king seized the opportunity to re-order the design and layout of the royal residence and promptly began a major rebuilding programme, which is partially documented in the exchequer records. (*ER*, iv, pp. cxxxv–cxxxix and *passim*; v, 10–11, 20–22).

The accounts show that operations had begun by 1424–25, when payment was made for the winning of stone (*ER*, iv, 391). Similar payments were made in the following year (*ER*, iv, 415) and by 1427–28 work was evidently in full swing. In 1430–31 payment was made to various masons and other craftsmen who had been brought to the work — their places of origin are not mentioned — and in 1433–34 materials were purchased for the king's painter at Linlithgow, which suggests that some portions of the fabric were well advanced by that date (*ER*, iv, 529–530, 579). Although the exchequer rolls are incomplete, it is evident that work continued until the spring of 1437, when the king's assassination brought operations to an abrupt halt leaving the new palace still unfinished.

The surviving accounts record expenditure of about £630 in each of the years 1429–30 and 1430–31, with indications of a broadly similar level of expenditure during the two preceding years. Accounts for the next two years are

C.1

5

missing, but some £1440 was spent during an eighteen-month period in 1433–34 and perhaps £550 in 1434–35; the account for the final year, 1436–37, amounted to £894. Clearly it is not possible to make an accurate computation of the total cost of the campaign on the basis of these figures, but when allowance is made for gaps in the accounts it seems reasonable to suggest that some £7000 was spent on the fabric during the period 1426–37. This is a very large sum, although modest by comparison with Henry V's expenditure of more than £8183 sterling (perhaps £14,000–£17,000 Scots) on the reconstruction of his palace of Byfleet and Sheen which, like Linlithgow, was still incomplete at the time of the king's death in 1422 (Colvin 1963–73, ii, 998–1000). Unfortunately, we do not know the full costs of the other main object of James I's architectural patronage, the Carthusian monastery at Perth.

What the accounts do not tell us is just how the new palace took shape, but it is generally agreed that James I's operations were concentrated on the erection of an east range, or quarter, containing a very grand entrance passage running beneath a great hall having a multi-storeyed kitchen block at its lower end. Adjacent portions of the north and south quarters also seem to belong, in part, to this phase, indicating that the main outlines of the existing courtyard plan probably go back to this period. We need not assume that the earlier residence was completely destroyed in 1424 for the king and queen made frequent visits to Linlithgow during the late 1420s, when the work of rebuilding was still in its early stages. Sometime during 1428–29 the archbishop of Reims was entertained for a night there upon his arrival from France and expenditure for the following year included the purchase of sheets and hand towels, some of which were to remain permanently at the palace (*ER*, iv, pp. cxxxvii–cxxxviii, 485, 512). It would seem likely that the buildings occupied at that time pre-dated the fire, in which case they may have stood on or near the site of the present west range, within the central area of the promontory summit.

The creation of the east entrance seems to have necessitated the acquisition of additional ground by the crown, for there is record of the purchase of 35 roods of land (about nine Scots acres) lying on the east side of the king's manor in 1427–28 (*ER*, iv, 450). This suggests that prior to *c.*1430 the main entrance to the palace was from the south, following the natural line of approach to the promontory. The east approach was more circuitous, but the ground on this side lay at a lower level, thus making it possible to construct a very showy gateway approached by a flying bridge. The south quarter of James's palace seems to have extended west for a distance of some 30m (i.e. to the present south porch), where the lowermost courses of the front wall terminate in a well-built corner perhaps intended to form one side of a subsidiary entrance on this side of the palace. The existence of latrine shafts at the base of the chapel wall suggests that the south quarter was originally designed for residential

1.1

use and it may well be that the upper floors contained a royal lodging opening off the upper end of the hall. Indeed, possible traces of such a lodging can be seen in this area, while the west wall of the chapel contains an earlier gable incorporating a disused flue.

The identity of James's designer is not known. The most likely candidate is the king's master-mason, but the previous holder of this post, Master Nicholas of Hane, disappears from the record in 1402 (*ER*, iii, 562) and the name of his successor is unknown. It is also possible that the king himself played a significant role in the project. Certainly he seems to have been well qualified to do so, for among James's many talents, as recorded by Walter Bower (1987–98, 8, 309), was an interest in drawing and painting and skills in the mechanical arts, which he had acquired in England. We are also told by Hector Boece

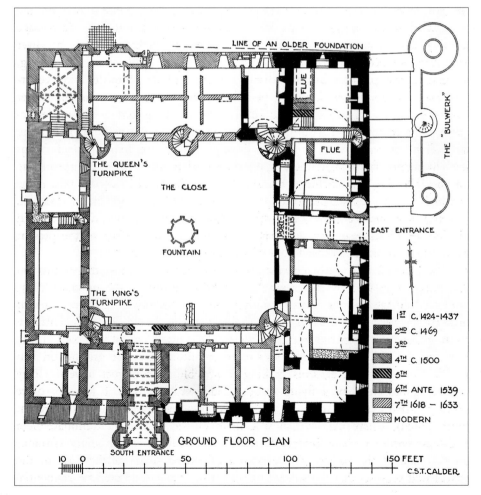

1.2 Linlithgow Palace. Ground-floor plan, 1929. The evidence suggests that a courtyard layout was envisaged from the outset.

7

(1938–41, ii, 393–394) that, because many native craftsmen had been killed in the wars, James brought craftsmen from England and Flanders 'to instruct his pepill in vertewis occupacioun'. It may therefore be significant that a group of craftsmen who are specifically mentioned in the accounts as having been recruited for work at the palace arrived in 1430–31, just when a five-year truce with England was being negotiated (*ER*, iv, 529–530; Brown 1994, 131). Initially the master of the fabric was John Waltoun, a Linlithgow merchant and collector of the king's custom dues for the burgh, but by 1434 responsibility had passed to Robert Wedale and Robert Livingstone. Another figure connected with the works at Linlithgow was the royal clerk, John Winchester (*ER*, iv, 555–556; v, 10), one of the auditors of the fabric books, who was also involved in building activities at the royal castles of Urquhart and Stirling and subsequently became master of the fabric at Inverness Castle as well as bishop of Moray (*ER*, iv, 498, 565; vi, 469, 521, 656).

Partly because James's palace was never finished and partly because those portions that were completed were subsequently remodelled, we cannot fully grasp the original conception. But the design was clearly a remarkable one. Neither a castle of chivalry of the kind depicted in the Duc de Berry's *Book of Hours*, nor a courtyard house of southern English type, the east portion of the palace, at least, seems to have been of simple U-shaped plan, without corner towers or gatehouse and with a show-front of almost entirely domestic appearance. If we are correct in supposing that the new approach from the east was deliberately contrived for visual effect, with the palace intended to be seen rising above the waters of Linlithgow Loch, the idea finds parallels in designed landscapes elsewhere in medieval Europe some of which, such as that at Bodiam Castle, Sussex, also made use of large expanses of water (Everson 1996).

Clearly, Linlithgow was built not as a castle, but as a princely dwelling-house, being in this respect more akin to the well-appointed residence erected by Robert I at Cardross almost exactly a century previously, of which nothing now remains (*ER*, i, 118, 123–136, 359–360). Linlithgow is first referred to as a palace in 1429 (*ER*, iv, 512) and this designation soon came to be adopted. It conveys a very different message from Robert II's reclusive tower-house at Dundonald and in some ways recalls the Duke of Albany's seat at Doune, where the planning of the frontal block offers a possible precedent for that of the east quarter at Linlithgow. The new palace was a symbol of a more self-confident style of monarchy and may have been intended to emulate Sheen, which James is likely to have visited during his time in England. Sheen has disappeared without trace, but is known to have had a great hall of similar size to that at Linlithgow (but wider), as well as a courtyard more than twice as large (James 1990, 139).

Another type of courtyard-plan residence that may have influenced the design of Linlithgow was the episcopal palace. If so, a likely point of contact would have been the queen's uncle, Cardinal Henry Beaufort, Bishop of Winchester (1404–47), one of the greatest builders of his day in England, who spent large sums in building or remodelling his several palaces.[1] In such palaces, as at Linlithgow, the needs of domestic planning always took priority over the needs of defence.

1.3 Linlithgow Palace. East entrance of c.1430 and part of bulwark of c.1500. The gateway was reached via a ramp and a drawbridge.

1.3
C.3

C.4

Other models have been proposed, notably the northern English courtyard castle of the type represented by Bolton, but these all had corner towers, whereas at Linlithgow the towers did not become a significant element in the design until the building campaigns of James IV and James V. There are parallels, however, between the entrance gateway of James I's palace, with its striking display of heraldry and sculpture, and the entrance fronts of certain late fourteenth- and early fifteenth-century castles in northern England, e.g. at Hylton and Lumley, and in France, e.g. at La Ferté-Milon and Pierrefonds. There is some doubt as to whether or not this sculpture, and that over the inner entrance of the pend, is contemporary with the rest of the gateway and Richard Fawcett has recently drawn attention to similarities between the cusped frames at Linlithgow and late fifteenth-century work at St John's Church, Perth (Fawcett 1994, 193, 308). But cusped arches of this kind occur over a very wide span of time and the structural evidence tends to suggest that the carved detail is integral with the remainder; on balance, therefore, it seems likely that the whole composition belongs to the 1430s.

4.2

4.7

Although the hall was extensively remodelled during the reign of James IV, the main elements of the original design are still discernible. Internally the hall measured at least 25m in length, and about 9m in width, making it about the same size as (but slightly narrower than) the late fourteenth-century ground-floor hall at Darnaway Castle (26.6 x 10.7m) and a good deal larger than the first-floor hall at Doune (20.4 x 8.2m). Like the latter it was reached by means of an external stair leading to a doorway at the lower, or service, end, but the Linlithgow doorway is much grander than the one at Doune, being designed as a major component of the courtyard elevation, like the great stairs (*les grands degrés*) that had been fashionable in France until the end of the fourteenth century (Mesqui 1991–93, ii, 90–93) and which are also found in a number of late medieval English first-floor halls, such as those at the castles of Kenilworth and Wressle. The lighting on both sides of the hall was always from high-level windows, as in many of the grandest English and French halls of the period, although the existing openings on the courtyard side date from James IV's time (Emery 1985, 291; Mesqui 1991–93, ii, 103). The clearstorey passage on this side of the hall was probably formed at the same time, but the similar passage at floor level is an original and highly unusual feature. Among other uses it may have facilitated the service of food from the kitchen at the north-east corner of the palace to the royal lodging in the south range. The chimneypiece at the south end of the hall appears to be an insertion of James IV's day and there may originally have been a central hearth with a louvre in the open timber roof, as in the halls at Doune Castle and Bothwell Castle.

THE COMPLETION OF THE PALACE BY JAMES III AND JAMES IV

The chronology of the next phase of construction at Linlithgow is more difficult to resolve, but the documentation is generally interpreted as indicative of two main building campaigns, one spanning the years around 1470 and the other extending from the accession of James IV in 1488 to his death in 1513. When the record evidence is looked at in the light of the changes in the financial administration of the royal works that took place during the late fifteenth and early sixteenth centuries (p. 212), however, a somewhat different picture emerges.

It would appear from the exchequer rolls that only minor building works were undertaken at the palace during the reign of James II and the early years of the following reign. Between 1465–66 and 1470–71, however, there is record of more substantial expenditure, including the purchase of timber, iron, slate and other materials, while we also have two accounts of the master of the fabric showing that some £770 was disbursed between March 1467 and October 1470. At this point a particular phase of work evidently came to an end and a horse and two iron-bound wheels which had been used to bring stone to the fabric were sold (*ER*, vii, 320, 404, 506, 585, 617, 638, 656–657; viii, 65, 134–135).

As we might expect, the exchequer rolls for the years after 1470 contain little mention of building activity either at Linlithgow or elsewhere. But they do demonstrate that work was in progress at the palace during the early 1480s, for there is reference at that time to the grazing of the palace meadows being allocated to horses employed on construction work (*ER*, ix, 16, 105, 172). If, as seems likely, the horses were used to transport building materials, this would suggest that fairly major operations were taking place.

It would have been helpful if Treasurers' accounts had been available for the middle and later years of James III's reign, but the only one to survive is that for 1473–74. This records expenditure of some £750 on artillery and workmen (*TA*, i, 74), but it is impossible to say whether any portion of this sum relates to building work at Linlithgow. The next surviving account, covering the period June 1488 to February 1492, records a payment made in early September 1488 to a wright travelling from Dundee to Linlithgow 'to see the Palis werk' (*TA*. i, 94), and this suggests that building operations were already in progress at the commencement of the accounting period. The same account specifically records expenditure of just over £500 on the fabric of the palace between May 1490 and February 1492, while the next one, running from February to August 1492, records an outlay of about £130, together with the purchase of £100 worth of timber (*TA*, i, 195, 204). Similar lump-sum payments may well have been made during the period June 1488–August 1490, for which the record is incomplete.[2] The surviving accounts for the years 1493–1501 (there are some gaps) contain no consolidated entries for expenditure on the royal castles and palaces, but it is clear from the numerous miscellaneous payments that work was in progress during at least some part of this period on several major buildings including Linlithgow, where some £200 was laid out in 1497–98 (*TA*, i, 354, 358–359, 367–370, 377, 384, 386, 390). The accounts from May 1498 to early 1501 are missing, but work evidently continued during this period (*ER*, xi, 365).

For the remaining years of James IV's reign we are on slightly firmer ground for, apart from a three-year gap in 1508–11, we have what looks like a fairly comprehensive series of fabric accounts of expenditure on the royal works for the whole of the period 1501–13. It would seem from these entries (*TA*, ii, 86–87, 269–281; iii, 82–89, 295–299; iv, 44–48, 275–284, 444–446, 523–530) and from the related entries in the *bursa regis* sections of the Treasurer's accounts and in the exchequer rolls (e.g. *ER*, xii, 174), that, in contrast to the extensive building campaigns being carried out at certain other royal residences, the work at Linlithgow was of a fairly minor nature, consisting mainly of repairs and modifications, together with a continuous programme of maintenance. Only in the last year or two of the reign did annual expenditure exceed £100 and between 1501 and 1508 it was usually less than half that. A good deal of this activity involved preparations for royal visits, which seem to have been even more frequent following the assignment of the palace to Queen Margaret in 1503 than they had been earlier in James IV's reign (*ER*, xiii, pp. xciv–xcv; *TA*, ii, 275; iii, 140, 146).

If this interpretation is correct, the significance of some of the individual entries in the accounts may need to be reassessed. In 1504, for example, there is a *bursa regis* payment to a mason 'for the bigging of the battaling of the west side of the Place of Linlithqw' (*TA*, ii, 440), which is often interpreted as marking the completion of the west front (RCAHMS, 1929, 225; McWilliam, 1978, 296). But the sum involved was £3 10s, which was only enough to pay the wages of a mason and his apprentice for five weeks (*TA*, iv, 279) and it could well be that the job in question was no more than a routine repair. Likewise the paving of the chapel in 1507 could be seen as part of a programme of refurbishment (*TA*, iii, 297–298; iv, 89).

So far as the years 1437–1513 as a whole are concerned, therefore, it may be suggested that the documentary evidence points to a period of fairly continuous, and at times substantial, building activity extending from the mid 1460s to about the turn of the century, with only minor works being carried out during the reign of James II and the latter part of the reign of James IV. Although the exact sequence of operations is far from clear, the late fifteenth-century building campaign evidently involved the reconstruction of the greater part of the palace, leading to the completion of the existing courtyard plan (*National Art Survey*, iv, Pls. 42–57).

First, perhaps, in the sequence came the erection of an L-plan block of which one limb completed the south side of the courtyard while the other formed the south half of a new west courtyard range. It is possible that the pause in building operations in 1470 that we have already noted marked the completion of this phase of the work. Curiously, the south limb of the block is on a slightly different alignment to that of the adjacent south range of c.1425–37 and its front wall is set back by more than 2m. This suggests the possibility that this south-west corner block preserves the ground plan, and perhaps even part of the fabric, of part of the pre-1424 palace, although there is nothing in the visible masonry to confirm this and excavation of the cellar forming the north limb of the block revealed no traces of earlier work (Caldwell and Lewis 1996, 829–831). The south-west corner of the block rises higher than the remainder, taking the form of a five-storeyed tower containing a single chamber on each of the upper floors. So far as we know this was the first of the corner towers to be built, the roof line of James I's palace being predominantly horizontal.

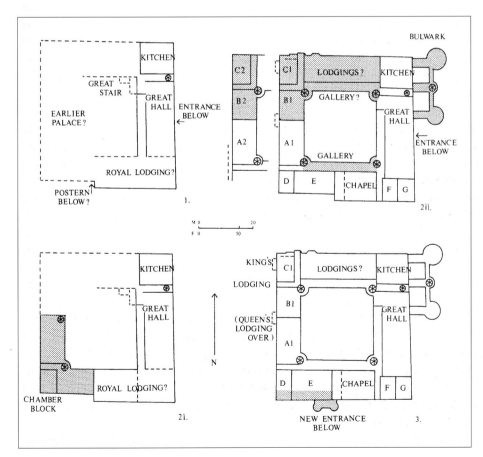

1.4 Linlithgow Palace. First-floor sketch-plans.
1. James I;
2i James III;
2ii James IV and
3 James V;
A1, B1, C1, King's Hall, Great Chamber and Chamber; A2, B2, C2, Queen's Hall, Great Chamber and Chamber;
D Lodging;
E Lords' Hall (?) or anteroom;
F Vestry (?);
G Chamber.

On the east side of the palace James I's great hall was remodelled, being equipped with new clearstorey lighting on the courtyard side and with a magnificent new chimneypiece at the upper (south) end. Above this fireplace a vault was constructed to support one of the gables of the south-east corner tower which, like its neighbour at the north-east corner of the palace, seems to have made its appearance during this phase of the work. Another addition to the east quarter was the triple-towered forework[3] at the north end known as the outer bulwark (*MW*, i, 127), which is now usually interpreted primarily as a sham fortification intended to enhance the appearance of the east front (Pringle 1989, 13). It may well have been designed to achieve this effect, but the word bulwark was generally used by contemporaries to describe a bastion or block-house (Saunders 1989, 246 and *passim*; *TA*, ii, 449) and its dumb-bell shaped gun-loops and postern doorway look quite businesslike. It was, of course, only a few years later that Falkland Palace was fortified with cannon to resist Queen Margaret (p. 24), while there are records of artillery being housed at Linlithgow itself

during the second half of the fifteenth century (*ER*, vi, 200, 204, 323, 385, 563; *TA*, i, 112, 181). The existing outworks at Linlithgow, however, are perhaps more likely to be a relic of Cromwell's fortifications. Another purpose of the bulwark was probably to reinforce the north-east corner of the palace, which seems to have been displaced by the thrust of the vault of the court kitchen.

The adjacent portion of the south range was also drastically remodelled, a new chapel (perhaps the first to exist in the palace) being constructed at first-floor level in the area formerly occupied by the royal lodging. We can be fairly confident in ascribing this latter operation to the early 1490s because there is record of timber for the chapel roof being purchased in 1492, while a payment of drinksilver the previous autumn 'for the pendin of thre voutis' could well relate to the reconstruction of the three cellars beneath the chapel (*TA*, i, 181, 204). The remodelling of the east and south quarters was completed by the erection of turnpike stairs within the north-east, south-west and south-east corners of the courtyard (the first of these replacing the original forestair to the great hall and the second an earlier spiral stair in a similar position) and the construction of superimposed corridors along the courtyard side of the south

1.6 Linlithgow Palace. View from the north-west showing north-east (kitchen) tower (left), north range, north-west tower and west range (royal lodging).

1.8

*1.7 Linlithgow
Palace. West
courtyard front
showing windows
of royal lodging.
The king's great
chamber has an
additional 'lying'
window.*

range in continuation of the scheme of internal communication already provided for the east range.

The abandonment of the old royal lodging in the south quarter made it necessary to find alternative quarters for the king and queen and this was achieved mainly by extending the south-west corner block northwards to complete the west courtyard range. The documents offer little guidance as to the timing of this operation, but the evidence of the fabric indicates that there was a gap of at least some years between the completion of the corner block, perhaps in 1470, and the erection of the new royal lodging. It is also clear that the extension of the west range northwards was carried out in two separate but consecutive phases of construction.[4] We shall consider the planning of the royal lodging in Chapter 5.

A good deal of work was probably also done on the adjacent north quarter, which may have contained lodgings for courtiers and officials, although most traces of these were obliterated by the reconstruction of the range in 1618–21. Some evidence remains, however, of what seems to have been a very grand

ground-floor loggia or corridor on the courtyard side, perhaps part of a super-imposed series of corridors like that on the opposite side. The arrangement may have been similar to that contrived in the late fourteenth century at Saumur (Mesqui 1991–93, ii, 33, 154), but with lintelled rather than arcaded openings at courtyard level. Operations in this area were probably concluded by the construction of the north-west turnpike stair, which is broadly similar to those in the other three corners of the courtyard, but more elaborately detailed internally. The mouldings of the stairhead are similar in character to those of the oriel windows of the royal lodging and one of the vaulting bosses bears the entwined initials IRM in roman capitals, presumably for James IV and Margaret Tudor, who were married in 1503 (although the wives of James II, James III and James V also had Christian names beginning with M). The north-west corner tower must also belong to the same period, although its upperworks seem to have been remodelled during the following reign.

1.6

We can identify a number of the principal craftsmen who worked on the palace during this period, although our information is far from complete. During the late 1460s the master-mason is named as Robert Jackson, who may have been related to the Nicholas Jackson employed there *c.*1502–04. By 1511 Stephen Balty was the senior mason at the palace and he continued to maintain the fabric until his death some five years later. Another name to be considered is that of John French, the earliest recorded member of a notable family of masons who had connections with Linlithgow over three generations. Although he is not mentioned in the surviving documents, the fact that he was buried in Linlithgow Church in 1489 suggests that he was employed either at the palace or the church, then also in course of reconstruction; indeed the similarity of certain details of the two buildings (e.g. the oriels) makes it possible that he had a hand in both, as his son did in the 1530s. Another prominent figure involved in the building operations at Linlithgow during the earlier part of this period was Friar Andrew Lesouris, the king's wright, who supplied timber for the works in 1469 (*ER*, vii, pp. xlix, 638, 657). The names of several of the masters of works are also on record, the most important of these being Henry Livingstone, Andrew Cavers, abbot of Lindores, who was also keeper of the palace, and Henry Forest (*ER*, vii, 656–657; *TA*, i, 368; ii, 86, 269). More is said about some of these tradesmen and officials in Chapter 7.

A good deal has been written in recent years about the origins and affinities of the various design features that can be identified at the palace during this period and this is not the place for an extended discussion of the subject. Two general points are worth making, however, the first being that there is ample testimony of the existence of widespread dynastic, political, cultural and economic links between Scotland and Continental Europe (and to a lesser extent between Scotland and England) during the reigns of James III and James IV.

We should therefore not be surprised to find evidence of the penetration into Scotland of architectural influences from countries such as France, Italy and the Netherlands. The second point, which relates more particularly to the situation at Linlithgow, is that if the interpretation of the documentary and structural evidence that has been put forward above is broadly correct, then there was no grand design for the palace of James III and James IV, but rather a programme of progressive enlargement, reconstruction and improvement pursued over a period of some 40 years. We know that the builders changed their minds more than once as the work progressed (e.g. in the development of the south and west quarters), so it is hardly surprising that changes were also made in the architectural vocabulary.

As we might expect, some of the salient features of the design, such as the use of corridors and the placing of newel staircases at the internal corners of the quadrangle, can be paralleled in late medieval courtyard-plan castles and houses in other Western European countries, including England and France.[5] External stair-turrets placed in one or more corners of a courtyard were especially popular in France — the house of Jacques Coeur at Bourges (c.1450) is a well-known example — and it is possible that this particular feature should, indeed, be seen as an import (Mesqui 1991–93, ii, 165–167; Evans 1952, 170).

4.7 Also perhaps of French inspiration is the magnificent triple chimneypiece of the great hall, the only one of its kind in Scotland. In France such chimneypieces were considered particularly suitable for royal and ducal palaces. The best known example is that in Jean de Berry's great hall at Poitiers (c.1385), but there were others at Angers, Bourges and Coucy (Evans 1952, 165). Another unusual feature, the umbrella vault of the north-west, or Queen's, stair at Linlithgow, may also have its origins in France, although a more direct source could have been the Northumbrian castles of Alnwick, Belsay, Bywell and Haughton (Mesqui 1991–93, i, 219; Wood 1965, 334–335; Emery 1996, 62, 100).

So far as other sources of foreign influence are concerned, Ian Campbell has made out a good case for seeing the Italian fortified palace of the later fourteenth and fifteenth centuries, with its rectangular courtyard and square corner-towers, as a possible model (Campbell 1994, 3–5), although it is clear that the Linlithgow towers did not assume their final form until the reign of James V. When account is also taken of the very English-looking appearance of the south courtyard front, we may well think that the designers of the royal works were decidedly cosmopolitan in outlook.

THE REMODELLING OF THE PALACE BY JAMES V

There is no record of any significant expenditure before the 1530s, but major works were evidently in progress between March 1534 and August 1536, at least £3855, and perhaps a good deal more[6] having been expended during that period.

Three separate masters of works' accounts appear to have been rendered for these operations, but only that for the twelve months from February 1535 survives (*MW*, i, pp. ix, xxiv–xxv, 115–131; *RSS*, ii, No. 2147). During the remaining six years of the reign total expenditure of some £900–£1000 is recorded in the Treasurer's accounts, together with a number of payments for routine maintenance (*TA*, vi, vii and viii, *passim*; *ER*, xvii, 170). In addition, certain unspecified, but possibly quite large, sums seem to have been advanced by Sir James Hamilton for the work prior to September 1539, when he was partially compensated for these by substantial grants of land (*RMS*, iii, No. 2021); part of the £4000 quit-claimed by Hamilton in November 1539 may also have been destined for Linlithgow (*RSS*, ii, No. 3199). Hamilton had been keeper of the palace since 1526 and he and his assistant, Thomas Johnson, had rendered the accounts for 1534–35 and 1535–36, although Hamilton seems not have held any formal appointment as master of works at that time (p. 221).

The evidence of the standing buildings gives a good indication of what was done, but the accounts themselves also furnish a number of useful clues. The chief undertaking was the transfer of the principal entrance from the east side

1.8 Linlithgow Palace. East and south courtyard fronts by R.W. Billings, c.1850 showing east entrance (left), with great hall windows above, south-east stair, superimposed corridors of south range and south entrance. The fountain was restored during the 1930s.

19

1.9 Linlithgow Palace. Outer gateway of c.1535. The badges over the gate represent the four orders of European chivalry to which James V belonged.

1.5   of the palace to its original position on the south. This involved cutting a new transe through the south quarter, equipping it with an entrance porch and erecting a handsome new outer gateway leading into the outer court from the kirkgate; within this outer court were stables and other offices. The porch and gateway were presumably complete by the spring of 1535, when the causeway connecting them was under construction (*MW*, i, 123). The old east entry was fitted with a wicket gate and remained in use until at least the middle of the seventeenth century (*MW*, ii, 345), but it was subsequently closed and the approach bridge removed. With the bulk of traffic now approaching the palace from the south it was decided to regularise the appearance of the south front by building a massive screen-wall between the new porch and the south-west corner. At the same time the south-west tower itself was enlarged and its upper-works remodelled to match those of the south-east tower. It is possible that the upperworks of the north-west corner-tower were likewise remodelled at this period in the interests of symmetry. These works must have accounted for a considerable proportion of the 2500 or so cartloads of freestone that were transported to the palace during 1535 (*MW*, i, 115–120).

The accounts also record the purchase of large quantities of timber, much of it probably required for the new floors and roofs of the south quarter. The chapel itself was re-ceiled and provided with new glass, some of it painted. Improvements were made to the king's kitchen and other offices and the royal lodgings were refurbished; it is possible that the tiled floor of the king's great chamber belongs to this period rather than to the previous reign as usually supposed (p. 167). The celebrated courtyard fountain, which first comes on record in 1542, can also be ascribed to this stage of the work[7] (*MW*, i, 115–131; *TA*, vii, 195, 472; viii, 72). Such fountains were a familiar feature of palace architecture in other countries and in 1535 Henry VIII had installed an elaborate example in the inner quadrangle at Hampton Court (Thurley 1988, 24–25).

The master-mason most closely associated with these operations was Thomas French (p. 227), son of the John French already mentioned. French was probably the principal devisor of at least the first stage of the work, but it is likely that Hamilton of Finnart, whose building activities have recently been highlighted by Charles McKean, also played some part in the design process (Mckean 1991). Indeed, Bishop Lesley specifically credits him with 'making new lodgings' (i.e. royal lodgings) both at Linlithgow and Stirling (Lesley 1830, 158). Whoever the designer, or designers, may have been the character of the work is predominantly late Gothic. The outer gatehouse and porch, the corbelled parapets of the corner-towers, even the form of the fountain, are all of traditional design and the medieval flavour of the work is further emphasised by the gun-ports that gave the palace a show of defence on the south side. It is only in the occasional detail — the cable moulded string-course of the gatehouse, the French-inspired chimneypiece in the king's presence-chamber (evidently from the same hand as those in the royal lodging at Stirling Castle) and the medallion heads and imperial crown that embellish the fountain — that Renaissance influence is apparent. In all these respects, and particularly in the retention and dramatisation of military features, James V's Linlithgow has more in common with the early palace architecture of Henry VIII than with that of Francis I.

C.2

Falkland Palace

THE CASTLE AND PALACE, 1424–88

The royal residence of Falkland was originally a castle of the Earls of Fife (RCAHMS 1933, 135–142; Gifford 1988, 212–217; Puttfarken *et al.* 1989). James I seized the castle from the Albany Stewarts in 1425, but showed little inclination to live there (Brown 1994, 73, 113). In 1451, however, James II granted the earldom of Fife, with the manor or castle of Falkland, to his queen, Mary of Gueldres, and Falkland became a favourite residence of the court for the remainder of the king's reign, being valued chiefly as a place for hunting and recreation (*RMS*, ii, No. 462; *ER*, vi, p. lxxviii). The castle lay immediately to the north of the existing palace and to judge from the remains exposed by the 3rd Marquess of Bute's excavations of *c.*1890, dated mainly from the late thirteenth century.

C.7

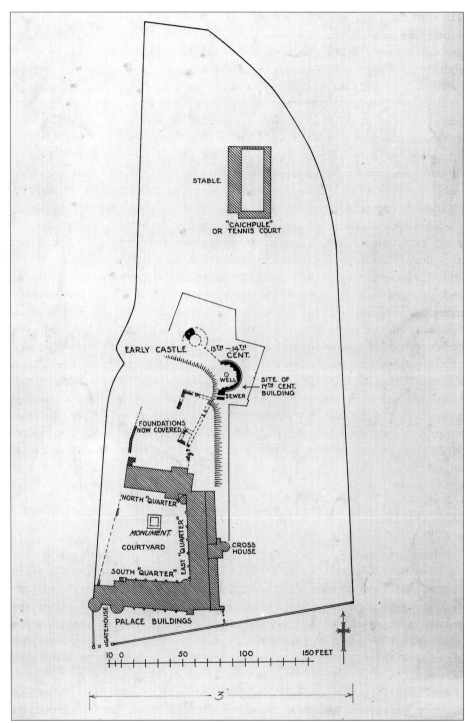

STABLE.

"CAICHPULE"
OR TENNIS COURT

EARLY CASTLE
13TH – 14TH
CENT.

WELL

SEWER

SITE OF
17TH CENT.
BUILDING

FOUNDATIONS
NOW COVERED

NORTH "QUARTER"

MONUMENT.

COURTYARD

EAST "QUARTER"

CROSS
HOUSE

SOUTH "QUARTER"

GATEHOUSE

PALACE BUILDINGS

10 0   50   100   150 FEET

*1.10 Falkland
Palace. Site plan,
1933, showing the
relationship of the
palace to the
earlier castle.*

The building was sometimes referred to as the tower of Falkland (*ER*, v, 534), which suggests that its most prominent feature was a great tower, or donjon, probably the one whose footings can still be seen in the north garden. From about the 1460s onwards, however, it was generally known as the palace of Falkland (*RMS*, ii, No. 714).

We learn from the exchequer rolls that a certain amount of building work was carried out at the castle during the 1450s, including repairs to the hall and to various chambers and offices, at a cost of some £52 (*ER*, vi, 565–566). Further improvements were made by Mary of Gueldres following James II's death in 1460. Indeed, the widowed queen proved to be a notable builder in her own right, funding major works at Ravenscraig Castle, Fife, and Trinity College, Edinburgh, as well as the more modest operations at Falkland.

These are not without interest, however, for we hear of a new chamber being made for the queen equipped with glass windows and an aumbry, as well as a door leading down to a newly made lawn. Like many of the buildings within the castle, this chamber seems to have been constructed mainly of timber and its erection was supervised by Andrew Lesouris, the king's carpenter. At the same time repairs were made to other structures, including the hall of Falkland, the great chamber of Falkland and the 'counthouse', while two chambers were partitioned off within 'le galry'. This appears to be the first known reference to this type of structure in Scotland and it is interesting to find that a French term is used to describe it. The fact that the gallery was wide enough to contain subsidiary chambers also suggests that it was something more than a corridor. The earliest references to galleries in English royal houses date from the reign of Henry VII (1485–1509), but they were not uncommon in fifteenth-century France and Burgundy and it is tempting to see the Falkland example as an innovation commissioned by the queen-mother, who had spent her early years at the Burgundian court (Colvin 1963–73, iv, 17; Mesqui 1991–93, ii, 154–161; Thurley 1993, 21). The total cost of these works, undertaken in 1461–62, was just over £35 (*ER*, vii, 75, 78–79, 106).

JAMES IV'S NEW PALACE

The loss of most of the Treasurers' accounts makes it difficult to know what, if any, building operations were undertaken at Falkland during the latter part of James III's reign and there are no indications of any architectural activity during the early years of the following reign, although James IV was a frequent visitor to the palace. The accounts from the end of May 1498 to January 1501 are missing, but those of 1501–02 show that by the spring of 1501 a start had been made on an extensive programme of works which seems to have continued until about the time of the king's death in 1513 (*TA*, ii, 103). In 1501–02 a quarry was opened within the burgage lands of Falkland 'for the construction of the said palace' and during the following year ground was purchased near the gates of the palace for the construction of a masons' lodge (*ER*, xii, 205, 524).

The surviving series of fabric accounts for the royal works contained in the Treasurers' books (*TA*, ii, 87–89, 269–281; iii, 82–89, 295–299; iv, 44–49, 283), supplemented by *bursa regis* entries (*TA*, ii, iii, iv, *passim*), enable us to trace the progress of these operations, except during the period 1508–11, when the accounts are missing. Considerable sums were also allocated to the work directly from the revenues of the lordship of Fife and the relevant entries in the exchequer rolls supplement the material in the Treasurer's accounts (*ER*, xii, 443, 523; xiii, 430, 504–505; xiv, 11).

Although the documents do not specify the location of the works, it is clear that these were focused primarily upon the erection of a group of new buildings on a site lying immediately to the south of the early castle and palace. These buildings were disposed round three sides of a rectangular courtyard, the largest of them, known as the new work (*ER*, xiv, 174), being on the east side. Payments for glasswork and plasterwork in 1505–06 may indicate that the shell of this range, which probably contained a new royal lodging, was approaching completion at that time (*TA*, iii, 85, 164, 179, 296, 355). The south side of the courtyard was probably occupied by a chapel and vestry, which were roofed in 1511–12 (*ER*, xiii, 430; *TA*, iv, 283). This chapel replaced or supplemented an earlier one, probably situated within the original castle of Falkland, which is mentioned in documents of the fifteenth and early sixteenth centuries[8] (*ER*, v, 686–687; xi, 303–304, 306; xii, 11). On the north side of the courtyard stood a great hall of which the masonwork was completed in 1511–12 (*ER*, xiii, 430) and the roof some two years later (*ER*, xiii, 504; xiv, 11). The entrance to this new complex of buildings was presumably on the west side of the courtyard, the approach from the adjacent burgh possibly continuing north to give access to the earlier palace.

The campaign was rounded off by the laying out of a new walled garden, which probably occupied much the same site as the existing one on the east side of the palace (*ER*, xiii, 504). The earlier palace remained in use, at least in part, and some of its buildings may have been refurbished, but the accounts make no specific reference to this. It may have been this earlier palace that was fortified against the dowager Queen Margaret in 1514–15 by the keeper, Archbishop James Beaton, who brought in a formidable array of artillery for this purpose (*ER*, xiv, pp. lxi–lxii, 163–164).

Expenditure seems to have been heaviest during the early years of the campaign, when the east range is likely to have been under construction and when masons were brought in from Dundee, Edinburgh and Perth (*TA*, ii, 88, 271, 418). It is not possible to make an accurate computation of costs, but at least

1.10

£3364 had been spent by 1508 and when allowance is made for the three-year gap in the Treasurer's accounts and for expenditure of at least £540 (including garden works) in 1511–14 it seems probable that the total outlay was not less than £5500–£6000.

At the beginning of the campaign the leading craftsmen were William Turnbull and John Brown, masons, and John Fendour, wright, best known for his work at St Nicholas' Church, Aberdeen (Fawcett 1994, 76, 162–165, 211). By the time that the chapel and great hall were completed, however, another mason, William Thom, who had previously worked at Stirling Castle, was in charge (*TA*, iv, 46). Timber for the roof of the great hall seems to have been obtained locally and its preparation was undertaken by John Drummond, the king's wright, who may also have designed and erected the roof (*ER*, xiii, 504–505). Andrew Wright, carver, was responsible for ceiling the chapel and great chamber (probably a new great chamber situated in the east range) and Andrew Laing, painter, was also employed in the work (*TA*, iv, 283, 380). The first master of works, Andrew Cavers, abbot of Lindores, who had held similar posts at Linlithgow and Stirling, resigned in 1503 and was succeeded by John Ramsay, vicar of Creich (*TA*, ii, 272). Another influential figure was James Beaton who, as well as being keeper of Falkland and chamberlain of Fife, held office as Treasurer for several years during this period (p. 237).

The relocation of the principal buildings to an adjacent site marked the foundation of what was virtually a new palace, comparable in many ways to the one that James IV was then erecting at Holyroodhouse. In both cases the new palace took the form of a courtyard attached to one side of an earlier residence, while a courtyard layout was also favoured, under rather different circumstances, in the contemporary works at Linlithgow, Stirling and Edinburgh. Given the opportunity presented by what seems to have been a fairly clear site, the layout of the new complex presents a decidedly piecemeal appearance and the planning of the courtyard is noticeably irregular. The oblique alignment of the hall, and its uncomfortable relationship with the north end of the east range, suggest that the hall may have stood on the site of, and perhaps even incorporated part of, the fabric of its predecessor or of some other building of the earlier palace.

The hall is now represented only by its excavated footings, which show it to have been of the same plan as the slightly earlier great hall at Stirling, i.e. with (nearly) opposed bay windows at the upper end. Although smaller than its likely model, James IV's hall at Falkland was nevertheless of a very respectable size (30.2m x 7.9m internally), being a little longer than his brother-in-law's hall at Hampton Court. As presently laid out, the footings of the hall appear to incorporate a fireplace in the east gable and this makes the building look like a ground-floor hall. The fireplace is not shown on the Bute excavation

plans (NTS drawings at Falkland Palace), however, and it seems more likely that the hall, like those at Stirling and Edinburgh, was built over an undercroft. The Bute drawings suggest that this undercroft was entered by a pair of opposed doorways towards the west end.

The adjacent east range, or quarter, was remodelled during the 1530s and accidentally burnt during Charles II's reign; after standing derelict for two centuries its roofless shell was partially restored by Lord Bute during the 1890s. Enough remains of James IV's work, however, to show that the building originally comprised an exceptionally long rectangular block (57m) having a centrally-placed tower on the garden side. Above a ground-floor cellarage there was a *piano nobile* and an attic, the latter lit on the courtyard side (the garden front has disappeared) by a row of small, squarish windows, several of which can still be identified, although blocked since the late 1530s. The first-floor windows, which seem to have survived intact, are much larger and more regularly disposed; they have simple chamfered margins and are surmounted by hood-moulds, a feature found also in James IV's work at Stirling. The medal-

1.11 Falkland Palace. East courtyard front of c.1502–13 as remodelled in the late 1530s.

lion heads, like the buttresses, are additions of the late 1530s. Comparison of the east range with the layout of other Scottish royal palaces suggests that this was the royal lodging, as it is certainly known to have been in the following reign, and its planning arrangements are discussed in Chapter 5.

Like the east range, the south quarter owes its present appearance mainly to alterations carried out by James V, but embodies the core of the building erected by his predecessor. All that can be said about the earlier building with any degree of confidence is that it probably contained a chapel and vestry (*TA*, iv, 283) above a vaulted cellarage. The account for roofing the chapel in 1511–12 (*ER*, xiii, 430) indicates that it required 13 roods of slatework, which suggests that the building measured very roughly 33m in length externally, about the same as the present chapel (33.5m).[9] The chapel may have been roofed at a lower level than the adjacent east quarter, for in 1512–13 payment was made 'for raising a wall between the new work and the chapel of Falkland to keep the wind out' (*ER*, xiii, 504). The structural evidence suggests that the south quarter originally extended west into the area now occupied by the east side of the gatehouse. Much of the early sixteenth-century cellarage survives, but the present north corridor evidently belongs to the 1530s, perhaps replacing an earlier one of timber.

THE REMODELLING OF THE PALACE BY JAMES V

Although efforts were made to maintain the fabric during the decade after Flodden, John Betoun of Creich, keeper of Falkland, found it necessary to make formal complaint about the condition of the palace in 1525 (*APS*, ii, 296a; *ER*, xiv, 161, 174, 402; xv, 118; *TA*, v, 79). Further repairs and maintenance were undertaken during the late 1520s (*ER*, xv, 351, 395; *TA*, v, 325–328, 389), while a master of works' account for 1531–32 records expenditure of some £88 on the erection of new stables and the repair of various buildings, including the new work and old chapel (*MW*, i, 73, 111–114). The operations on the new work, or east quarter, centred on the repair and roofing of the 'new galryis and corssis' (cross-house) — the first mention that we have in the accounts of these structures. We know from later entries in the accounts that the cross-house was the central tower of the east quarter, while the galleries were evidently the passages that flanked the garden side of the building to north and south of the cross-house. They are clearly depicted on Alexander Kierincz's painting of *c.*1640, where it can be seen that they rose to the full height of the east range, being capped with flat lead roofs within balustraded parapets. The upperworks of the galleries were remodelled in 1616–17, however, (*RPC*, x, 517–518; *MW*, ii, p. c) and the roofs that were constructed in 1531–32 were of slate, perhaps of lean-to type with somewhat lower wall-heads.

These galleries are interesting and unusual features and it is important to

1.13

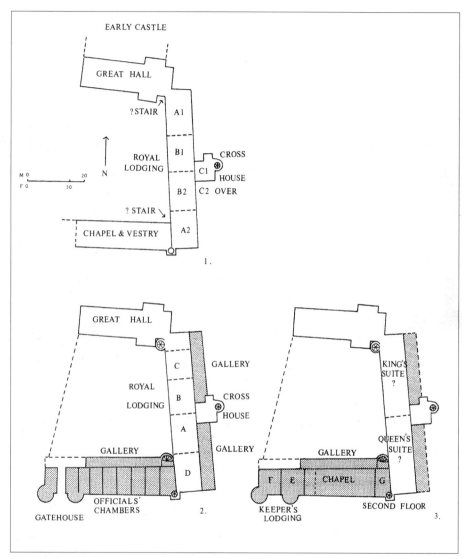

*1.12 Falkland
Palace. First-floor
sketch plans.
1. James IV: A1,
B1, C1, King's
Hall (?), Great
Chamber (?) and
Chamber (?);
A2, B2 C2,
Queen's Hall (?),
Great Chamber (?)
and Chamber (?).
2 and 3: James V;
A Outer Chamber
(?), B Mid
Chamber (?), C
Inner Chamber (?),
D Lords' Hall (?)
or anteroom,
E Outer Chamber,
F Inner Chamber,
G Vestry.*

know when they were erected. Unfortunately, it is not clear from the accounts whether they were being roofed for the first time in 1531–32, or merely repaired. We know from the evidence of their exposed foundations, however, that while the cross-house itself was constructed, or at least commenced, at the same time as the remainder of the east range, the flanking structures were later additions. They could therefore have been erected at any time between about 1506 and 1531, perhaps during one of those periods for which we lack Treasurers' accounts. On balance, however, it seems likely that the operations of 1531–32 represented the final stage in the construction of the galleries and that these had been begun

in the previous year, for which a volume of masters of works' accounts is known to be missing (*MW*, i, pp. ix, 111).

While some further work seems to have been undertaken during the mid 1530s (*TA*, vi, 232), James V's main programme of improvements at Falkland was commenced only in 1537, following his marriage to Madeleine de Valois, eldest daughter of Francis I, in Paris at the beginning of that year. Continuous and detailed masters of works' accounts survive for the period December 1537 to September 1541 (*MW*, i, 196–234, 235–263, 264–292), by which time the work seems to have been almost complete. There is also reference to an earlier account, now missing, probably covering the greater part of the year 1537 (*MW*, i, 218, 234; *TA*, vi, 349). The peak year of activity was 1539, when there were often more than 60 masons on site and monthly building costs averaged as much as £390. Expenditure during 1538 totalled about £2450 and during 1539 about £4670, while the 21 month period from December 1539 to September 1541 saw an outlay of some £4540. When allowance is made for the missing account for 1537 it seems likely that the overall outlay was in the region of £14,000.

1.13 Falkland Palace. Detail of view from south-east by Alexander Kierincz, c.1640. The galleries of the royal lodging in the east range are clearly visible.

STABLE

THE PENT-HOUSE

PLAN OF STABLE & TENNIS COURT

10 0 10 20 30 40 50 60 70 80 90 100FEET

CHAPEL

FIRST FLOOR OF GATEHOUSE AND SECOND FLOOR OF "QUARTERS"

C.S.T.C.

1.14 Falkland Palace. Plan of 1933 showing gatehouse, chapel, second floor of east range (royal lodging) and tennis-court.

1.12

During these five years the royal lodging in the east quarter was remodelled and provided with a stylishly revamped courtyard front. The adjacent south quarter seems to have been almost completely rebuilt above the cellarage, while retaining the main features of the early sixteenth-century layout. Both the external and the courtyard fronts of this range were almost entirely renewed in ashlar, the latter comprising superimposed corridors covered with a lean-to roof. The main accommodation comprised a series of first-floor chambers, presumably designed as lodgings for courtiers and senior officials of the household, with a new chapel and vestry on the second floor and another series of chambers above. At the west end of the south quarter a gatehouse, or fore-entry, was built to provide a new entrance to the palace with lodgings for the keeper on the upper floors, while prominent, extruded newel-stairs were built, or rebuilt, at the north-east and south-east corners of the courtyard. Other new buildings included a 'cachepell', or tennis court (p. 207), situated to the north of the early palace, a bakehouse, a brewhouse and a fountain (*MW*, i, 261). Whether this last stood in the principal courtyard, like its counterpart at Linlithgow, is uncertain and it does not appear in Slezer's views.

Parts of the early castle and palace, including the tower (*MW*, i, 219) seem to have remained in use and we hear of certain other buildings, such as the wester lodging (*MW*, i, 260), whose location is not known. The old chapel, presumably the one known to have been in existence prior to 1511–12, was still in use in 1538, but a reference to the 'redding and away hawing of the auld chapel ground' in the following year suggests that it was demolished shortly afterwards (*MW*, i, 217, 280). Curiously, nothing is heard of the great hall after 1535, when it was equipped with new tables (*MW*, i, 182). Possibly its role as a communal dining-room, except for use by the lower ranks of the household, was in decline by this time (p. 109).

The work force at Falkland comprised a remarkable array of talent, including no less than four royal master-masons. The first to be named in the accounts were John Brownhill and Moyse (Moses) Martin. Brownhill, who had been appointed in 1532, had previously been employed at Holyroodhouse; his seniority

1.15 Falkland Palace; south range. Gatehouse and part of chapel by R.W. Billings, c.1850.

*1.16 Falkland
Palace; south
range. South
courtyard front of
c.1540 by R.W.
Billings, c.1850.
The façade was
evidently to
continue across the
rear of the
gatehouse.*

is attested by the fact that he had personal responsibility for the receipt of certain of the tax revenues earmarked for the work. Martin was a Frenchman who had worked for some years in Scotland before apparently accompanying James V on his French visit of 1536–37, during which he had been appointed a royal master-mason (p. 228). The timing of this appointment, coming as it did when arrangements for the royal couple's return to Scotland must have been under discussion, suggests that Martin was being groomed to play a leading role in any building operations that might be required to prepare the Scottish royal castles and palaces for the reception of the bridal pair. He and Brownhill probably worked at Falkland from the commencement of operations on the east range in 1537 — the date is inscribed on the buttresses — until his death in the spring of the following year. Brownhill continued on site and in 1540–41 was paid £400, jointly with Henry Bawte, for completing the gatehouse and roofworks of the south quarter (*MW*, i, 279).

It was probably to replace Martin that Thomas French, who had recently worked at Linlithgow and Holyroodhouse, was brought to Falkland in July 1537.

In 1539 he and another master-mason, James Black, received bounties for their work on the south range and its new corridor-galleries (*MW*, i, 256). By this time another French mason, Nicholas Roy, had arrived at Falkland with three assistants, having been dispatched thither by the Duchess of Guise at the request of her daughter, Marie of Lorraine, whom James had married as his second wife in 1538, following the death of Madeleine de Valois. On his arrival in Scotland in the spring of 1539 Roy was appointed a royal master-mason; he began work at Falkland in July and remained there until the summer of 1541 (p. 228).

Other prominent craftsmen included the Dutch carver, Peter Flemishman, who sculpted the statues for the chapel buttresses (*MW*, i, 256) and the French pargeoner, Hector Beato, — his modest wage-rate suggests that he undertook plain, rather than ornamental plasterwork (*MW*, i, 213). Several highly experienced wrights were employed, particular mention being made of Richard Stewart, who was paid £216 in 1540–41 for fitting out the chapel (*MW*, i, 281; *TA*, vii, 219–220, 274). No doubt the fittings of the royal apartments were of equally high quality, but here the accounts are less informative. We learn, however, that two notable Scots carvers, John Drummond, who had worked on the roof of the great hall a quarter of a century earlier, and Robert Robertson, were employed at Falkland for many weeks during 1538, when the east quarter was being fitted out. It is interesting to find that Drummond, who was king's wright and gunner, spent part of the spring of that year in France on duties connected with the artillery (p. 234). Patrick Pow, painter, was responsible for the painting of ceilings and wainscoting, as well as the external ironwork, while in February 1542 following the completion of the main building programme, the queen's painter, possibly Pierre Quesnel, is known to have been employed at Falkland (*TA*, viii, 59; Apted and Hannabuss 1978, 115). Surprisingly, there is very little in the way of glazing accounts for the royal apartments.

Building operations were supervised by the king's principal master of works, Mr John Scrymgeour, whose longstanding Fife connections — he was the owner of the nearby castle and estate of Myres — may have prompted him to exercise a more personal degree of oversight at Falkland than at some of the other royal castles and palaces. His good services to the crown were recognised in 1542 by a confirmation charter of his lands of Myres, which made specific mention of the works at Falkland Palace and Holyroodhouse (p. 220).

The most remarkable feature of James V's palace is the contrast in style between the external and internal elevations of the principal buildings. The gatehouse, which looks like a smaller version of the king's great tower at Holyroodhouse, has a decidedly military appearance, while the adjacent chapel likewise has a late Gothic exterior. This last is sometimes explained by supposing that the shell of the building belongs mainly to James IV's reign (Gifford 1988,

1.15

*1.17 (a) Falkland
Palace. Detail of
south courtyard
front showing
French-inspired bay
design.*

1.17 (b) Detail of south front of château of Villers-Cotterêts from F. Gebelin's Les Châteaux de la Renaissance *(1927).*

1.16

1.17

214), but the wide-mouthed gun-ports that pierce the base of the south wall can hardly be earlier in date than *c.*1530 and appear to be integral with the rest of the facework. As we have already seen, similar gun-ports were constructed in the new entrance front of Linlithgow Palace at about the same period. In fact, the external appearance of the chapel, with its tiered buttresses and statue niches, was probably intended to proclaim the ecclesiastical function of the building. The courtyard façades of the palace, on the other hand, are up to the minute essays in the style of the Parisian region, being generally recognised as among the earliest examples of coherent Renaissance design in Britain. In all probability the bay design of these façades derives from those of Francis I's châteaux of Fontainebleau (Cour Ovale, *c.*1531) and Villers-Cotterêts (1533–37), while the medallion heads, statuary and prominent dormer windows, perhaps the earliest in Scotland, are doubtless also of French inspiration (Dunbar 1991, 4). There are indications that the courtyard elevation of the south quarter was intended to continue behind the gatehouse as an arcaded screen with a gallery above, again very much in the French manner.

C.9

These differences in style probably result, in large part, from the allocation of different tasks to different masons. So far as we can judge from the accounts, the specific assignments of John Brownhill, James Black and Thomas French related mainly to the gatehouse and south quarter and the character of their work there is very much in line with what we know of their output elsewhere. For example, the design of the principal front of the gatehouse could well owe a good deal to Brownhill, who had worked on James V's great tower at Holyroodhouse in the early 1530s, while some of the details, such as the cable-moulded string-courses, strongly recall French's work at Linlithgow. Martin, on the other hand, had recently been with the king in France and is likely to have visited Villers-Cotterêts and other châteaux around Paris, as well as in Normandy and the Loire Valley. It seems likely that he was the principal designer of the internal elevations, sharing responsibility for the very tricky recasting of the east courtyard front with Brownhill. The accounts do not specify the nature of Nicholas Roy's work, but bearing in mind that he seems to have been the highest paid mason of the entire building operation (p. 228) it seems reasonable to credit him with the medallions and other carved detail of the north courtyard front, which is dated 1539; Black and French, as we have seen, were also involved in the construction of the corridor galleries of the north front.

Beyond these personal idiosyncrasies of style is the probability of a deliberate intention to create a contrast between exterior and interior, so that a visitor approaching the palace by way of the businesslike looking south front and gatehouse would be surprised to find, on entering the courtyard, that all was ease and splendour within. The idea, which is perhaps a fairly obvious one, had already been employed in a number of Italian and French châteaux, either by rebuilding within the shell of a genuine, medieval castle, as at Amboise, or by deliberately building a new château in contrasting styles, as at Bury (Bentley-Cranch 1986). At Falkland, where much of the early castle still stood, a mixture of these two methods was adopted. The planning of the royal lodgings also has French overtones and these are discussed in Chapter 5.

NOTES

1 The More, Hertfordshire, Bishop's Waltham and Wolvesey, Hampshire. *Cf.* also Faulkner 1970, and Hare 1988.

2 The discharge of the accounts for the period June 1488 – August 1492 is in three parts. The final summation of the first part of the discharge, June 1488 – May 1490 (*TA*, i, 88–165) is missing, but on comparison with the expenditure totals of the other two parts of the discharge (*TA*, i, 169–195, 198–208) Dr Athol Murray has suggested to me that some £3700 may be unaccounted for and that much of this is likely to have been expended upon the royal works. If so, it is probable that some of this expenditure was incurred at Linlithgow.

3 There may originally have been four towers.

4 In 1939 a bronze seal matrix of probable fourteenth-century date was found in the first-floor room known as the king's outer chamber or presence chamber. Although it has been suggested that this discovery could point to the survival of significant remains of fourteenth-century work in the west wing of the palace, it has to be said that there is nothing in the appearance of the standing masonry to confirm this suggestion (Caldwell and Lewis 1996, 832, 854).

5 Corridors occur at Bishop's Waltham Palace *c.*1440 (Hare 1988, 237); Herstmonceaux 1440s, Knole 1450s–60s (Faulkner 1970, 138–142); Saumur 1370s, Angers 1430s–50s (Mesqui 1991–93, ii, 149–161); corner stairs occur at Lumley late fourteenth century (Pevsner 1953, 181–183); Coucy late fourteenth century, Le Plessis Bourré *c.*1465–73 (Mesqui 1996, 63–64).

6 The total expenditure in 1534–35 is not known, but the superexpenditure (i.e. the excess of discharge over charge) amounted to some £1200 (*MW*, i, 130).

7 The lead feed-pipe of the fountain is said to have been inscribed with the date 1538 (MacWilliam 1978, 297.

8 The location of this chapel is uncertain, but an account for its repair in 1516, by which time it had become known as the old chapel, shows that it

lay within the precincts of the palace (*ER*, xiv, 174–175). There was also a chapel of St Mary at Birkinside, near Falkland, whose chaplain was supported from the crown lands in Fife (*ER*, xii, 197, 285, 448).

9 This calculation allows for a building about 9.1m in width with a roof pitch of 45°. James V's chapel required a similar quantity of slatework when it was roofed in 1539–41 (*MW*, i, 285).

Chapter 2

STIRLING CASTLE AND HOLYROOD PALACE

Stirling Castle

THE CASTLE, 1424–88

Stirling has an even longer history as a royal centre than either Linlithgow or C.10
Falkland and the castle's outstanding military and political importance ensured
that its principal buildings were subject to frequent replacement and change
(RCAHMS 1963, i, 179–223; Cross 1994, 546–562; Fawcett 1995). Of the castle
that James I took possession of in 1424 almost nothing now survives and it is
only in the late fifteenth and early sixteenth centuries that the majority of the
buildings that we see today began to make their appearance.

The indications are that James I himself did not undertake any major works
at Stirling. The castle was by no means neglected, however, for entries in the
exchequer rolls reveal an average expenditure of about £60 per annum on the
fabric for the greater part of the reign, with no less than £176 being disbursed
during the year spanning the crisis of the king's assassination in February 1437
(*ER*, iv, 403, 435, 468, 502, 528, 565, 605; v, 3–4). Possibly the unsettled state
of the kingdom made it necessary to put the castle into a higher state of defence
than usual at that time, while the earlier payments mainly involved repair and
maintenance. We simply do not know, because the records give little indication of the nature of the work done. For the greater part of this period the
master of the fabric was Alexander Guild, one of the custumars of the burgh
of Stirling.

For much of James II's reign the exchequer records again give no indication of major building activity at Stirling, although we hear of repairs to various
buildings, including the king's and queen's chambers, the kitchen and certain
other offices (*ER*, v, 266, 274, 478; vi, 326, 415). It looks as if more extensive
operations were planned towards the end of the reign, however, for in 1458–59
a new quarry was opened for the king's work in the castle of Stirling and in
that, and in the following year, the revenues of the Earldom of Lennox,
amounting to about £200 per annum (of which perhaps £150–£175 would have

been actually available for expenditure on the fabric[1]), were allocated to the work (*ER*, vi, 543, 548–550, 607.). It may be that these operations, which were directed by Thomas Bully, were abandoned or postponed following the king's unexpected death in August 1460, for during the early years of James III's reign the exchequer rolls record only minor works and repairs[2] (*ER*, vi, 495; vii, 26, 59, 189, 367, 392). By the mid 1460s, however, there are indications that, because of changes in the administration of the king's finances (p. 212), expenditure on the royal works was being handled in part by the Treasurer and therefore recorded in the Treasurer's accounts rather than in the exchequer rolls (*ER*, vii, 425).

Since the surviving series of Treasurer's accounts does not (with minor exceptions) commence until the beginning of James IV's reign in 1488, there is a period of some 20 years during which scarcely any information is available about building activity at Stirling. Before the information derived from the exchequer rolls finally dries up in about 1470, however, there is a sprinkling of entries which suggest that fairly large-scale works were in progress at that time. In 1466–67 we hear of the rebuilding of part of the castle wall and between then and 1468–69 several payments were made for work on the chapel, including repairs to the roof and the provision of paving stones. The roof works were undertaken by Andrew Lesouris, the king's carpenter, while operations were again directed by Thomas Bully, who is described as master of the fabric of the chapel of the castle of Stirling (*ER*, vii, 448–449, 452, 501, 544, 660).

These payments probably relate to the building, or rebuilding, of the chapel that preceded the existing one of 1594 and whose footings are thought to lie on the north side of the upper square, partly underlying the present chapel but following a somewhat different alignment. These footings show that the chapel was a large and substantial building, but apart from the fact that it was oblong on plan and possibly incorporated side-aisles and a south porch we know nothing of its outward appearance (Fawcett 1995, 28–31). We may speculate, however, that behind James III's building activities was the intention to establish a new chapel royal at Stirling, an aim eventually fulfilled by his son.

Looking at the period 1424–88 as a whole it has to be admitted that our information about architectural activity at the castle is seriously deficient. In particular, the latter part of the reign of James III, who is traditionally credited with important undertakings at Stirling, could well have witnessed major works that have gone unrecorded.

THE REMODELLING OF THE CASTLE BY JAMES IV

Fortunately, we are much better placed to assess the activities of James IV, for the surviving series of Treasurer's accounts covers about three quarters of the reign. Admittedly, some of the gaps come at awkward times, but against that

2.5

the consolidated entries for what were evidently some of the busiest years contain more specific information than is available for most of the other royal castles and palaces at this period. The king was a frequent visitor to Stirling Castle, often spending Easter there. In 1495 he received Perkin Warbeck, a pretender to the English throne, there and for part of the following year he lodged his mistress, Margaret Drummond, within the castle (*TA*, i, pp. cxxiii, cxxxiii).

Apart from routine maintenance, the first mention of building activity at the castle relates to the chapel, where the new king continued his father's work by further enhancing the fabric. James IV also erected the chapel into a collegiate church known as the chapel royal at Stirling, final approval for the new foundation being given by the pope in 1501. So far as we can judge, the improvements made to the building between about 1494 and 1502 mainly involved redecoration and the provision of new fittings and furnishings, including a set of bells (*TA*, i, 228, 238, 331, 357, 370; ii, 61–69).

As well as the chapel royal, there was another, probably much smaller, church known at this period as 'the ald kyrk within the Castell of Strivelin'. This was rebuilt in 1504–05 by a mason called John Yorkstoun, following which James IV increased the number of chaplains serving it to a total of three (*TA*, ii, 280; iii, 82; *ER*, xiii, pp. xciv, 59). It is uncertain where this church stood, but it is possibly to be identified with a building, subsequently remodelled for use as a kitchen, situated at the south-west corner of the upper square, or inner 2.5 close. This structure, within which a number of burials came to light during excavations conducted in 1997–98, follows approximately the same alignment as the early chapel royal on the opposite side of the close.

More important than either of these undertakings was the erection of a building described in the accounts as the 'king's house', which Richard Fawcett has convincingly identified as the so-called King's Old Building now occupying 2.1 the west side of the inner close. Although it was greatly altered during the eighteenth and nineteenth centuries, recent investigations have shown that this originally contained what was almost certainly a spacious royal apartment placed over a vaulted cellarage (Fawcett 1990b and 1995, 35–39). The building seems to have been constructed with considerable speed, for the earnest money for the masonry contract was paid only in June 1496 and the house was ready for slating by mid November (*TA*, i, 277–306, 310). Possibly preparations had begun rather earlier, however, for the Treasurer's accounts are incomplete, apparently lacking entries for the period November 1495–April 1496.[3] Payments made in the following year (1497) for the construction of a gallery — seemingly a timber structure on a stone footing and with a slate roof — may relate to the completion of the same building (*TA*, i, 336, 357, 370; Fawcett 1995, 37–38). The master mason of the royal lodging was Walter Merlioun, one of the leading

2.1 Stirling Castle. Conjectural reconstruction of King's Old Building (royal lodging) of mid-1490s by David Pollock (1995). It is now thought unlikely that the lodging had a second floor, as suggested here.

practitioners of the day and a member of a well-known family of masons, at least one of whom, John, assisted him in the project. It was no doubt in recognition of his services at Stirling, as well as at other royal castles and palaces, that Merlioun was paid an annual fee of £40 (p. 224).

As well as refurbishing the chapel royal and building a new lodging for himself, James IV reconstructed the principal defences on the south and east sides of the castle. As rebuilt, these comprised, on the south side, a central gatehouse flanked by a high curtain wall terminating at either end in a residential tower, the west one now known as the Prince's Tower and the east one as the Elphinstone Tower. The whole is described in the records as the forework and still bears that name today. From the Elphinstone Tower another length of curtain extended along the east side of the castle to connect with an earlier gatetower, now known as the Mint, which gave access to the nether bailey.

Entries in the Treasurer's accounts enable us to follow the progress of this massive undertaking in considerable detail. Unfortunately, the accounts for the period May 1498 – February 1501 are missing and the first identifiable reference to the forework is a payment for drinksilver at the founding of a building described as the kitchen tower in June 1502[4] (*TA*, ii, 149). This is probably the Elphinstone Tower, which has a kitchen on the first floor, and the accounts show that work continued on its fabric until 1504 (SRO, E 21/6, ff.59^r, 60, 61^v, 62^r). In August 1502 we hear of the heading (i.e. completion of the upperworks) of the foretower (*TA*, ii, 85), probably to be identified as the prominently sited Prince's Tower, and it seems reasonable to assume that this had been begun in

1500 or 1501. By 1502 the central gatehouse, or fore-entry, was also under construction and by the summer of 1504 this was sufficiently advanced for the portcullis to be installed; final payment was made two years later (*TA*, ii, 269–270, 277; iii, 88). With the end towers and gatehouse approaching completion the emphasis shifted to the intervening sections of curtain and the two smaller intermediate towers (one apparently called the Red Tower), which were under construction between about 1505 and 1508 (*TA*, iii, 84, 87–89, 296–297; iv, 44). There is then a three-year gap in the accounts, during which the east curtain is likely to have been completed, following which the project seems to have been rounded off in 1511–12 by the recasting of what is described as the 'gret towre — in the northtest nuk of the Castele of Striveling', probably to be identified as the north gateway, or Mint (*TA*, iv, 281).

Responsibility for the work was divided between several masons. John Lockhart had charge of the gatehouse and north-east tower, John Yorkstoun built the foretower and John Masoun the kitchen tower. Both Lockhart and Yorkstoun also worked on other parts of the forework, while a third mason, Adam Reed, is credited with the construction of a gateway on the other side of the castle, described as the 'Nethir gait undir the Crag', or west gate, in

2.2 Stirling Castle. Conjectural reconstruction of forework of c.1500–08 by David Pollock (1995) showing Prince's tower (left), gatehouse and Elphinstone Tower.

2.3

1501–12 (*TA*, ii, 83–85, 141). This may be the gateway, now blocked, on the W side of the nether bailey, overlooking the King's Park.[5] Lockhart's contribution was evidently especially noteworthy and this was recognised by the grant of an annual pension in November 1508, a date which may have marked the completion of the forework.

No mention has so far been made of the grandest of the buildings associated with James IV's operations at Stirling, namely the great hall. The difficulty is that the documents contain very few identifiable references to the construction of the hall. In April 1501 there is a payment to 'the quareouris of Mowtrais toure that wynnys the allowring to the Hall of Strivelin' and in July 1503 there is a payment to an English plasterman travelling to Stirling 'to plaistir the new hall' (*TA*, ii, 82, 103, 274, 381). The first of these entries may refer to the dismantling of an earlier tower — perhaps on the site of the forework — to obtain stone for re-use in the parapet-walk of the hall, while the second probably refers to internal plasterwork rather than harling, because it is clear that the material used was of high quality, being made from imported English alabaster or gypsum.

It looks, therefore, as if the external fabric of the hall was approaching completion in 1501 and the interior in 1503 and we know that hooks for hangings were installed in November of the latter year (*TA*, ii, 408). If so, the main period of construction probably spanned the immediately preceding years, but the absence of the Treasurer's accounts makes it impossible to confirm this. It may be significant, however, that the accounts for the autumn and winter of 1497–98 contain references to quarrying operations and to the recruitment in St Andrews of men for the Stirling workforce (*TA*, i, 359–361, 377). The dates now proposed for the main period of construction also fall fairly neatly between the completion of the king's house in 1497 and the probable commencement of the forework in 1500–01. Another possibility is that the great hall was built, or at least, begun, during the latter part of James III's reign where again the accounts are missing. This seems unlikely, however, for as Dr Fawcett has pointed out, the great hall was very awkwardly sited in relation to James III's chapel royal (Fawcett 1995, 30). It should also be noted that some of the carved detail of the hall, such as the external hood-moulds, can be closely paralleled in the forework.

This leads on to the question of the identity of the craftsmen responsible for the hall. Here the evidence is extremely tenuous, but we can probably rule out Walter Merlioun as master-mason because shortly after completing the king's house in 1496–97 he moved to Dunbar Castle to begin work there (*TA*, i, 331) and as soon as the castle was finished he embarked upon another major enterprise at Holyroodhouse. In November 1497, just about the time that the design of the hall is likely to have been under active discussion, the master mason of Linlithgow visited Stirling 'to gif his devis to the werk' (*TA*, i, 367). If, as is possible, the master mason of the palace at that time was a member of the French family, it may be significant that a certain Thomas French (Franch) was at Stirling in April 1501 (*TA*, ii, 102). Perhaps the most likely candidate, however, is John Lockhart, who was certainly the leading mason at the castle in the years after 1501 and who remodelled the wall-walk of the hall in accordance with the king's particular instructions in 1512 (*TA*, iv, 372). So far as the carved timberwork of the hall is concerned, including the remarkable hammerbeam roof, the candidates include David Kervour, who had worked on the roof of the chapel, John Kervour, younger, who recruited part of the workforce in 1497 (*TA*, i, 360) and the resident carpenter, David Borg, a member of a distinguished family of wrights (*ER*, xi, 223, 370).

In addition to these major works, there is record of some minor projects, including the remodelling of a building described as the 'old hall', possibly the predecessor of the great hall of *c.*1498–1503. This was undertaken by John Lockhart between 1502 and 1508, while in 1507–08 his colleague John Masoun was refurbishing 'the ald chameris in Strivelin on the west part of the ald clos' (*TA*, ii, 269, iv, 44, 46). We do not know the precise location of these buildings, but it seems likely that some of them stood in the area now occupied by the palace block of James V.

The cost of these works was considerable and probably higher than that incurred by James IV on any other single castle or palace. The form of the accounts, and the fact that they are incomplete, makes it impossible to give precise figures or to estimate the costs of individual buildings, but between the probable commencement of the king's house in the spring of 1496 and the probable completion of the forework in the late summer of 1508 the overall recorded expenditure amounts to some £12,300, excluding identifiable work on the gardens and the furnishings of the chapel royal (*TA*, i, 273–311, 319–394; ii, 81–85, 96–161, 269–281, 340–479 and SRO, E 21/6, ff.54–63; *TA*, iii, 82–89, 126–210, 295–299, 329–417; iv, 44–48, 71–141; *ER*, xi, 297). The peak years seem to have been 1501–12 when — if the above analysis of the building programme is broadly correct — the overlap between work on the great hall and that on the forework raised the annual outlay to about £1600. This declined to about £700 by 1507–08. If these figures are then revised upwards to allow for the gap in the accounts between May 1498 and February 1501 total expenditure for the period 1496 to 1508 rises to more than £16,000. The loss of the accounts for the three years commencing August 1508 makes it impossible to estimate expenditure during the latter part of the reign, but the fact that some £412 was spent between August 1511 and August 1512 shows that this was not inconsiderable (*TA*, iv, 281–282, 293, 357).

The organisation and financial administration of these operations was controlled by successive masters of works, some of whom, like Andrew Cavers,

2.3 Stirling Castle.
Great hall of
c. 1498–1503
showing south
gable and bridge
to palace.

abbot of Lindores, who subsequently filled similar posts at the palaces of Linlithgow and Falkland, held office for only a short time. The other two named masters of work during the mid 1490s were Thomas Smith and William Betoun (*TA*, i, p. cclxvi). Towards the end of 1497, however, the office passed to Andrew Aytoun, who was also chamberlain of the king's lands in Stirlingshire and for a time keeper of the castle (p. 217). He held the post of master of works throughout the main period of building activity, surrendering it to Robert Calendar in or after 1508 (*ER*, xiii, p. xcii).

Clearly James IV spared no expense in his building operations at Stirling, where major works were in progress throughout the greater part of his reign. As we have seen, he not only replaced or refurbished most of the principal domestic buildings of the castle, but also renewed the main defensive walls and gateways. We shall discuss the planning of the royal lodgings in Chapter 5 and it is sufficient here to note that whereas at Linlithgow and Falkland James provided new lodgings both for himself and his queen, the king's house at Stirling (built some seven years before his marriage), was precisely what its name implied. The queen's chamber, whose location at this period is unknown, seems not to have been rebuilt, although, as previously, it continued to be kept in repair (*ER*, vii, 59; *TA*, ii, 441). So far as we can judge, the architectural character of the king's lodging was late Gothic, the mouldings being similar to those found in the great hall (Fawcett 1990b, 190, fig. 9).

The hall itself is probably the grandest secular building to have been erected in Scotland during the later Middle Ages. Certainly there is no other surviving building to match it. At present in course of restoration to something approaching its original condition, the hall is constructed above an undercroft and was formerly approached from the inner close by means either of a forestair or of a flying bridge. It measures about 38.6m by 11.1m internally and rises to a height of some 16.5m. The building is lit by pairs of externally-splayed high-level windows in the side- and end-walls and by large bay windows flanking the dais. The vast interior space was heated by five fireplaces, while circulation was provided by two principal and two subsidiary stairs, all of spiral form. Kitchen and service facilities for the hall were provided close to the north gateway and in a range laid against the inner face of the adjacent east curtain (p. 186).

James IV was clearly out to impress for this was a big building by any standards, fully comparable in scale with all but the very largest great halls in England and the Continent (Colvin 1963–73, i, 44; Mesqui 1991–93, ii, 78–80). So far as we know, the elongated plan, with prominent bay windows placed at the upper end, was unprecedented in Scotland and the formula seems to have been repeated only once, namely at Falkland Palace a few years later. These features are typical of late medieval great halls in England, however, while the original hammerbeam roof, known only from eighteenth-century drawings, was also of a type that had been developed in England. It has to be said, however, that we know very little about late medieval carpentry techniques in Scotland and that one of the few earlier timber roofs on this scale to survive, that erected at Darnaway Castle, Morayshire, during the late 1380s, shows features that could foreshadow fully developed hammerbeam construction (Stell and Baillie 1993, 176–178). If the architect of the Stirling hall, whoever he was, did indeed draw some of the main elements of his design from England, a likely model would have been Edward IV's highly prestigious, but slightly smaller, hall at Eltham

4.4

Palace, Kent, completed in about 1480 (Colvin 1963–73, ii, 936–937; Fawcett 1995, 39–45). Scottish, and perhaps also some French, influence can be seen in the upperworks of the Stirling hall, with their corbelled wall-walks and angle-rounds and prominent cap-houses, while the mouldings and other details are for the most part typical of native late Gothic work. The hood-moulds that surmount the doorways and smaller windows are more English than Scots, however, and may also derive from Eltham (Pugin 1831–38, i, Pl. 48).

As it happens, a certain number of high ranking and influential Scots were probably familiar with the hall at Eltham, for the palace's position a little to the south of London made it a convenient place for the reception of delegates to the English court. It is known that the embassy sent by James III to conclude a peace agreement with Henry VII in 1486 was entertained there. Among the party on that occasion, some of whom took part in a hunt in the surrounding forest park, were Bishop William Elphinstone, Abbot Bellenden of Holyrood, John Ross of Montgrenan and the king's Secretary, Archibald Whitelaw (Campbell 1873–77, i, 229, 484; Macfarlane 1995, 136–37).

2.5 The placing of the king's lodging and the great hall roughly parallel to each other on opposite sides of the inner close was probably part of a scheme to regroup the principal domestic buildings round a spacious courtyard, as at Linlithgow and Falkland. In order to achieve a more or less regular quadrangle, however, it would have been necessary to remove James III's chapel royal from the north side of the inner close and rebuild it on a slightly different alignment a little further to the north. Possibly, as Dr Fawcett has suggested, James IV would have done this had he not met an untimely end at Flodden (Fawcett 1990b, 180–182 and 1994, 315). In the event it was left to James VI to complete the project in the 1590s, the west side of the upper square having by that time been occupied by part of James V's palace.

As a piece of military architecture, the forework was of conservative design, being essentially a high screen wall punctuated by a gatehouse and flanking towers of rectangular and circular projection. Only the exceptional thickness of parts of the curtain-wall and the provision of gun-loops in the gatehouse (there may have others at parapet level) indicate an awareness of the needs of artillery defence (Stell 1981, 41–45). Most of the surviving gun-loops are of a distinctive dumb-bell shape, first seen in Scotland at James III's castle of Ravenscraig and found also in the east bulwark of Linlithgow Palace.

As a number of scholars have recently pointed out, however, the forework was conceived as much as a showfront as a defence and the more exotic components in its design have to be understood in that context (Fawcett 1995, 50–51; Campbell 1995, 312 and n.74). Clearly there was a deliberate attempt to achieve both symmetry and elegance and it is remarkable that the entire facework was of ashlar. In its original, much loftier form, the multi-turreted gatehouse must

The Prospect of their Maties Castle of Sterling. Arcis regiæ Sterlinensis prospectus.

have made a most imposing entrée to the new domestic buildings within. Although certain features of the gatehouse recall Early Tudor gateways in England — the hoodmoulds, however, possibly deriving directly from the great hall at Stirling — , the main external elements in the design are probably of French origin. The cap-houses and wall-walks of the angle-turrets, for example, as seen in Slezer's views, are characteristic of late medieval military architecture in that country. The distinctive triple portal, however, has been seen by Aonghus Mackechnie (1991) as a reworking of the Roman triumphal-arch motif and therefore as an early example of Italian Renaissance influence. All in all, then, James IV's work at Stirling, like that at Linlithgow, appears to have been highly eclectic, which is perhaps no more than we should expect of that most European of monarchs.

JAMES V'S NEW PALACE

There is no record of any significant building activity at Stirling during the minority of James V, although it has to be remembered that the Treasurer's accounts for this period are not complete. A small amount of work was done between August 1529 and September 1531 (*TA*, v, 389, 436; *MW*, i, 55), while between September 1531 and August 1532 some £200 was spent on refurbishing the royal lodgings and certain other buildings within the castle, as well as the

2.4 Stirling Castle. View from southeast by John Slezer, c.1693, showing forework and great hall.

stable beneath the walls (*TA*, vi, 34, 49; *MW*, i, 105–111). Certain other works, again probably of a minor character, were carried out during the mid 1530s (*TA*, vi, 84, 232, 267; *ER*, xvi, 585; *MW*, i, 227–228), but all these activities are overshadowed by the erection, during the closing years of the reign, of the building described in the records as the new work in Stirling (*TA*, vii, 482) and now generally known as the palace. This was constructed in the space between the inner close and the west end of the forework in order to provide new lodgings for the king and queen together with accommodation for courtiers and officials.

Unfortunately, no detailed masters of works' accounts for the building of the palace survive and we have to work out the timing and costs of the project, as best we can, from other sources. The arrival of Sir James Hamilton of Finnart at 'the place of Striveling' and his entry to the work there in or about May 1538 probably marked the commencement of the building programme (*MW*, i, 227–228) and dendrochronological analysis of the first-floor joists of the palace has recently demonstrated that some of the timber was felled in that year[6]. Hamilton, whose role at Linlithgow has already been noted, evidently played a leading part in the construction of the palace, temporarily supplanting James Nicholson, who had been appointed master of work within the castle of Stirling early in 1530 (*RSS*, ii, No. 487). In September 1539 Hamilton was appointed principal master of works, an office which evidently ran in parallel with that already held by Scrymgeour, albeit with a vastly inflated salary, and he seems to have continued in post until shortly before his sudden downfall and execution in August 1540 (*RSS*, ii, No. 3144). As explained in Chapter 7, Hamilton seems to have financed a large part of the construction costs of the palace from his own resources in exchange for favours from the king.

Following Hamilton's death, work at Stirling continued under the direction of James Nicholson, some £1460 having been expended between July and December 1540 (*TA*, vii, 474). In August 1541 Nicholson was succeeded as master of work by Robert Robertson, a wright and carver, and this appointment, taken in conjunction with a reference to the roofing of the tofall (lean-to) of the queen's chamber in December of the same year, suggests that the building was now approaching completion (*RSS*, ii, No. 4191; *TA*, viii, 47). There are no identifiable references to the construction of the palace after 1542 and it seems likely that the work was substantially complete by the time of the king's death at the end of that year. The former existence of dormer windows behind the palace parapet, one bearing the date 1557 and another the initials MR, suggests that further work was carried out during the regency of Mary of Guise (MacGibbon and Ross 1887–92, i, 475; Fawcett 1995, 64).

Miscellaneous payments by the Treasurer between 1539 and 1542 that probably relate to the construction of the palace (including some for debts incurred

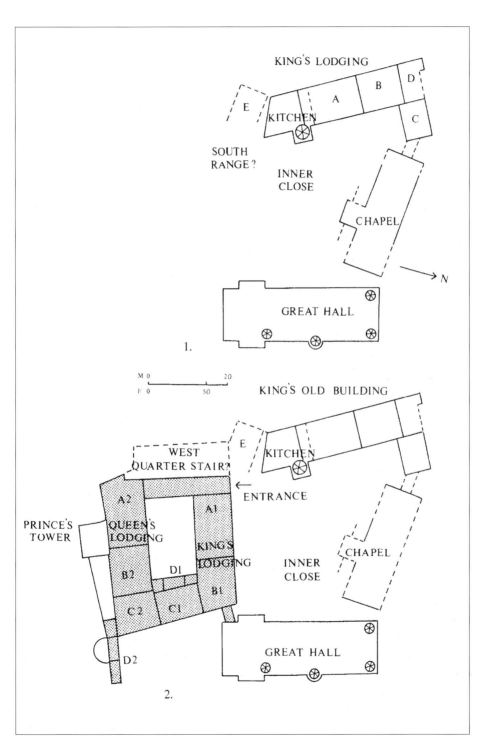

KING'S LODGING

E

KITCHEN

A

B

D

C

SOUTH
RANGE?

INNER
CLOSE

CHAPEL

N

GREAT HALL

1.

M 0   20
F 0   50

KING'S OLD BUILDING

WEST
QUARTER STAIR?

E

KITCHEN

ENTRANCE

A2

A1

PRINCE'S
TOWER

QUEEN'S
LODGING

KING'S
LODGING

CHAPEL

INNER
CLOSE

B2

D1

B1

C2

C1

D2

GREAT HALL

2.

*2.5 Stirling Castle.
First-floor sketch-
plans.
1 James IV; A, B,
C, King's Hall,
Great Chamber
and Chamber,
D King's Closet
and Wardrobe (?),
E Early Chapel.
2. James V: A1,
B1, C1, D1, King's
Hall, Outer
Chamber,
Chamber and
Closets; A2, B2,
C2, D2, Queen's
Hall, Outer
Chamber,
Chamber and
Closets, E Early
Chapel.*

by Hamilton) amount to £783 (*TA*, vii, 159, 470–471, 482; viii, 31, 37, 47, 55), bringing the recorded expenditure to some £2243. To arrive at the overall total it would be necessary to add in the very large sums that must have been accounted for separately by Hamilton, but these are unquantifiable. Bearing in mind what we know of the scale of Hamilton's operations and having regard to the known expenditure on contemporary works at Holyroodhouse and Falkland, however, it would be surprising if the palace, with its abundant carved detail in stone and timber, cost less than £10,000 to complete.

There is almost no direct evidence as to the identity of the craftsmen and designers employed at the palace. If the dates of construction proposed above are broadly correct, however, the work at Stirling must have overlapped with operations at the palaces of Linlithgow and Falkland. Between them these two projects are likely to have absorbed a high proportion of the skilled craftsmen that were available locally and one of the attractions of contracting the Stirling project out to Hamilton may have been that he would be responsible for recruiting his own labour force.

Be that as it may, we know that Robert Robertson, the carver who was master of work during the closing stages of the building campaign, had been employed at Falkland in 1538. Of his fellow craftsman there, John Drummond, the king's wright, it was recorded in a history of the Drummond family compiled in 1681 that 'he wrought for King James the Fyfth the fine timber work in the Castle of Stirline' (Drummond 1831, 62). Either or both of these may have had a hand in the design and execution of the fittings of the royal apartments, about which more is said in Chapter 5. Another name that has been suggested is that of Andrew Mansioun, the French carver and wright, who is known to have been active in the royal works at this time (p 162).

So far as master-masons are concerned, we do not know the identity of any of the Stirling operatives and with one or two obvious exceptions, such as the chimneypieces in the royal chambers, which resemble one at Linlithgow, there is nothing either in the overall design or detail of the palace to suggest close links with any other royal house. In view of the markedly French character of much of the detail, however, it is worth recalling that of the six French masons apparently sent to James V by the Duke and Duchess of Guise in the spring of 1539 only three (initially four) appear to have been employed at Falkland (*TA*, vii, 48, 184, 330; *MW*, i, 252–256, 277–278; *Balcarres Papers*, i, 20, 33.). Possibly the others were assigned to the work at Stirling. It is also of interest to find that the French master-mason, Nicholas Roy, who was probably responsible for some of the best of the carved detail at Falkland, was a member of the household of Mary of Guise, the Queen Dowager, at Stirling Castle *c.* 1543–44 and was employed by her on works in the royal park (Marshall 1993, 139; NLS MS. 29.2.5, fol. 9).

There is evidence that Sir James Hamilton took a close interest in the progress of the work, spending a great deal of time on site (*TA*, vii, 482) and on occasion apparently personally transporting building materials (*TA*, viii, 37). Knowing what we do of his career and reputation, it seems likely that Hamilton also had some input to the design, but the extent of this contribution, as of any made by the king himself, must remain uncertain.

The design of the palace is in several respects a remarkable one. The most economical way of providing new royal lodgings at Stirling would have been by refurbishing, and if necessary extending, the existing accommodation, as was done in similar circumstances at Linlithgow and Falkland. Instead, the king chose to retain his father's lodging on the west side of the upper square — perhaps the initial idea was that this would serve as a separate state suite as at Holyroodhouse and Falkland — and build a completely new pair of lodgings on a cramped and steeply sloping site partly occupied by existing buildings.

The ingenious solution adopted to overcome these difficulties was to set out the royal lodgings, all on one level, round three sides of a very tight hollow

2.6 Stirling Castle. Prince's Tower of c.1500–02 (left) and palace of c.1538–42.

2.7 Stirling Castle.
South-east corner
of James V's palace
showing sculptured
figures of St
Michael (left) and
Jupiter.

square. This inner court, known as the Lions' Den, is too small and secluded to permit much architectural elaboration, but externally there are two show-fronts overlooking the approach with a third facing on to the inner close. Here the designer has turned the disparity of levels to advantage by placing the principal entrance at the upper corner, where it could give direct access to the royal apartments without the use of steps. Elsewhere there is an undercroft of varying height, while above the very grand royal rooms there is a low and inconspicuous second storey probably intended for courtiers and officials.

The Stirling show fronts are divided into bays in which large, iron-grilled windows alternate with shallow, cusp-headed recesses containing sculptured figures supported on candelabra columns. Above, smaller columned figures perch on a cornice of winged cherubs' heads, the whole scheme possibly symbolising the four quarters of the heavens and the influence of the planetary deities (Shire 1996a, 72–84). The carving is exuberant, but coarser than that seen in contemporary work at Falkland and the way in which the bay design turns the corners of the principal façade is more than a little awkward. Much of the carved detail is most closely paralleled in near contemporary French architecture, including two buildings associated with Mary of Guise, namely the north wing of Châteaudun, the residence of her first husband the Duke of Longueville, and the palace of her uncle, the Duke of Lorraine, at Nancy, where a magnificent circular staircase, now demolished, incorporated buttresses decorated with sculptured figures, together with a further series of smaller figures at parapet level not unlike those at Stirling and Falkland[7] (Babelon 1989, 73–76, 96–89). It is also interesting to find that the planning of the Renaissance château built by Mary's father, the Duke of Guise, at Joinville during the late 1530s and early 1540s was similar to that of the palace of Stirling in that it comprised a very grand principal storey set over a service basement with only subsidiary accommodation above (Babelon 1989, 394–399).

2.6
C.11

Holyrood Palace

THE LATE MEDIEVAL ROYAL GUEST-HOUSE

Unlike the palaces of Linlithgow, Falkland and Stirling, Holyroodhouse originated not as a purpose-built royal residence, but as a guest-house within a conveniently placed monastery (Harrison 1919; RCAHMS 1951, 144–153; Gifford *et al.* 1984, 125–148; Fawcett 1988; Gow 1995; Cross 1994, 249–268) As in the parallel case of Dunfermline, the royal connection was important from the beginning for the Augustinian abbey of the Holy Rude had been founded by David I and he and his successors are likely to have been regular visitors. But it was not until the Stewart kings made Edinburgh the capital of Scotland in the

C.12

fifteenth century that the attractions of the abbey as a royal residence came to be fully appreciated.

The nearby castle of Edinburgh, of course, offered greater security, but there was not a great deal of space on the rock summit and, as Bishop Gavin Douglas remarked, living conditions there were 'wyndy and richt unpleasand' (RCAHMS 1951, 144). The abbey was no less well situated for the conduct of government business and its pleasant gardens and orchards provided welcome relief from the smell and bustle of the adjacent burgh. So it is not surprising that we find increasing evidence of royal use from about the beginning of the fifteenth century onwards. James II, for example, was born at Holyroodhouse in 1430, crowned in the abbey church seven years later and eventually buried there (Dunbar 1906, 195–200).

At first the cost of accommodating the king and his household seems to have fallen almost entirely upon the abbot and convent, with the royal exchequer occasionally contributing towards provisions or specific expenses (*ER*, i, 202, 224; ii, 418, 521; iii, 515; v, 382, 619; vii, 615). Likewise the fabric of the lodging was maintained by the abbey, although there were occasions, such as the preparations for the wedding of James II to Mary of Gueldres at Holyrood in 1449, when the king appears to have funded a certain amount of structural work (*ER*, v, 346–347). Initially, royal visitors were presumably housed in one or other of the monastic guest-houses, but during the second half of the fifteenth century there is evidence to suggest that they were occupying specific accommodation on a permanent or semi-permanent basis. In 1473 the Treasurer paid 5s to a glazing wright in the abbey to install or repair a window in the queen's chamber (*TA*, i, 46), while during the 1490s we hear of the 'king's chamber in the abbey of Holyrood' and likewise of the king's closet (*Prot. Bk. Young*, 113, 173, 214; *TA*, i, 355). The precise whereabouts of the royal lodging are not known, but it probably lay a little to the west of the abbey church and conventual buildings. Indeed, as suggested below, there is some reason to think that it may have stood close to the site now occupied by the great tower of James V.

JAMES IV'S NEW PALACE

James IV was a particularly frequent visitor to Holyrood, sometimes holding Yule there (*TA*, i, *passim*) and it was he who decided to convert the royal lodging into what was described in a document of 1503 as 'the king's palace near the abbey of Holyrood' and in 1513 as the palace of Edinburgh (*Prot. Bk. Young*, 310; *TA*, iv, 528). While this decision can be seen as the logical response to the Stewart's growing preference for Holyrood as their principal residence in the Edinburgh area, the actual timing of events seems to have been dictated by the king's desire to provide suitable premises for the reception of his long-awaited English bride, Margaret Tudor, whom he was to wed in the abbey church in August 1503.

Possibly because of the pressure of building activity at the other royal castles and palaces and consequent difficulties in obtaining men and materials, operations were slow to get under way. The first we hear of building at Holyroodhouse is in October 1501, just when the Scottish Commissioners were leaving for London to conclude the formal negotiations for the royal alliance (*TA*, ii, pp. liii–vi, 83–84), and work did not begin in earnest until the autumn of 1502. As a result the palace was not completed until more than a year after the wedding.

Although a complete series of Treasurer's accounts survives for the period February 1501 to February 1505, the entries are brief and selective and this makes the record difficult to interpret (*TA*, ii, 87, 139, 145, 269–281,[8] 344, 369–370, 374, 380–383, 392–393, 398). We hear of the construction of a forework and new chapel under the direction of the king's master-mason, Walter Merlioun, who had only just completed a major project at the castle of Dunbar[9] (*TA*, i, 328, 364; ii, 86). He began work in October 1502, almost simultaneously with the start of construction on a windowed gallery by another mason, William Turnbull, who had been transferred from the labour force at Falkland Palace. Turnbull was subsequently joined by another Falkland mason, John Brown, while Michael Wright (probably a wright by trade as well as by name) was responsible for the erection and fitting out of the queen's great chamber, which may have been largely of timber construction. Stone for these works was no doubt obtained locally, but great quantities of timber were imported from the Baltic. Glass, too, had to be imported, although we are not told its origin, while plaster was shipped from France.

The pace of work increased throughout the early summer of 1503, reaching a peak in July, when the monthly expenditure amounted to £867. Following the royal wedding on the 8th August, operations continued throughout the autumn and winter and to a lesser extent during the summer of 1504 and the grant of an annual pension of £40 to Mr Leonard Logy, the master of works, in September of that year for 'his diligent and grete laboure made be him in the building of the palace beside the Abbay of the Holy Croce' indicates that the building was by then more or less complete (*TA*, ii, pp. lxxxi–lxxxii; *RMS*, ii, No. 2752). The final payment for fitting out the new chapel, however, was not made until January 1505.

As usual, the form of these accounts is such that it is not possible to make an exact calculation of costs, but recorded expenditure amounted to about £3800, excluding furnishings, which seems cheap in comparison with the £6125 spent on the wedding celebrations themselves (*ER*, xii, p. liv).

Since almost nothing now remains of the buildings mentioned in the documents, we cannot be certain of the layout of James IV's palace. We know from the masters of works' accounts of the 1530s, however, that the new chapel stood on what was eventually to become the north side of the inner quadrangle of Holyroodhouse and that the queen's lodging occupied all or part of the south side of that quadrangle, with her great chamber at the west end (*MW*, i, 188, 191; *TA*, v, 220). So it looks as if the new palace included two wings pushed out westwards at right angles from the west claustral range of the medieval abbey. The accounts of 1501–05 make no mention of work on the king's chambers, which suggests that the existing royal lodging may in part have been integrated within the new palace. If so, it probably occupied what was to become the west side of the inner quadrangle, because we know from John Young's account of the royal wedding that the queen's chambers communicated with the king's and that the king's chambers lay adjacent to the chapel (Leland 1770, iv, 300; *TA*, v, 219). We shall consider the possible planning of the royal lodging in more detail in Chapter 5.

It would seem likely, therefore, that James IV's palace of Holyroodhouse, like those of Linlithgow and Falkland, was of quadrangular plan and that it occupied roughly the same position as the present inner quadrangle of the palace. All the principal rooms, including the chapel and royal lodging, appear to have been at first-floor level. There was also an outer court, described by

2.8 Holyrood Palace. James IV's gatehouse from the west by Thomas Sandby. To the rear stands the great tower of the palace.

John Young in 1503 as the 'basse Courte' (Leland 1770, 298), to the west, while the forework mentioned in the accounts is probably the gatehouse at the north-west corner of the present forecourt, of which part still survives. This was being completed in July 1503, when plaster was purchased 'to the turatis of the forzet in Halyrudhous' and Thomas Galbraith, one of the clerks of the chapel royal in Stirling and a skilled painter, was paid for illuminating the king's arms set over the outer gate[10] (TA,, ii, 273–274, 383, 416; Apted and Hannabuss 1978, 40–41). It is possible that this entry superseded an earlier abbey gatehouse occupying a similar position. The new gatehouse, described as the Abbay Yet in documents of the 1530s, seems to have served both the abbey and the palace (*RSS*, ii, Nos. 1535 and 2360). The outer court was sometimes used for tilting and it is possible that the windowed gallery mentioned above was used to accommodate spectators at events of that kind[11]. At the royal wedding of 1503 'Jousts war apoynted in the basse Courte before the Wyndowes'. The king's party occupied one group of windows, while the queen's party looked out of the windows of her great chamber at the south-west corner of the inner court (Leland 1770, iv, 298). It has to be said that no gallery is visible in the forecourt as depicted in the bird's eye view of 1544 (Harrison 1919, opp. 34).

So far as we can judge from the surviving series of Treasurers' accounts — those for the period August 1508 to August 1511 are missing — only minor works were carried out at Holyroodhouse during the latter part of James IV's reign. The most important of these was the erection of a tower, perhaps the one subsequently known as the south tower, by Walter Merlioun in the latter part of 1505 at a cost of £133 (*TA*, iii. 84–86). Then in 1511–13 we hear of the building, or rebuilding, of the queen's gallery and of a lion house, as well as of repairs to the chapel, royal chambers and kitchen (*TA*, iv, 100, 275–276, 372, 375, 377, 528–529). In 1503 canvas was purchased for the windows of the queen's gallery in Edinburgh, but it is not clear whether this was situated at the castle or the palace (*TA*, ii, 410). The south tower seems to have contained additional accommodation for the sovereign (*MW*, i, 27) and to have stood near the south-east corner of the forecourt, close to what later became known as the south garden (Mylne 1893, opp. 169). Indeed, it is possible that the south garden was actually formed at this time, for we know that in 1507 a loch lying beside the abbey was drained to provide garden ground (*TA*, iii, 299; iv, 44). It was no doubt within the royal gardens that the king's growing menagerie was housed (p. 209).

Many of these features recall those created by James's father-in-law, Henry VII, at the royal palaces of Richmond and Windsor, and also at the Tower of London, in the early 1500s (Thurley 1993, 27–34). There the new works were designed to provide additional private living-space for the king and queen within a recreational setting and it may well be that the south tower and queen's gallery at Holyroodhouse were intended to serve a similar purpose.

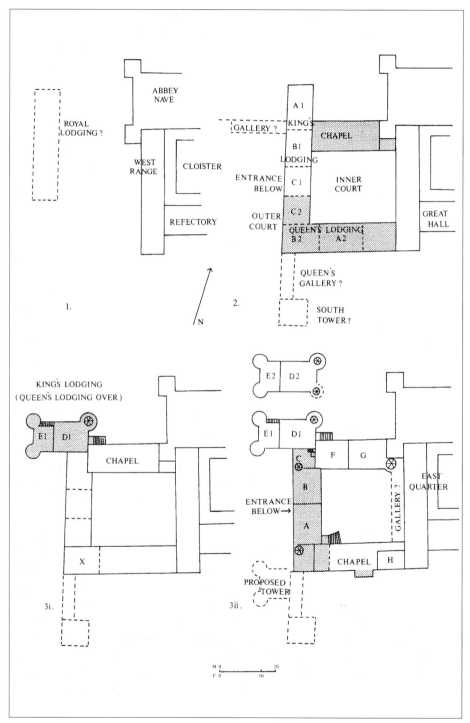

*2.9 Holyrood
Palace. First-floor
sketch plans.
1 before 1500.
2. James IV: A1,
B1, C1, King's
Hall (?), Great
Chamber (?) and
Chamber (?); A2,
B2, C2, Queen's
Hall (?), Great
Chamber and
Chamber (?);
3i James V 1532–35
and 3ii James V
1536 onwards;
A Outer Chamber,
B Mid Chamber,
C Inner Chamber
and Wardrobe,
D1, E1, King's
Outer Chamber
and Inner
Chamber, D2, E2,
Queen's Outer
Chamber and
Inner Chamber;
F North Chamber,
G Council House,
H Vestry, X Hall
for Household.*

Other named buildings include the treasure house (*TA*, iii, 390) and the hall, which was big enough for the king to practise shooting in with his culverin on winter days (*TA*, iv, 98, 103). This is presumably the building described in 1486 as 'the great hall of the monastery of Holyrood' (*Prot. Bk. Young*, 14), but subsequently appropriated for royal use. It seems to have stood on the south side of the abbey cloister, which suggests that it originally served as the monastic refectory[12] (*MW*, i, 72, 103, 193). There is also mention of various chambers allocated to the king's secretary and other officers of the household (*TA*, iv, 528–529; v, 114). Some of these may have been situated in the west claustral range of the abbey, although it is only in the next reign that there is specific evidence to suggest that all or part of this range had been absorbed within the palace.

THE REMODELLING OF THE PALACE BY JAMES V

Following James IV's death at Flodden, court life continued on a much reduced scale. The Duke of Albany, who held office as governor for the first ten years or so of the young king's minority, spent a good deal of time at Holyroodhouse during his periodic visits from France. A wide-ranging programme of refurbishment was carried out at the palace at the time of Albany's first arrival in 1515 and steps were subsequently taken to ensure that the fabric remained in good repair (*TA*, v, 10–16, 37, 78–82, 93, 95–96, 115, 219–221, 325–328; *ER*, xiv, 162).

Between James V's assumption of the royal prerogative in 1528 and his death 14 years later major building campaigns were undertaken at nearly all the principal royal castles and palaces. So far as Holyroodhouse is concerned, three schemes of work can be distinguished (Dunbar 1964). The first, undertaken between 1528 and 1532, saw the erection of a new royal lodging at the north-west corner of James IV's palace. This took the form of a massive rectangular tower 2.10 with engaged rounds at the corners, which still survives as the dominating feature of the palace frontispiece. During the second scheme, from 1535–36, the west range of James IV's palace was replaced by a new forework housing additional reception rooms, while the north and south quarters were extensively remodelled, the south one being converted to accommodate an entirely new chapel royal. Our knowledge of the third scheme derives mainly from an outline sketch and accompanying note scribbled on Mylne'e survey of 1663, which 2.13 indicates that it was 'the old desyne off King James the 5' to erect the front of a second great tower at the south-west corner of the palace[13] (Mylne 1893, opp. 148). This ambitious proposal to create a symmetrical façade with matching towers was presumably cut short by James's premature death and it was left to his great-great grandson, Charles II, to implement the scheme to the designs of Sir William Bruce.

2.10 Holyrood
Palace. Great
tower of c. 1528–32
from the west. The
sash windows were
installed during the
1670s.

62

James V's building operations are recorded in a number of masters of works' accounts. The series is not complete, but those accounts that do survive are quite full, making it possible to chart the progress of the work in considerable detail. The erection of the 'tour and new werk of Halyrudhous' (*MW*, i, 1–55, 56–103) was probably begun in the late summer or autumn of 1528, but the first years' accounts are missing and when the second book commences in late August 1529 the main fabric of the ground floor was already complete and the masons were working 'abone the woltis', i.e. on the first floor. The construction of the great tower evidently required the dismantling of part of the north-west corner of James IV's palace, where the king's suite was situated, so James V took up temporary residence in the south tower. Other contingency arrangements included the erection of a masons' lodge in the abbey churchyard and the utilisation of the great hall as a joiners' shop (*MW*, i, 17–18, 27, 69–73). The south tower remained standing until the 1670s (*MW*, i, 332, 336; ii, 398; *TA*, xii, 348) and may be the building depicted at the south end of the west front of the palace on Gordon's view of 1647.[14]

By May 1530 the walls had been carried a storey higher and joists to cover the first floor were arriving on site. Scottish oak was employed for this purpose, but most of the timber required for the construction of the tower, comprising mainly oak and pine, seems to have been imported from the Low Countries and the Baltic, while some of the wall-plates for the angle-rounds were made up of old ships' timbers. The demands of the masons were such that several quarries were at times worked simultaneously. Unhewen rubble for the main body of the walls was obtained from the nearby quarry at Salisbury Craig, but freestone and ashlar for external facework and dressings had to be brought from Leith Hill, Ravelston, Niddrie, Stenhouse and Culross. Lime was carted from Cousland and Gilmerton to be mixed with sand from Leith Links to make mortar while oyster shells were gathered, presumably from the foreshore of the Forth Estuary, to be used as pinnings for ashlar masonry (*MW*, i, 2–4, 7, 11, 26, 29, 35, 38, 55, 76, 91, 96).

The accounts for the next twelve months are missing, but good progress was evidently made on the two upper floors, for by the time the fourth book opens in September 1531 the tower was ready to be roofed. The roof itself seems to have been partly prefabricated and when it was finally placed in position in mid November eight workmen were needed for a whole week 'lyftand the grete plaitform ruyf and wynnand the samen to the hous heid'; the roof was then covered with lead. The upperworks of the tower were next completed and as a final touch the conical roofs of the two west rounds were capped with ornamental finials in the form of lions and miniature turrets, all brightly painted and gilded. Meanwhile work was proceeding on the fitting out of the interior, the principal chambers being lined with Baltic pine and enriched with panelling and other carved decoration.[15] (*MW*, i, 64, 71, 74, 76, 79, 87, 91). The existing compartmented timber ceilings on the second floor of the tower, although subsequently refurbished, are probably survivors of this scheme. Christmas celebrations at the palace were not allowed to disrupt operations, although the wrights had to vacate the great hall to enable the traditional Yule festivities to take place. By this time virtually all the tower windows had been fitted with iron bars or grilles and when spring came these were given a protective coating of red lead and paint. Most of the iron required for these fittings, as also for the tradesmens' tools and equipment, appears to have been imported from France and Spain, but some use seems also to have been made of the products of the emerging native iron-smelting industry of Wester Ross[16] (*MW*, i, 2, 5–6, 59, 68, 74, 86; Macadam 1886–87, 102).

Among the last accounts to be made up were those of Thomas Peebles, the king's glazier. Peebles had been looking after the glasswork of the royal palaces since the beginning of the century and occupied his own house within the precincts of Holyroodhouse (p. 235); in all probability he had fitted out James IV's palace thirty years previously (*MW*, i, 93–95). As we shall see when we consider the planning arrangements of the royal lodging in Chapter 5, his accounts are of particular interest in that they enable us to identify many of the rooms. The other principal craftsmen employed included John Ayton, king's master-mason, who probably designed the tower. He died before January 1532, when he was succeeded by John Brownhill (p. 227). The wrights and carvers were headed by John Drummond, king's wright, and included Richard Stewart, Alan Carvour, and Robert Robertson, most of whom, like Brownhill, subsequently worked at Falkland. The master of works was Mr John Scrymgeour, then just beginning his long and distinguished career as principal master of works.

In the original arrangement the principal approach to the tower appears to have been by way of a forestair leading to a first-floor doorway in the east wall. This doorway, which gave direct access to the royal lodging, was secured by an iron yett and drawbridge, while several of the internal doorways of the tower were provided with yetts and draw-bars (*MW*, i, 18, 24, 29, 33, 40). The drawbridge may have continued in use until the construction of the north gallery in the 1570s (*TA*, xiii, 150–151, 162). It is noticeable that the great tower is set obliquely to the main axis of the palace, which appears to be governed by the

2.9   orientation of the abbey church. This may have come about accidentally, but is more likely to arise from the fact that the tower was laid out at right angles to the west range of James IV's palace which itself reflected the alignment of an earlier building on the site, perhaps the late medieval royal lodging.

The great tower seems to have been substantially complete by the late summer of 1532. The master of works' account for 1531–32 records expenditure of about £1608 on new work, together with some £200 on repairs to the earlier palace. To this can be added the £1567 recorded in the 1529–30 account and the £2273 noted in the Treasurer's accounts as having been expended between October 1530 and September 1531 to give a total of about £5448 for the three years for which at least rough figures are available (*MW*, i, 55; 56–114; *TA*, v, 389, 433; vi, 33). When allowance is made for the missing account for 1528–9 total expenditure on the great tower can be estimated at at least £7000.

The second scheme of work was carried through with a much greater sense of urgency than the first, the entire operation apparently being completed between June 1535 and the late autumn of the following year. As in the case of James IV's building programme, the time scale was probably geared to the progress of the king's matrimonial negotiations, which culminated in his wedding to Madeleine de Valois in Paris on 1st January 1537. The king brought his young bride home to the newly refurbished palace in May, only to see her die there a few weeks later.

With time evidently at a premium the early summer of 1535 saw the rapid assembly of a large labour force in and around Holyroodhouse. Additional masons were recruited throughout Lothian and Fife, as also from Dundee and Perth, and by October more than 80 masons and nearly 20 wrights and carvers were employed on site (*MW*, i, 153–167, 170–175). For the most part materials were obtained from the same sources as in the previous phase of operations, but additional stone quarries were worked and roofing slates were shipped from Caithness and lead from Dundee, whither it may have been imported from Hull, or one of the other eastern English ports. Lochaber is specifically mentioned as a source for the supply of native timber (*MW*, i, 136, 138, 181–182, 188, 194).

It was evidently decided at the outset that, while the north and south quarters of James IV's palace could be adapted for new uses, the west range would have to be entirely rebuilt. Accordingly, the start of building operations saw workmen engaged in taking down the walls of the west quarter and preparing the foundations of the new forework, or fore entry. Much of the face work was no doubt re-used in the construction of the new building, while the rubble core of the old walls was ground down to make aggregate for mortar (*MW*, i, 134, 167–168).

The work advanced rapidly and by late September 1535 the quarriers at Ravelston were furnishing lintels for the first-floor windows of the state rooms. A month later 'ane gret stane to the gret armis of the new werk' was quarried at Preston and carted to St Paul's Work, Edinburgh, where it was carved to a design by John Kilgour, the heraldic painter, candlelight being provided for the masons during the dark December days. Following a short break for Yule, the masons cut stone for parapets and battlements and by May 1536 the stonework of the new work seems to have been virtually complete. One of the final tasks was to place the great stone panel bearing the royal arms over the central

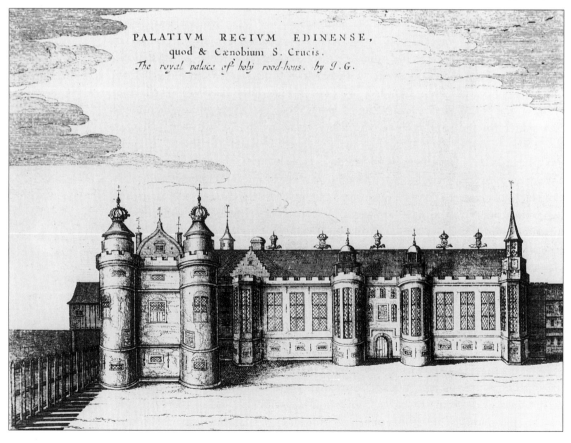

2.11 Holyrood
Palace. West front
of James V's palace
by James Gordon,
c.1649. The west
range contained a
suite of three
reception rooms
linked to the king's
and queen's private
quarters in the
great tower.

gateway, where it can be clearly seen in Gordon's view of *c.*1649, drawn about 25 years before the building was demolished (*MW,* i, 138, 144, 162–165, 170, 185; Fawcett 1988, 5).

Internally, the new state rooms were expensively fitted out with timber linings or panelling, compartmented ceilings with ornamental finials, and large quantities of plain and painted glass. The floors seem to have been paved with a mixture of local freestone and imported tile (*MW,* i, 136, 184, 190–191). More is said about the fittings of these rooms in Chapter 5. Among the other works carried out at this time the most important was the construction of a new chapel on the first floor of the south quarter, occupying part of the area formerly taken up by the queen's lodgings. The chapel, which was roofed in December 1535, was approached by an elaborate stone stair so placed as to give access also to the adjacent state rooms. The fittings of the chapel are described in Chapter 4.

In the north quarter James IV's chapel was dismantled and a new first-floor room, known at first as 'the north chalmer nixt the tour', and subsequently as

PALATIVM REGIVM EDINENSE,
quod & Cænobium S. Crucis.
The royal palace of holy rood-hous. by J.G.

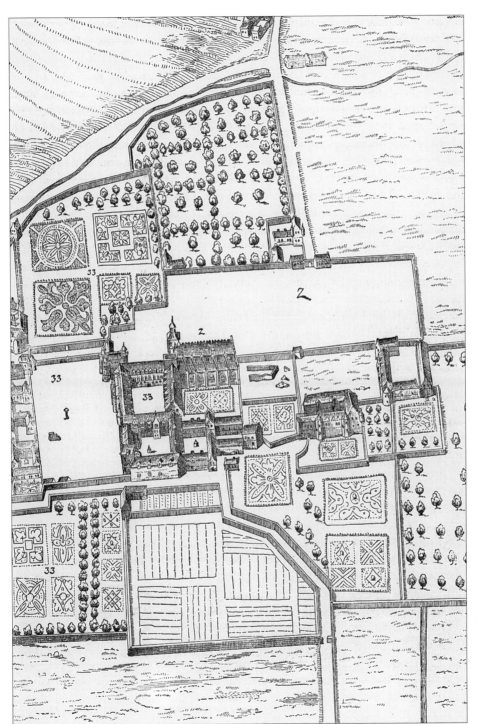

2.12 Holyrood
Palace. Bird's eye
view from the
south by James
Gordon, 1647. The
forecourt and inner
court of the palace
(both numbered
33) are clearly
visible, while to
the east is the nave
of the abbey
church, with the
former cloister laid
out as a garden.
To the south are
subsidiary courts,
two of them
containing wells.
Among the
buildings to the
east of the main
complex are the
commendator's
house and the
dean's house.

the privy chamber, was constructed. The remainder of the range at this level was remodelled to contain a single, large room known as the council house, which was used for meetings of the council and certain other formal occasions. Elsewhere in the palace two coats of arms, made of lead, were provided for the west front of the great tower while another, of carved stone, seems to have been affixed to the east quarter. This east quarter was in all probability the former west range of the abbey cloister (p. 61) and the fact that it begins to appear in the documents under its new name at this period indicates that it was by now regarded as forming part of the royal palace. The east range was probably occupied, at least in part, by chambers allocated to household officials and others having frequent business at court. Other parts of the palace mentioned at this period include the governor's tower, 'the auld quenis lach — chalmeris' (perhaps part of Queen Margaret Tudor's former lodging in the south quarter), the long gallery, the armoury, the forging house, the tapiser's house (tapestry-maker's house), the cunyiehouse (mint) and various kitchens and other ancillary buildings (*MW*, i, 166, 170, 186, 188, 190–194, 223–225, 242, 290; *TA*, viii, 173).

2.12   Some of these buildings were probably grouped round lesser courts lying to the south and south-east of the principal court, or inner close. Although these courts are depicted on the bird's eye view of 1544 (Harrison 1919, opp. p. 34), it is difficult to identify individual buildings. Further work was also carried out on the royal gardens at this time under the direction of a French gardener (*MW*, i, 191–192). The reference is probably to the garden on the south side of the palace, for it would seem that the north garden, also depicted on the view of 1544, did not pass into the possession of the crown until the late 1550s (*TA*, x, 394).

The building operations of 1535–36 cost about £5680, a small part of which was spent on repairs and minor alterations (*MW*, i, 132–195). The principal craftsmen were mostly the same as in the first phase, but with the addition of a certain 'Andreis Francheman', perhaps to be identified with Andrew Mansioun, a French carver afterwards employed in the royal service (p. 162). As before, Mr John Scrymgeour acted as master of work, subsequently receiving specific recognition of his services. There is also record of small works on various parts of the palace during the closing years of James V's reign, including preparations for the reception of the king's second wife, Mary of Guise, in the summer of 1538 (*MW*, i, 219–227, 242, 288–290).

James V's building programme at Holyroodhouse was the first major project undertaken by the royal works since his father's death some 20 years previously. We do not know what part, if any, the king himself played in the design process, but the distinctive character of the architecture may indicate that the on-site master-masons, John Ayton and John Brownhill, played a predominant role. Nor can we be certain whether the three phases of building, or proposed building, that have been described were conceived from the outset as components of a single design or whether the final scheme evolved over a period of years. It seems likely, however, that the erection of the great tower was initially undertaken as a self-contained operation and that its successful completion encouraged the king, firstly to remodel the remainder of the palace, and then to contemplate the construction of a second tower. Even without this final phase, total expenditure on new works and associated alterations must have amounted to well over £12,000.

Within this wide-ranging programme of building we can recognise a number of familiar elements and others that are decidedly novel. Although no other Scottish royal palace of the sixteenth century could boast a residential tower like that at Holyroodhouse, great towers of a similar kind were a characteristic feature of late medieval castles and palaces in several Western European countries. While such towers had a particular function — usually that of providing separate residential accommodation for the lord —, they were also seen as status symbols and great importance was attached to giving them an impressive external appearance. English examples include Tattershall, Lincolnshire (*c.*1430–50) and Ashby de la Zouche, Leicestershire (*c.*1470–80), while in Scotland David's Tower at Edinburgh Castle (*c.*1368–72) can be seen as a forerunner and Bishop Stewart's magnificent tower at Spynie (*c.*1460–80) as a mature specimen of the type.

With its circular angle-turrets, however, Holyroodhouse is closer to some prominent French examples, such as Vincennes (*c.*1360–70) and the Tour Maubergeon at Poitiers (*c.*1395–1400), and its bossed window-grilles (*MW*, i, 68), tiered upperworks and steep, conical roofs are also decidedly French in character.[17] Nearer home a number of these features had recently appeared in James IV's impressive gatehouse at Stirling Castle. It may also be significant that great towers remained fashionable in Early Tudor England. Henry VII re-housed himself in great splendour within the early fifteenth-century donjon at Richmond (1498–1501) and erected an entirely new tower at Greenwich (*c.*1500–04), while as late as *c.*1530 Henry VIII built a small donjon at Hampton Court (Thurley 1993, 27–52).

The great tower at Greenwich was entirely domestic in character and structurally integral with the remainder of the royal suite. In contrast, James V's tower at Holyroodhouse provided a high degree of security and access to the rest of the palace was strictly controlled. As well as being equipped with a drawbridge and numerous iron grilles, there is evidence to suggest that the tower was originally protected by a moat, at least on the north side (Harrison 1919, 58), In addition, the ground floor was provided with gun-ports (now mostly blocked), as was the new forework of 1535–36. These features were not installed simply for show, for we know that Holyroodhouse continued to be used as an

2.13 Holyrood
Palace. Part of
first-floor plan by
John Mylne, 1663.
Note the dotted
outline of the
second great tower
proposed by James
V, but not
implemented until
the 1670s.

artillery park at this period and it would seem that the upperworks of the tower
were equipped with 'certane small munitioun' — presumably small cannon —
which were serviced on the premises. Despite these precautions, the palace seems
to have offered no resistance to the devastating English raid of 1544, although
it may be significant that the interior of the great tower appears to have escaped
the fire that engulfed the remainder. (*MW*, i, 185; *TA*, v, 259, 266; vi, 420,
438; vii, 350; viii, 236). We do not know how the tower, when first built, communicated with the rest of the palace. After the alterations of 1535–36 there was
direct communication between the tower and the west range at first-floor level.
On the ground floor the tower and west range were separated by a passage

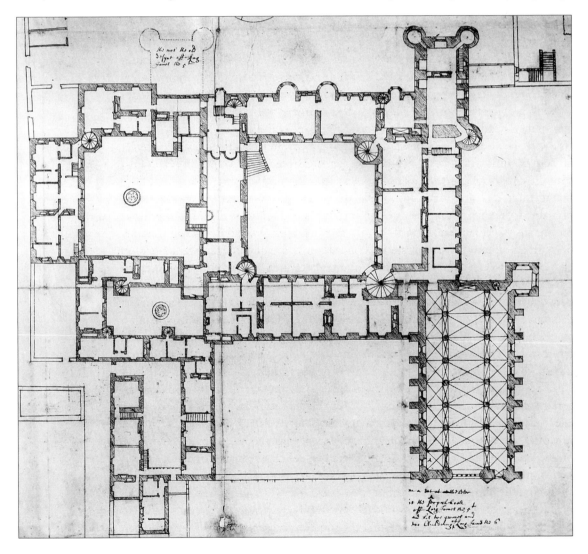

which may have communicated with the stair in the south-east corner of the tower.

While the first phase of James V's programme was essentially conservative in character, the second introduced several important new elements. The construction of a series of new state rooms in the forework, or west quarter, made it possible to separate public and private space more effectively than in the earlier palace and these arrangements are discussed in Chapter 5. The great scale stair in the south-west corner of the inner court was also an unusual feature in that it broke away from the tradition of extruded spiral stairs. As depicted in Mylne's plan of 1663, this has the appearance of an open forestair, like the much earlier one at Linlithgow, but with a balustraded landing having separate doorways to the chapel royal and the state rooms. Whatever its precise construction, the unusual form of this staircase may reflect the influence of current fashions for processional stairs both in France, e.g. at Fontainebleau (Babelon 1989, 201–204) and Early Tudor England, e.g. at Hampton Court (Thurley 1993, 53–54, 118). The Holyroodhouse stair had no immediate successors, however, and other stairs erected there later in the century, were of spiral type.

There is also an intriguing reference in the masters of works' account for 1535–36 to a payment of £13 6s 8d to a certain Alexander Mure 'for ane patrown of ane dowbill turngrece' (the pattern of a double spiral stair) (*MW*, i, 191). This is a very substantial sum to pay for a design and it raises the possibility that the original intention at Holyroodhouse was to build an elaborate double or twin spiral staircase of the kind occasionally found in France and Germany during the late medieval and early Renaissance periods, the best known example being that of *c.*1517–18 at Francis I's château of Chambord (Guillauame 1985, 28, 33–34, 202–203, 210). Alexander Mure does not appear to be mentioned elsewhere in the building accounts, but it is possible that he was the Danish herald of that name who made a number of trips between Scandinavia and the Scottish court at that period (*TA*, v, 440; vi, 46, 153, 263).

Although the great hall on the south side of the cloister was repaired and refurbished at this time (*MW*, i, 189, 191), it had probably by now lost its traditional role as the principal dining room of the king and household (p. 109). The building appears to have been damaged during the English raid of 1544 and following this event the roof was stripped of its lead[18] (*TA*, ix, 44). The later history of the old great hall is uncertain (*TA*, xiii, 81; *MW*, i, 306), but it would seem that from about the middle of the sixteenth century onwards public and ceremonial events were generally held in the new council chamber in the north quarter of the palace, which is described variously as the council chamber, the great hall and the north hall[19] (*CSP*, i, 562; Melville 1827, 179; *MW*, i, 306, 331–332, 340; *Diurnal of Occurrents*, 331).

While the great tower of 1528–32 probably owed a good deal to French prototypes, the design of the west front of the palace may reflect influences from Early Tudor England. The double-towered gateway with its exotic open-work cap-houses, the battlemented parapets, prominent bay-windows and large expanses of glass strongly recall Henry VII's and Henry VIII's palaces of Richmond and Hampton Court, while the fittings of the state rooms and chapel, so far as these can be judged from the documents, seem also to have been mainly of Tudor character. This mingling of French and English elements at Holyroodhouse would have been even more marked had the third and final phase of work been realised, although the nobility of James V's 'grand design' — modest in scale as it was — would have been hard to match in either country.

NOTES

1 I owe this estimate to Dr A. L. Murray.

2 Between the time of the king's death and that of the queen mother late in 1463 the castle was in the hands of Mary of Gueldres and expenditure on works was funded by her exchequer.

3 Dr A. L. Murray has pointed out to me that the running totals in the extant portion of the account for April 1496–31 January 1497 (SRO E/21/4, *TA*, i, 273–311) represent only about two thirds of the total expenditure.

4 The account is defective and the location of the tower is not certain, but the king is known to have been at Stirling at the date in question (*TA*, ii, pp. xxv–xxvi).

5 It may be from this gateway that a passage was made down to the park in 1531 (*TA*, v, 436).

6 Information from Dr Richard Fawcett.

7 Other parallels include cusped arches at Blois and Gaillon (Babelon 1989, 45, 89); twisted columns at Blois, Meillant and Saint-Ouen-de-Chemazé (Babelon 1989, 46, 66, 144–145); winged cherubs' heads at Villers-Cotterêts (staircase ceiling) (Babelon 1989, 217); wreathed candelabra at Blois and Chenonceau (Prinz and Kecks 1985, figs. 336, 349); ribboned branch at Bonnivet (Prinz and Kecks 1985, fig. 340d).

8 See also SRO E 21/6 fols. 54–63.

9 A single reference to Merlioun's work on 'ye foirwerk and ye new hall' is possibly a clerical error (SRO, E 21/6, fol. 54^r), since there is no other evidence to suggest that a new hall was erected at this time.

10 The royal arms are clearly visible in Thomas Sandby's view (NGS D 17^r; copy in NMRS EDD/3/142). Cf. also Sinclair 1904–5.

11 In the accounts the structure is described as 'the gallory and windois' (*TA*, ii, 269).

12 It may have been replaced by the 'New-frater de Halyruidhous' mentioned in a charter of 1564 (*RMS*, iv, No. 1567).

13 The original drawing is in the Bodleian Library, Oxford (Gough Maps, 39, fol. l^v). The note is confirmed in a memorandum, dated 19 October 1663, drawn up by John Mylne for the government of the day (Leicester Record Office. Buckminster Papers 4/10/83).

14 Gordon's view suggests that the tower was obliquely aligned to the west front, like the great tower of James V at the north-west corner. These irregularities are not shown on Mylne's plan of 1663.

15 Gordon's view of 1649 shows that the original tower finials had by then been replaced by imperial crowns. 2.11

16 This assumes that 'Ros irne' (*MW*, i, 6) did, indeed, come from Ross-shire.

17 For French examples of this plan-form see Mesqui 1991–93, i, 148, 157–160, 207–208. For iron grilles see illustration of Saumur in the various editions of *Les Tres Riches Heures du Duc de Berry*.

18 The old great hall may be the large building with a damaged roof shown to the south of the abbey church in the bird's eye view of 1544 (Harrison 1919, opp. 34).

19 Later on there were both an outer and an inner council house (*MW*, ii, 205).

*3.1 Edinburgh
Castle. General
view from the
south east showing
(left to right)
barracks, Queen
Anne Building,
great hall, palace
block and Half
Moon Battery.*

Chapter 3

THE CASTLES OF EDINBURGH AND DOUNE, DUNFERMLINE PALACE AND THE LESSER RESIDENCES

Edinburgh Castle

THE CASTLE, *c.* 1370–1488

Edinburgh Castle was a major royal residence by the time of Malcolm III and Queen Margaret, if not before, and the earliest standing building, St. Margaret's Chapel, belongs to the twelfth century (RCAHMS 1951, 1–25; Gifford *et al.* 1984, 85–102; Fawcett 1986; MacIvor 1993; Cross 1994, 211–37). Since the castle also contains, in the fragmentary remains of David's Tower, what appears to be the earliest surviving royal lodging in Scotland, it is worth going back a little beyond the reign of James I in order to consider this particular building (Oldrieve 1913–14). The structure is poorly documented, but by virtue both of its position, immediately adjacent to the later residential complex, and of its name, which goes back at least to the mid fifteenth century, we can be fairly confident that this was indeed the tower erected by David II during the closing years of his reign (*ER*, v, 311; *TA*, i, 83; v, 120–121). The architectural characteristics of the tower also point to a late fourteenth century date.

Entries in the exchequer rolls between 1368 and 1372 record payment of some £145 for the erection of a building described as the new tower of Edinburgh (*ER*, ii, 308, 364, 393). A further series of entries, extending from 1375–79, records payments for the construction of a tower described as the tower built at the gate of the castle of Edinburgh at a cost of some £580 or more (*ER*, ii, 473, 475–476, 520, 551, 554–555, 557, 608, 621). Although some scholars have taken these latter entries to refer to the completion of David's Tower, it seems more likely that they relate for the most part to the erection of a separate gate-tower, afterwards known as the Constable's Tower. The customs accounts for 1370 and 1371 are missing and either for this, or for some other reason, the

C.13

sum of £145 is unlikely to represent the full cost of David's Tower, which was probably still unfinished at the time of the king's death within the castle in February 1371.[1]

We know little of how David's Tower stood in relation to the hall and other major buildings of the day, but in 1382–83 a kitchen and other offices, all apparently vaulted, were built alongside it (*juxta magnam turrim in castro*) (*ER*, iii, 89). As first built, the tower was of L-plan, comprising a vaulted ground floor and an unknown number of upper storeys, some of which may also have been vaulted; subsequently the re-entrant angle was filled in to make the building almost square on plan. The upper floors of the tower were destroyed during a siege in 1573 and thereafter the surviving stump was immured within the Half Moon Battery, being rediscovered only in 1912. Although it contained a postern doorway on the ground floor, it seems likely that the tower was designed primarily as a royal lodging and its erection can be seen as the first step towards the creation of the palace complex that we see today. This also appears to be the earliest documented example in Scotland of the construction of what we now call a tower-house, and the fact that it was built by the king himself is likely to have contributed a good deal to the increasing popularity of this type of residence among the nobility. The planning arrangements within the tower are discussed in Chapter 5.

3.1

Although the fifteenth century saw a gradual decline in the importance of Edinburgh Castle as a royal residence in favour of Holyrood Abbey, James I and his two immediate successors all spent a good deal of time there. When James regained control of the castle in 1424 he probably found the place in good condition, for a number of the principal buildings, including David's Tower and St. Mary's Chapel, were fairly new and expenditure on repairs and maintenance had continued during the years of the king's captivity.

James I continued to make repairs and improvements to the castle, the bulk of the expenditure being incurred during the latter part of his reign. An account of Robert Gray, a prominent Edinburgh burgess, who was master of the mint as well as master of the fabric at Edinburgh Castle and Leith Palace, records expenditure of some £736 in 1433–34, of which the greater part was evidently laid out on the castle (*ER*, iv, 579). The exchequer rolls for the two previous years are missing, but reference is made to what seems to have been another sizeable account presented during that period (*ER*, iv, 579). Gray's next account, for 1434–35, records expenditure of another £88 at the castle, while other references show that operations continued up to and beyond the time of the king's death in 1437 (*ER*, iv, 599, 601, 603, 611, 619, 623, 625–27; v, 36, 66). The customs accounts for 1436 are missing.

Among the items specifically mentioned, the most interesting is the construction of a new great chamber, which was roofed with lead shipped from

Berwick-on-Tweed. As Iain MacIvor has suggested, this chamber was probably situated adjacent to the king's lodging in David's Tower and part of it may survive within the fabric of the existing palace block (MacIvor 1993, 40). Payment for roofing the great chamber was not made until 1444–45 (*ER*, v, 180). Other works undertaken at this period included the repair and renewal of the kitchens serving the young Duke of Rothesay (the future James II) and the captain of the castle. A herb garden was also formed within the castle at a cost of £8.

James II continued to lay out sizeable sums on the upkeep both of the domestic buildings and of the defences of the castle. Following a siege in 1445, repairs were made to various buildings, including David's Tower and the nearby king's kitchen, while in 1458 we hear of the refurbishment of the hall in preparation for a meeting of parliament (*ER*, v, 98, 104, 274, 311, 347, 687; vi, 4–5, 385, 387). In the absence of the Treasurers' accounts, our information about the building activities of James III is largely confined to the first ten years or so of his reign and even for this period it is very far from complete. There is, however, sufficient evidence to demonstrate that the fabric continued to be kept in a good state of repair. There are also indications that the castle was now beginning to assume an enhanced role as an arsenal for the royal artillery, with on-site facilities for the manufacture and repair of guns (*ER*, vii, 33, 285, 294, 424. 427, 501).[2]

THE REMODELLING OF THE CASTLE BY JAMES IV

Although James IV was responsible for important works at the castle, his building activities there are less well documented than at the other major royal castles and palaces. The architectural evidence suggests that it was James IV, more than any previous monarch, who shifted the residential focus of the castle southwards from the summit area, where the earliest buildings seem to have stood, to the steeply sloping ground overlooking the precipitous south and south-east faces of the castle rock. This move necessitated the construction of a complex series of vaulted cellars and undercrofts to create a level platform for the new buildings. This was a major task and part, at least, of the substructure had probably been formed earlier in the century, in connection with the erection of James I's great chamber. Further work may have been done in the latter part of James III's reign, for which the documentary record is lacking.

The first stage of James IV's building programme seems to have involved the reconstruction of the great chamber to provide a new and more spacious royal lodging. The second was centred on the erection of a new great hall, replacing an earlier one whose location is not known. When complete the new royal lodging and hall formed the east and south sides of a roughly square courtyard (the present Crown Square), of which the north side was occupied by the refurbished chapel of St Mary, originally built, or rebuilt, in the late

3.1

3.2

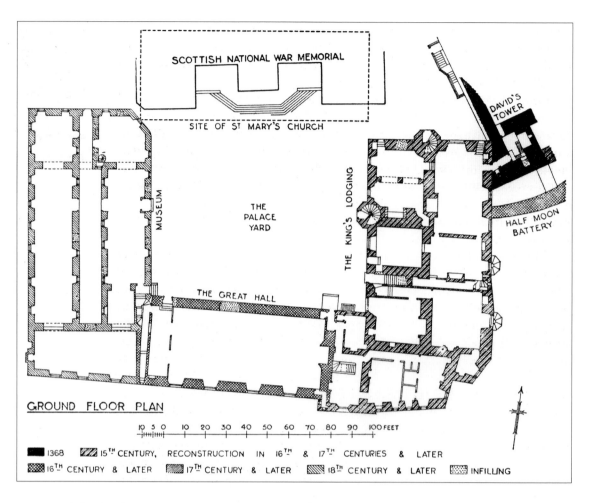

SCOTTISH NATIONAL WAR MEMORIAL

SITE OF ST MARY'S CHURCH

DAVID'S TOWER

MUSEUM

THE KING'S LODGING

THE PALACE YARD

HALF MOON BATTERY

THE GREAT HALL

GROUND FLOOR PLAN

10 5 0   10   20   30   40   50   60   70   80   90   100 FEET

■ 1368   ▨ 15TH CENTURY, RECONSTRUCTION IN 16TH & 17TH CENTURIES & LATER
▩ 16TH CENTURY & LATER   ▨ 17TH CENTURY & LATER   ▨ 18TH CENTURY & LATER   ▨ INFILLING

3.2 Edinburgh Castle. Plan of Crown Square, 1951. James IV's lodging occupied the east half of the palace block ('The King's Lodging') and communicated at its north end with David's Tower.

fourteenth century and now superseded by the Scottish National War Memorial. The general arrangement was thus broadly similar to that of the other palaces constructed by James IV. The west side of the courtyard at Edinburgh may have been occupied by one or more of the arsenal buildings, which were probably approached not from the courtyard itself, but from the lower ground to the north (MacIvor 1993, 59–60).

Although the documentary evidence is too sketchy to furnish anything approaching a full chronology of these operations, it does offer a number of clues as to the timing of events and the identity of the principal craftsmen involved. An instalment payment to John Maware, younger, for roofing 'the gret hous in the Castel of Edinburgh' in February 1497 suggests that the royal lodging was approaching completion at that time (*TA*, i, 319). The roof structure of the king's quarters — perhaps including a ribbed or panelled timber

78

ceiling — was evidently handsome enough to make it worth imitating, for later in the same year one of the wrights employed on the construction of Dunbar Castle was sent to Edinburgh 'to tak the mesure of the ruf of the Kingis chamir to mak Dunbar sic lik' (*TA*, i, 338–339).

Other works under way in 1496–97 included the roofing of the castle chapel — the reference is probably to St Mary's Chapel on the north side of the square rather than to St Margaret's Chapel on the summit — and the construction or reconstruction of the arsenal workshop. Among the carpenters employed were the two John Mawares, father and son, of whom the former had distinguished himself during the reign of James III and continued to receive a royal pension until his death in the early 1500s (p. 234). The names of the master of works and master mason are not recorded. (*TA*, i, 279, 281, 289–290, 301–303, 307, 310, 357, 362).

This phase of work seems to have been concluded by about the turn of the century, for when the Treasurer's accounts become available again in 1501 (there is a gap from mid-May 1498 to February 1501), they show no evidence of any major building activity at the castle — a situation in marked contrast to that which prevailed at Falkland, Stirling and Holyroodhouse. The second stage of James IV's programme was probably commenced some time during the years 1509–10, because when the accounts resume again in August 1511, following a three-year gap, work was evidently in full swing. During the following twelve months or so the very large sum of £1521 (excluding identifiable expenditure on artillery) was laid out on the fabric of the castle, including a final payment, in August 1512, to John Kelso for slating the great hall (*TA*, iv, 278–279). This probably marks the completion, or near completion, of the existing structure. Further references in the accounts, some of them specifically to work on the arsenal, indicate that operations continued into the spring of 1513, when the record again fails (*TA*, iv, 293, 306, 313, 329, 459, 508–520).

The master of works was Thomas Kincaid, who was also constable of the castle (*TA*, iv, 445–446). The master mason is not named, but in view of the markedly Italianate character of the roof corbels of the great hall it may be significant that an Italian mason named Cressent was in the employment of the Crown during 1511–12 (and perhaps earlier) and that his monthly wage of £7 made him one of the highest paid royal craftsmen (p. 229).

There is also an isolated reference in the accounts of the king's chamberlain of the lordship of Fife for 1512–13 to the transport and dressing of timber for the roof of the new chapel of the castle of Edinburgh (*ER*, xiii, 504–505). This may be the building, subsequently used as the garrison chapel, that stood alongside the earlier chapel of St Margaret (MacIvor 1993, 55, 60) and it should not be confused with another new chapel which had been built a few years earlier beneath the south wall of the castle to serve the tournament field, or tiltyard, situated near the king's stables (p. 203). The timber for the chapel roof of *c.*1512 was prepared by John Drummond, the king's carpenter, who probably also erected it. Since Drummond is also known to have played a similar role with regard to the roof of the contemporary great hall at Falkland Palace (p. 25), he appears to be the most likely craftsman to have designed the roof of the Edinburgh great hall.[3]

The only buildings of James IV's time that survive today are the royal lodging and the great hall, both of which have been greatly altered since that time. The lodging, now forming part of the early seventeenth-century palace, seems to have been about the same size as the contemporary king's lodging at Stirling and its internal layout may well have been similar. The windows of the principal chambers looked east, commanding splendid views over the neighbouring burgh and what was then open countryside to the south. Although rebuilt in the seventeenth century, these windows were evidently originally constructed as oriels and a carved fragment recovered during building operations within the palace in 1997 indicates that they were similar in design to those in

3.3 Edinburgh Castle. Palace block and Half Moon Battery from the east. The stumps of the oriel windows that originally lit James IV's lodging can be seen.

the contemporary royal lodging at Linlithgow Palace. Within, two surviving
5.6 chimneypieces have moulded jambs and capitals similar in character to those
in the great hall at Stirling.

Of the three great halls that James IV erected within the first decade or so
of the sixteenth century, Edinburgh is the smallest by a considerable margin
(25.1m x 10.1m internally).[4] Possibly the cramped nature of the site prevented
the construction of a longer building and this may also have been a factor in
the decision to dispense with bay windows at the upper end. Otherwise the
plan is similar to that adopted at Stirling and Falkland, with the hall standing
above an undercroft. As at Stirling there was a lean-to corridor running along
4.5 the lower part of the building on the courtyard side. The big, mullioned and
transomed windows that light the hall from the south look as if they might be
4.6 of French or Flemish inspiration, while the fine hammerbeam roof, like the
slightly earlier one at Stirling, may to some extent have been based on English
prototypes.

While the overall design of the hall is typically late medieval, the wall-posts
of the roof are supported on carved stone console-brackets of Italianate

*The Castles of
Edinburgh and
Doune,
Dunfermline
Palace and
the Lesser
Residences*

*3.4 Edinburgh
Castle. Renaissance-
style consoles from
the roof of James
IV's great hall.
Photographed
during the restor-
ation of 1887–91.*

Renaissance character which, as already suggested, may tentatively be associated with the presence of an Italian mason in the contemporary royal work force. Until quite recently scholars have been reluctant to ascribe these corbels — and the hall itself — to a date as early as the reign of James IV because of what Christopher Wilson has described as their 'unequivocally Renaissance character' (Gifford *et al.* 1984, 97), but in view of the fact that some of the corbels actually bear the king's initials (JR 4) there seem to be no good grounds for not accepting them at face value.

All in all then, James IV's buildings at Edinburgh Castle can be seen to exhibit as great a stylistic diversity as those at Linlithgow Palace and elsewhere. Nor was such eclecticism confined to works of architecture, for it is found equally in the other visual arts of the period and no doubt figured prominently in the products of the royal arsenal and shipbuilding yards, which we know were manned by craftsmen recruited from many countries of western and southern Europe (*TA*, ii, iii, and iv, *passim*; Kemp and Farrow 1990, 33–34).

THE CASTLE UNDER JAMES V

With the completion of the first palace of Holyrood in 1502–05 the castle finally lost its position as the premier royal residence of the Scottish capital. Henceforward it was used mainly as a fortress and arsenal and as a place for the safe custody of records and other valuables. So far as personal use by the sovereign was concerned, the castle was seen primarily as a place to visit on state occasions and as a refuge in times of insecurity.

It was no doubt because it provided a high degree of security that the castle was chosen as the residence of the young James V during the early years of his reign. We do not know exactly where he was accommodated, but in 1517 repairs were made to what was described as the 'Kingis chamir' and it seems likely that this was situated somewhere within the new royal lodging. At the same time the king's kitchen and the court kitchen were refurbished and some £6 was spent on the refurbishment of the schoolroom where the five-year old king was instructed by his tutor, Gavin Dunbar, the future archbishop of Glasgow (*TA*, v, 129; *ER*, xiv, pp. civ, 350). Some of these works were undertaken in conjunction with alterations made to David's Tower under the direction of John Drummond, the king's wright; the master-mason was John Kirk (*TA*, v, 120–122). This scheme seems to have involved the conversion of the old royal lodging to other purposes, the main first-floor chamber in the tower now becoming the lords' hall (p. 110).

Unlike the other major royal castles and palaces, Edinburgh was the scene of only small-scale building operations during the latter part of James V's reign. The most important of these was the conversion of St Mary's Chapel into a munition house in 1539–41, the leading mason being William Cadislie (*TA*, vii,

214–227; 342–359; 489–490). With St Margaret's Chapel by now adapted for secular use this seems to have left the adjacent chapel of c.1512–13 as the only ecclesiastical building within the castle (MacIvor 1993, 60). Contemporaneously with the creation of the munition house a repository for the state records was built in the south-east corner of Crown Square. The new register house, which replaced an earlier repository elsewhere in the castle, was erected under the direction of John Drummond, wright, and John Merlioun, mason, at a cost of just under £400 (*TA*, i, 184; vii, 337, 474, 493, 499; viii, 93, 132–134). The master of works at the castle during this period seems to have been Mr John Scrymgeour, but only one account in his name survives and this deals mainly with artillery operations (*MW*, i, 229–234).

Little is heard of the domestic buildings of the castle, but repairs were made to the great hall from time to time (*MW*, i, 232; *TA*, vii, 218, 350; viii, 132–133). As at Holyroodhouse and Falkland, however, the great hall was by now seldom required for ceremonial occasions and sometime before 1583 it seems to have been adapted for temporary use as a workshop (*MW*, i, 312).[5]

Doune Castle

When first erected about the turn of the fourteenth and fifteenth centuries the castle of Doune in the lordship of Menteith, was not, strictly speaking, a royal residence for its builder, Robert, Earl of Menteith and Fife, and from 1398 Duke of Albany, was the third son of King Robert II and thus a younger brother of King Robert III. It was Albany, however, a more forceful character than either his father or his brother, who was the effective ruler of Scotland from his appointment as guardian of the kingdom in 1388 until his death in 1420. The castle is poorly documented and we do not know exactly when it was built (Fraser 1881; MacGibbon and Ross 1887–92, i, 418–429; Simpson 1982; Pringle 1987; Cross 1994, 144–147). There was evidently a lordly residence of some kind at Doune in 1381, because a document was issued there (*apud Dwne in Meneteth*) in that year, but we cannot be sure that this was the present castle (Fraser 1879, ii, 237). After 1406, however, when the young James I was taken captive to England and Albany began to grant great seal charters in his own name, these were often issued from Doune (*apud castrum nostrum de Doune*) and we can be fairly confident that the castle was in full residential use by that time (e.g. *RMS*, i, No. 914; Murray 1996, 176). For some unknown reason, however, the structure was never completed for it is clear from the appearance of the existing fabric that not all the accommodation originally specified was actually built.

Since there is no mention of any payments for the construction of the castle in the exchequer rolls (which are not, however, complete), it seems likely that

C.17

the work was funded from Albany's own ample revenues rather than from those of the crown, although we can speculate that the king's mason, Master Nicholas of Hane (p. 223), may have been called in to advise on its design. Whoever its designer was, the castle is remarkable more for its impressive appearance and high standards of domestic amenity than for its defensive capability, the large, outward-facing windows, in particular, making the building vulnerable to assault. Albany was also keeper of the royal castle of Stirling, only a few miles from Doune, and spent a good deal of time there on affairs of state, as he did also at Perth. Doune Castle is much smaller than that of Stirling and it seems likely

3.5 Sketch-plans of royal castles and palaces.
1. Edinburgh Castle; A, B, C, King's Hall (?), Chamber (?) and Closet (?), D Hall (?), E Great Chamber (?), F Chamber.
2. Doune Castle: A1, B1, C, Duke's (King's), Hall, Chamber and Closet; A2, B2, D, Duchess's (Queen's) Hall (?), Chamber (?) and Closet/ Oratory (?).
3. Dunfermline Palace; A, B, King's Hall (?) and Chamber (?), C Transe or Gallery, D Queen's House, E Constable's and Bailie's houses; F West Claustral Range.

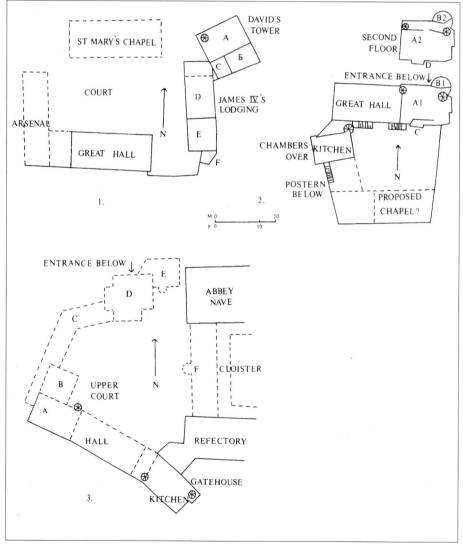

that it was built not as an official residence, but as a retreat from the pressures of high office and as the administrative centre of the earldom of Menteith. Certainly that is how the kings of Scots regarded it after James I took possession of the earldom and castle following the execution and forfeiture of Albany's son in 1425.

James II was a frequent visitor to Doune and to the nearby forest of Glenfinglas and he and his two successors also used the castle as a dower house. From the reign of James V onwards the keepership of the castle was held by the Stewarts of Beath and it eventually became the property of their kinsmen, the Stewart Earls of Moray. The castle was kept in repair by the crown up to the reign of James VI and thereafter the fabric was maintained by the Earls of Moray, a major scheme of restoration having been carried out by the 14th Earl in 1883–86. Unlike nearly all other surviving royal residences, however, no fundamental alterations were made to the structure during its long history and the castle that we see today is substantially the one erected by the Duke of Albany about the turn of the fourteenth and fifteenth centuries. Since it also seems to

3.6 Doune Castle. Conjectural reconstruction by David MacGibbon, 1887. The windows in the south curtain wall were intended to light a range of buildings on that side of the courtyard, but this seems never to have been completed.

85

❧

*3.7 Doune Castle.
View from the
north showing
residential gate
tower and great
hall. The louvre of
the (restored) great
hall roof served a
central hearth.*

have been built on a clear site, the castle, albeit unfinished, gives us some insight into current ideas about the appropriate design specification for a semi-royal residence of middle rank.

The castle was built round a courtyard, the principal accommodation being incorporated within a massive, frontal block, part of which rose two storeys higher than the remainder in the form of a residential tower. The first floor contained a good-sized great hall (20.4 x 8.2m) with an adjacent hall and chamber, or chambers, for the duke. With its tiled floor, lofty barrel-vault and handsome double-arched fireplace, the duke's hall must have been a particularly impressive room and the Victorian restoration successfully captures something of the spirit of the original. Each hall had its own forestair from the courtyard, while above the duke's hall, which straddled the castle gateway, was a second hall of similar size, again with its own chamber. As we shall see

4.1

5.3

The Castles of
Edinburgh and
Doune,
Dunfermline
Palace and
the Lesser
Residences

3.6

when we come to discuss the planning arrangements in Chapter 5, it seems likely that this suite was intended for the duchess, subsequently functioning as the queen's lodging.

The first-floor kitchen, placed at the lower end of the great hall, was reached from the same forestair via a lobby which also functioned as a servery. Above the lobby and kitchen were a number of chambers probably to be identified as lodgings for junior members of the duke's family and for guests and senior officials (p. 200). It is also clear from the tusking on the south wall of the kitchen tower and from the large windows piercing the south curtain wall that it was originally intended to erect two-storeyed ranges along the west and south sides of the courtyard. It is likely that the aim was to provide additional residential accommodation, together with a chapel, and it seems surprising that neither the duke himself, nor successive kings of Scots, took the trouble to complete the full scheme as planned. It is possible, however, that some of this space was made habitable by the construction of internal walls of timber, although there is no visible evidence of these. A charter of 1581 mentions the existence of two chapels at Doune, both dedicated to St. Fillan, of which one was situated outside the castle and the other inside it (*RMS*, v, No. 280).

In an analysis of the plan published some 60 years ago Dr W. D. Simpson interpreted the gate tower as a self-contained seigneurial residence deliberately isolated from the remainder of the establishment in the interests of security, and he went on to draw a close comparison with the great French castle of Pierrefonds, constructed by the Duc d'Orléans in about 1390–1400 (Simpson 1938a, 77–80).[6] The concept of bastard feudalism is no longer fashionable and today we would be more likely to take a contrary view of the planning of Doune, emphasising its integrated nature and drawing parallels with castles such as Bolton in England and La Roche-Jagu in France (Faulkener 1963, 225–230; Mesqui 1991–93, ii, 57–58, 132). Other features of the design that can be paralleled in contemporary France include the superimposition of twin suites for the duke and duchess and the placing of the siegneurial lodging above the principal entrance, as for example at the Breton castles of Suscinio and Vitré (Meirion-Jones 1993, 178–179; Mesqui 1991–93, i, 344–345; ii, 71–72, 110, 122–123).

Dunfermline Palace

The royal palace of Dunfermline, like that of Holyrood, originated as a monastic guesthouse. (MacGibbon and Ross 1887–92, i, 514–519; RCAHMS 1933, 106–121; Gifford 1988, 43, 175–185; Fawcett 1990; Cross 1994, 193–194). It was Queen Margaret and her youngest son, David I, who established the Benedictine community at Dunfermline and made the abbey a royal burial-place, and the practice of offering hospitality to the family of its founder probably went back to the

*3.8 Dunfermline
Palace. Site plan
of 1933 showing
relationship of
abbey and palace.*

earliest days of the monastery. The connection was maintained by succeeding sovereigns, including Robert I, who helped to fund the rebuilding of the abbey after its partial destruction by Edward I (*ER*, i, 215). The early Stewart kings are known to have resided at Dunfermline from time to time and James I was born there in 1394 and in later years sometimes housed his own children there (*ER*, iii, 290, 342, 699, 701; iv, 24; Dunbar 1906, 182). In 1429, for example, payment was made to one of the king's servants for the expenses of his infant daughters at Edinburgh and Dunfermline, while a few years later three barrels of barley were provided for the use of the royal nurse there (*ER*, iv, 437, 508, 627).

There is nothing to suggest that either James II or James III spent much time at Dunfermline, but James IV and Queen Margaret were frequent visitors and James V and his second wife occasionally stayed there (*TA*, ii, 459, 463; iv, 308; vi, 419, 421–422). But it was only at the end of the sixteenth century,

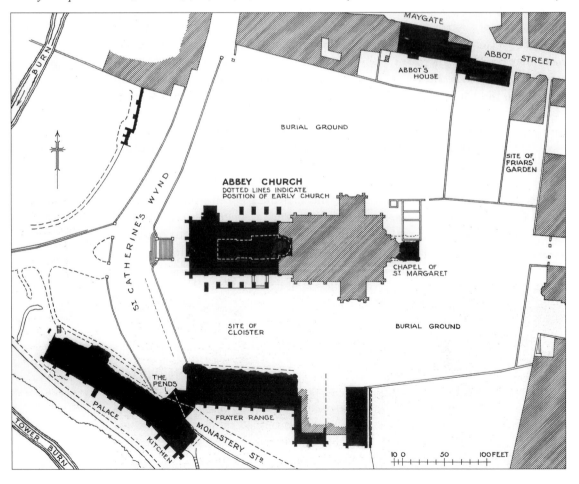

when the abbey was annexed to the Crown and then, with what remained of the lordship of Dunfermline, granted by James VI to his wife, Anne of Denmark, that the palace came into its own as a royal residence. An extensive programme of reconstruction appears to have been undertaken at that time, including the erection of a new building, known as the Queen's House.

Unfortunately, the palace of Dunfermline is less well documented than almost any other of the major royal residences and the existing remains are fragmentary. During the lifetime of the abbey, i.e. up to about 1560, responsibility for the provision and upkeep of the royal accommodation appears to have been borne mainly by the monastic community, whose records are for the most part lost. As we should expect, the records of the royal exchequer contain few references to building activity at Dunfermline during this period. In 1428–29 a quantity of timber boards was supplied for the king's work in the monastery of Dunfermline (*ER*, iv, 482), which suggests that, as in similar circumstances at Holyrood, the crown occasionally funded structural work on the royal lodging. In the following century the Treasurer's accounts show that in the summer of 1507 and again a few months later James IV gave gifts of drinksilver to the masons and other craftsmen at Dunfermline (*TA*, iii, 412; iv, 113). While these references provide a strong indication that building operations were then in progress at the abbey, they do not necessarily relate to work on the royal

3.9 Dunfermline Palace. View from the south west by John Slezer, c.1693 showing (left to right) the Queen's House, the ruinous north-east wing and the south-west range. Behind are the abbey church and part of what was probably the west claustral range of the abbey.

lodging. Even beyond the period that is dealt with here, when the abbey had passed under direct royal control, the documentation remains extremely scrappy.

As at Holyrood, the main buildings of the palace were grouped round a courtyard immediately to the west of the abbey. Because of the configuration of the ground, which falls steeply to Pittencrieff Glen on the south west, the courtyard is irregular and the principal, or south-west, range was perched on the lip of the glen, with its main axis running roughly north west and south east. From the north-west end of this range a wing extended at right angles (i.e. north east) towards the Queen's House, to which it seems to have been linked by a transe or gallery. The Queen's House stood close to the west front of the church and incorporated an arched pend giving access to the court.[7]

The best, and almost the only, description of the palace is that contained in Macky's Tour, published in 1723, but probably compiled a few years earlier (Macky 1723, 173–176). 'This Palace', he writes 'consists of Two Courts, the Upper and Lower; the Lower was a Meuse (mews) as large as that at *London*, for Stables, Hawks and Hounds, and the Officers belonging to them; the Upper Court makes the Palace, the Royal Apartments are to the *South* and *West*, Queen *Anne's* Jointure-house to the *North*, and the Church and Remnants of the ancient Monastery to the *East*.' Speaking of the jointure-house he notes that the queen 'built an Apartment for her self, at top of the Entry or pen'd, with a Gallery of Communication with the Royal Apartments.' The author of the *Statistical Account* records that the Queen's House incorporated a Latin inscription stating that it had been rebuilt and enlarged by Queen Anne in 1600, and the form of wording used in this inscription suggests that the building occupied the same position as the north gatehouse of the medieval palace (*Stat. Acct.*, xiii, 448).[8] Between the Queen's House and the west front of the abbey church stood the houses of the constable and bailie of the regality of Dunfermline, both probably of post-Reformation date, but perhaps replacing earlier structures in the same position[9] (Chalmers, 1844–59 i, 108 and map in ii, plate 1).

The east side of the upper court was bounded by a building apparently occupying the position of the west claustral range of the abbey (Howard 1995, 28). As depicted by Slezer in the late seventeenth century (Slezer 1693), this comprised two main storeys, the west front being divided into windowed bays by tall buttresses terminating beneath a crenellated parapet; towards the centre of the façade stood an extruded stair-tower with a conical roof. Whether or not this building, whose appearance recalls James IV's and James V's work at Falkland, formed part of the palace is uncertain. Possibly, like the similarly-placed range at Holyroodhouse, it had been adapted from monastic use to provide lodgings for courtiers and officials. At the south-east corner of the courtyard stood a medieval gatehouse, originally serving the abbey, which gave access to the lower court of the palace. To what extent the other monastic buildings were

3.9

incorporated within James VI's palace is uncertain, but according to Macky the cloister itself was turned into a tennis court (Macky 1723, 175).

The palace is said to have remained habitable until 1695, although Slezer's views indicate that much of the north-west side of the upper court was already ruinous by that date. In 1708 the roof of the main part of the south-west range fell in and its inner, or north-east, wall was pulled down in 1736. A few years later the remaining, or north-west, portion of this range, together with the adjacent north-east wing, collapsed. The Queen's House, which was inhabited until about 1780, was demolished in 1797, although part of its entrance pend could still be seen almost a century later (*Stat. Acct.*, xiii, 448; Chalmers 1844–59, i, 108; Gordon 1868, i, 415–416; Henderson 1879, 254, 536).

All that survives today is the incomplete shell of the south-west range, which probably originated as part of the late medieval royal guest-house. It has been much altered, but seems originally to have comprised a large hall set over a rib-vaulted undercroft, with a chamber at the upper, or north-west, end and a kitchen at the lower (south-east) end. The hall, which was lit by five hand-

3.10 Dunfermline Palace. View from the south east by John Slezer, c.1693, showing south-west range of palace (left) and monastic refectory. Behind is the abbey church.

3.11 Dunfermline
Palace. Exterior of
south-west range.
In their present
form the upper
floors date mainly
from the mid and
late 16th century.

some, arched windows overlooking Pittencrieff Glen, appears to date from the fourteenth and fifteenth centuries, while the chamber and kitchen, both also at first-floor level, seem to have been built, or rebuilt, about the turn of the fifteenth and sixteenth centuries. The hall was probably entered at its lower end, where the level of the ground on the north-east side would have allowed direct access to the first floor. The undercroft contained a big, canopied fireplace, which suggests that part of it, at least, may originally have functioned as a lower hall. The chamber at the upper end of the hall may have been an associated reception room. Beneath is another heated chamber, originally unvaulted but latterly subdivided by barrel vaults. This seems at one stage to have been adapted for use as a kitchen, perhaps to serve the royal family's private rooms, which may have occupied the adjacent north-east wing.

Subsequently, the entire south-west range was reconstructed and heightened, the hall and chamber windows being renewed with mullions and transoms and an upper floor being added or largely rebuilt. This second floor was lit in part by prominent oriel windows. Opinions vary as to the date of this reconstruction

and it is possible that it was implemented in two main phases. Some work was evidently carried out during the middle decades of the century, for Macky noted that the royal apartments bore the arms both of James V and Mary of Guise (1538–42) and of James Hamilton, Earl of Arran, who was regent of Scotland from 1542 to 1554 (Macky 1723, 175–176). Partial confirmation of this statement is provided by the existence (in the abbey museum) of a carved stone panel bearing the impaled arms of James V and Queen Mary, which could well have stood above an external doorway or gateway of the palace. In 1812 a stone (now also preserved in the abbey museum) bearing a carving of the Annunciation and the arms of the last abbot, George Durie (c.1530–60) — he was also commendator —, was discovered built into the ceiling of the south-east oriel of the south-west range[10] (Chalmers 1844–59, i, 92–83; RCAHMS 1933, 120–121). If this stone was *in situ*, as appears to have been the case, the chamber or chambers above the hall are likely to belong to this phase. The subject matter of the carving suggests that the oriel may have contained an oratory or closet not unlike the one in the second-floor hall at Doune Castle. Further work was undertaken towards the end of the sixteenth century, possibly during the years after 1590, when at least £400, and probably £533 or more, was allocated to William Schaw, the king's master of works, for repairs in preparation for Queen Anne of Denmark's first visit to the palace (SRO, E 21/67/110–111, 113). James Murray, the king's master-wright, is known to have been working at Dunfermline in 1599 (*MW*, i, 320). Possibly the remodelling of the north-west portion of the range, with its large, central oriel window, should be attributed to that period.

The only detailed information that we have about the accommodation provided by the palace comes in a glazing estimate of 1654 (SRO, GD 28/1705). This lists some seven dwelling-chambers in what is described as the new work — probably the Queen's House —, including a low and high hall, a dining-room, a chamber of dais and wardrobe. The 'uyer wark' (other work) — probably the south-west range and adjacent wing, contained about a dozen rooms, including a king's apartment of five main chambers. There was also a long transe, which apparently incorporated — perhaps on an upper floor — various other rooms, including a painted chamber; mention is also made of a bowling alley (p. 205). It is difficult to relate these arrangements, which probably dated mainly from the late sixteenth and early seventeenth centuries, to the existing fragments of the palace, but the king's apartment may well have occupied the first floor of the south-west range and adjacent wing. The long transe, which evidently ran roughly north and south, is possibly to be equated with the gallery of communication mentioned by Macky as connecting the Queen's House with the principal royal apartments. If so, it can perhaps be identified as the ruinous, two-storeyed building shown on one of Slezer's views as occupying the north-west side of the upper court.

3.12 Dunfermline Palace. Interior of south-west range showing undercroft with hall windows above.

Despite our imperfect understanding of so many aspects of its development, Dunfermline Palace is a structure of the greatest interest. For of the several royal guest-houses and lodgings that are known to have existed in Scottish religious houses — and these include Holyrood, the Dominican Friary at Perth and probably the Augustinian priory at Scone — this is the only one to survive. Unlike Holyrood and all the other major palaces, it seems not to have been provided with its own chapel, so the king presumably worshipped in some appointed part of the abbey church.

At Holyrood the monastic refectory seems to have been appropriated to serve as the great hall of the palace, but at Dunfermline the royal lodging was provided with its own great hall from the beginning. So, at least, we may infer from the very large size of the first-floor hall in the south-west range (28.6 x 8.8m) which, even allowing for a servery at the lower end, is as big as James I's great hall at Linlithgow Palace. Indeed, the whole arrangement, with kitchen, great hall and chamber *en suite*, is very similar to that found both there and in the royal castle of Urquhart (Simpson 1929–30, 214–239; Tabraham and Stewart 1994).

94

The Castles of
Edinburgh and
Doune,
Dunfermline
Palace and
the Lesser
Residences

The Lesser Residences

Adopting a broadly chronological approach, some brief mention should first be made of the castle of Kindrochit in the braes of Mar (Simpson 1922–23; 1928; 1949, 42–44, 60, 68). Although the earldom of Mar was not annexed to the crown until 1435, evidence for the use of Kindrochit as a royal residences comes mainly from the 1370s and 1380s, when Robert II was an almost annual visitor during the hunting season. More than a dozen royal charters were issued from Kindrochit during this period and the exchequer rolls contain records of expenditure incurred by the king and his household (Murray 1996, 173; *ER*, ii, 364, 543; iii, *passim*).

The existing remains are fragmentary and our knowledge of the site derives primarily from excavations carried out by Dr W. D. Simpson in 1925–26. These suggested that the castle occupied by Robert II was a huge, rectangular hall-house (about 30.5 x 9.1m internally) having quadrangular turrets projecting from at least three of its corners. Above an unvaulted ground floor there was probably a spacious hall, approached from a forestair, together with one or more chambers. Subsequently, an oblong tower-house (13.1 x 6.7m internally), built on a different alignment, was intruded into one end of the hall-house, a considerable portion of which was removed to accommodate it. The remainder of the hall-house seems to have continued in occupation, the central portion possibly having been adapted to form a small, open court. There was also an outer court on the south side which seems to have contained one or more buildings. The angle-turrets are difficult to interpret and little of them can be seen today. The two north ones seem to be original, although their size and shape are uncertain and neither communicated with the main block at ground-floor level. The south-east turret looks as if it belongs to the second phase of work.

We do not know when, or by whom, the hall-house was built and its chief interest in the present context is that it represents a building-type not otherwise found among surviving late medieval royal residences. The closest architectural parallels are with a group of Scottish and northern English baronial halls of the thirteenth and early fourteenth centuries, such as Edlingham and Haughton, Northumberland, some of which have square or multangular angle-towers (Dixon 1992; 1993, 27–32). The tower-house was probably built shortly after 1390, when Robert III granted a license authorising his brother-in-law, Sir Malcom Drummond, husband to the Countess of Mar, to erect a tower at Kindrochit (Simpson 1922–23, 91, n.2).

The fashion for tower-houses no doubt owed a good deal to recent royal building activity at Edinburgh Castle, where Robert II had completed the new residential tower begun by David II, as also at Clunie and Dundonald. At the ancient royal castle of Clunie, in south-east Perthshire, Robert II appointed his

3.15

95

*3.13 Dundonald
Castle. Robert II's
tower-house from
the west.*

kinsman, John of Roos (Ross) to be keeper of the castle in 1377 and gave him considerable financial support towards the construction of a tower there over the next few years (*RMS*, i, No. 596; *ER*, ii, 585, 621; iii, 80, 98). The king issued a number of charters from the castle, of which almost nothing now remains apart from what are probably the footings of the solidly built tower, measuring about 15m square (Murray 1996, 173; Salter 1994, 80; RCAHMS 1994, 105–106).

3.15   Dundonald formed part of the ancestral Stewart lands in northern Ayrshire and there in the late thirteenth century the family had built a great courtyard castle with twin-towered gatehouses on a plan not unlike that seen in Edward I's castle of Rhuddlan, in north Wales. (Simpson 1947–49; Ewart 1994; Cross 1994, 177–178). This was partially destroyed during the Wars of Independence and it may have been in the aftermath of Robert Stewart's accession to the throne in 1371 that the new building campaign was begun. The east gatehouse was abandoned and the courtyard considerably reduced in area, while upon the stump of the west gatehouse there was reared a large, oblong tower-house. The work is not documented, but the tower bears the royal arms as well as those of the Stewarts.[11] Both Robert II and Robert III are known to have resided at Dundonald and the former died there in 1390.

The plan of the tower is puzzling. As it stands today it contains two main vertical divisions, each covered with a barrel-vault. The lower incorporated an unheated and poorly lit ground-floor chamber evidently designed for storage and service purposes. The floor above was the main entry level and contained a hall heated by braziers vented by mural chimneys; there was an entresol floor at the north end. In the absence of a separate great hall this could have provided accommodation for public and ceremonial functions as well as for the day to day needs of the royal household. The upper division contained a handsome, mock-rib vaulted hall some 15.0m in length and 7.6m in height, having a servery at its lower end and what seem to have been a closet and a latrine and its upper end, both contained within the thickness of the gable wall. This may have been the king's hall. Since there is no provision for a royal chamber at this level, nor any identifiable accommodation for the queen, we must suspect that the tower originally rose a storey higher than it does today and clearly the stair in the south-east corner formerly continued upwards. If the tower originally incorporated an additional storey, its wall-walk is likely to have been about 21m above ground, a height occasionally reached in major towers, such as Threave, Alloa and Borthwick. Subsequently, additional chambers were constructed on the south side of the tower, while recent excavations have revealed traces of a number of buildings within the courtyard, including what may have been a chapel and a cistern. Presumably the kitchen also lay thereabouts, but it has not yet been identified.

Another ancestral castle of the Stewarts was that of Rothesay, in the Isle of Bute (Hewison 1893–95, ii, 105–132; Simpson 1937–40; Pringle 1995; Cross 1994, 489–492). By about the end of the thireenth century this had become quite a sizeable establishment, containing a great hall, probably also a chapel, and several drum-towers, of which the largest may have incorporated the royal lodging. Both Robert II and Robert III spent a good deal of time at the castle, but neither is known to have carried out any major building operations there. In 1512, however, James IV began to erect a new royal lodging, described in a document of 1520 as a great tower called 'le dungeoun' (*TA*, iv, 335, 345; *ER*, xiv, 362). The first phase of work cost £191 7s, but the structure seems to have been left unfinished following the king's death at Flodden the following year. The principal masons are named as John and Huchone Cowper. Accounts for the completion of the lodging cannot be identified in surviving exchequer records, but according to Pitscottie, James V, following a visit to Rothesay, commissioned his principal master of works, Sir James Hamilton of Finnart to 'reforme his castell and palice thairof' so that 'he might remaine thair sum tyme of the yeir at his plesour witht his court and quen' (Pitscottie 1899–1911, i, 389). The sum of three thousand crowns (about £3000 Scots) is said to have been assigned to the project, which may have included the rebuilding of the chapel and work

5.4

3.15

on other parts of the castle, as well as the completion of the lodging. The work was presumably commenced in 1539–40, when Hamilton briefly held the office in question (p. 221).

What the early sixteenth-century clerk described as a dungeon we would call a residential gate-tower or barbican, for James IV's lodging was built directly above the main gate of the castle and its ground floor included an extended entrance passage and guardroom. The concept was very similar to that found a century and a half earlier at Doune Castle, although there the work was

3.14 Rothesay Castle. Gate house from the west. The royal lodging occupied the upper floors.

executed on a much larger scale. The upper floors of the lodging are incomplete, but the first floor contained a good-sized chamber (about 14.6 x 6.4m) with its own latrine; this was probably the king's hall. The main approach was from the castle courtyard by means of a forestair and anteroom, this last also serving as a portcullis chamber. The second floor contained at least two chambers, perhaps to be identified as the king's outer and inner chambers, and there were others in the attic. The lodging communicated with the two adjacent drum-towers by means of the earlier wall-walks. These planning arrangements are considered in more detail in Chapter 5.

When the castle of Newark, in the Forest of Ettrick, came into the hands of the crown following the forfeiture of the Douglases in 1455, it was already a place of some importance (MacGibbon and Ross 1887–92, i, 247–250; RCAHMS 1957, 61–65). We know nothing about the buildings of the Douglas occupation, apart from the fact that they included a great hall in which the earls held their baronial courts (*Roxburghe MSS*, 25). From the middle of the fifteenth century onwards the kings of Scots maintained the castle as the administrative centre of the Forest of Ettrick, while at the same time making frequent use of it as a hunting seat. In 1456 the exchequer rolls record payment for the repair and roofing of various houses 'in le Newark', while three years later £22 was laid out on the building and repair of a hall and two chambers at the time of the king's visit, as also on the repair of various other houses there (*ER*, vi, 227, 545). In 1465–68 payments amounting to about £100 were made to Thomas Joffrey, master of the fabric at Newark, for work on the building, including the provision of iron, lime and timber, and mention is made for the first time of the tower of Newark (*turris de Newwerk*) (*ER*, vii, 422, 452, 477–478, 498, 501, 525, 528). In 1472–73 two chambers were built within the manor of Newark and various houses were repaired there, while about five years later the tower itself was equipped with a new stone chimney (*ER*, viii, 143, 477). In 1490 Alexander, 2nd Lord Home, was appointed keeper of the Forest of Ettrick and of the castle of Newark and in the same year received payment of £200 for work on the tower and on the other houses there (*ER*, x, 98, 166, 170, 173–74).

It is difficult to draw any firm conclusions about the nature of the late fifteenth-century castle from these entries in the exchequer rolls, but it may be inferred that it contained a number of residential buildings, some perhaps taking the form of hall and chamber blocks, together with the earlier great hall, a tower-house and associated kitchens and offices, although these last are not specifically mentioned in the accounts. While the tower itself was certainly built of stone and lime some, at least, of the other buildings were probably constructed of less durable materials. Almost all of them probably occupied the present site, a low, flat-topped mound overlooking the bank of the Yarrow Water, and this is likely to have been enclosed either by a wall or a ditch and bank.

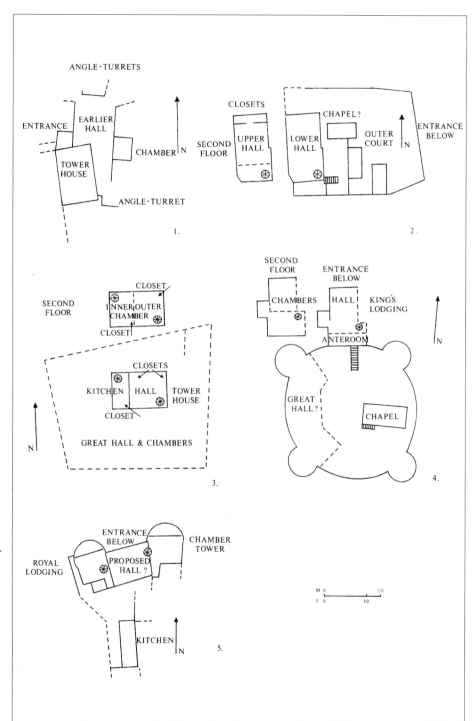

3.15 *Sketch-plans of royal castles.*
1. Kindrochit.
2. Dundonald.
3. Newark (Selkirkshire)
4. Rothesay.
5. Ravenscraig.

3.16 Newark Castle. Tower-house from the north. The royal lodging probably occupied the second and third floors.

The principal feature of the existing remains is the tower-house and this stands within a mid sixteenth-century barmkin wall which evidently replaces the earlier courtyard or enclosure. Almost nothing now survives of the court-yard buildings, although the larger of the two barmkin towers contains what may have been a ground-floor kitchen. Although it has sometimes been argued that the lower part of the tower belongs to the Douglas occupation, its appear-ance suggests that, apart from the cap-houses, the whole building dates from the late fifteenth century. Incomplete as they obviously are, the accounts seem to indicate that the tower was begun in the late 1460s, but it may well not have been finished until Lord Home's building campaign of *c.*1490 and the plan shows similarities with those of Elphinstone and Comlongon, both prob-ably erected about the turn of the fifteenth and sixteenth centuries (Maxwell-Irving 1996).

Only the lowest part of the tower is vaulted and this contains a storeroom with an entresol chamber above. The latter was lit by large windows equipped with bench seats and was heated by a small fireplace at one end. Like the rather similar chamber at Dundonald, this could have been a hall for members of the household, although major public events, such as the forest courts, were presumably held in the nearby great hall. The principal entrance was on the first floor, which contained what may have been the king's hall, together with several mural closets and a kitchen. The king's and queen's chambers probably occupied the second and third floors, while there are another two storeys above, each containing one or more chambers. The planning arrangements of the royal suite are discussed in more detail in Chapter 5.

*3.17 Ravenscraig
Castle. View from
the north east
showing (left to
right) east tower,
central block with
gun platform and
west tower.*

Approximately contemporary with Newark, but designed primarily for purposes of defence, is the castle of Ravenscraig, on the north shore of the Firth of Forth (Simpson 1938b; Cross 1994, 476–477). The construction of this new castle seems to have been initiated by James II, who granted the site, with certain neighbouring lands, to his wife, Mary of Gueldres, a few months before his death in August 1460 (*RMS*, ii, Nos. 746 and 747). The queen already

possessed the adjacent lordship of Fife as part of her jointure lands (*RMS*, ii, No. 462), so it was administratively convenient that Ravenscraig should be held in her name, but following her husband's unexpected death she took a close personal interest in the project, which seems to have been financed entirely from her own revenues.

The exchequer rolls show that building operations began in or before 1461 and continued at a brisk pace until about the time of the queen's death in December 1463, when they were quickly brought to an end (*ER*, vii, 59, 63, 77, 84, 138, 153, 171–172, 174–175, 189, 197, 216–217, 243); the evidence of the fabric indicates, however, that the building was left unfinished. The recorded expenditure amounts to about £630, but the accounts of the queen's lands for the first term after the king's death are missing, so this figure may well be an underestimate. Although incomplete, the castle was evidently at least partly habitable during the queen's lifetime, for in 1461–62 her steward and other staff spent more than three weeks there and in the following year the larder at Ravenscraig was stocked with marts (*ER*, vii, 78, 82, 86, 168).

The construction of the castle was superintended by the master of works, David Boys, and some of the timber used was supplied by the king's wright, Andrew Lesouris, who may also have been involved in its fabrication. Although he is not actually described as such in the accounts, the master mason appears to have been Henry Merlioun, the earliest known reference to a family which was to give faithful service to the crown for some three generations (p. 230). James III took no interest in the castle and in 1470 granted it to William Sinclair, Earl of Orkney and Caithness, in exchange for the castle of Kirkwall and his right to the Earldom of Orkney. The castle was eventually completed on a smaller scale than that originally envisaged and interpretation is hampered by the difficulty of distinguishing the royal work of the 1460s from that carried out by the Sinclairs during the late fifteenth and sixteenth centuries (Stell 1981, 41–42; Fawcett 1994, 286–288).

The plan was determined mainly by defensive considerations and comprised a central block flanked by D-shaped towers laid across the neck of a coastal promontory, with a kitchen and other ancillary buildings at the rear. Following a study of the distribution of masons' marks at the castle, it has recently been suggested that only the east tower, together with the lowest portion of the central block, belong to the first phase of construction and that the west tower and upper portion of the central block should be attributed to the Sinclairs (Zeune 1992, 63–64). As the castle stands today, the west tower reads as an independent unit with a series of vertically stacked chambers providing the same sort of accommodation as an equivalent-sized tower-house; this may have been designed, although perhaps not built, as the royal lodging. The east tower contains a number of individual chambers, while the central block comprises a

*3.18 Ravenscraig
Castle. West tower,
possibly designed as
royal lodging, from
courtyard.*

gun-platform set over a vaulted cellarage which is pierced by the entrance passage. Whatever the precise sequence of building may be, it is clear that the gun platform is of secondary construction and it is possible that the original scheme allowed for a first-floor hall linked at its upper end to the royal lodging, an arrangement which recalls that found at Doune and in the first phase of Linlithgow.

NOTES

1   By way of comparison John Lewyn, the English master-mason, contracted to build a new gatehouse at Roxburgh Castle for 550 merks (£366–13s–4d or about £490 Scots) in 1378 (Colvin 1963–73, ii, 820; Gemmill and Mayhew 1995, 117).

2   The castle's role as an arsenal is described in Caldwell 1981.

3   It may be significant that Drummond's emoluments were augmented at about this time and that he is first described as king's carpenter in 1513–14 (p. 233).

4   In addition to the great halls at Stirling, Falkland and Edinburgh, the king also built a hall at Lochmaben Castle (*TA*, ii, 278) and in 1509 ordered the construction of another at Inverness. This was to measure 100 feet in length and 30 feet in width (about 30.5m by 9.1m), with walls of the same height; these were probably external dimensions (*RMS*, ii, No.3286).

5   Iain MacIvor has suggested that it was an earlier great hall, standing on the rock summit, that was converted into a workshop (MacIvor 1993, 51, 54, 60).

6   Macgibbon and Ross (1887–92, i, 421–422) had already put forward a similar view.

7   Fig. 3.5 is a conjectural sketch-plan based on plans and drawings published in RCAHMS 1933, Figs. 240–241 and 253, supplemented by a ground plan in Chalmers 1844–59, ii, plate 1, John Slezer's drawings (1693) and various drawings of the Queen's House.

8   The inscription is given in full in Howard 1995, 28.

9   These houses, as also the Queen's House, are depicted in a drawing reproduced in Howard 1995, 29.

10 Visiting Dunfermline in 1732, John Loveday noted what seems to have been a second stone bearing Durie's coat of arms, together with the date 1555,

built into what he described as 'a Tower' of the palace (Loveday 1890, 128).

11 Other shields on the tower appear to represent the earldom of Carrick, granted to the future Robert III in 1368, and the earldom of Fife, which passed to Robert Stewart, third son of Robert II and the future builder of Doune Castle, some time after 1371 (Dunbar 1906, 166, 172).

Chapter 4

HALL AND CHAPEL

The Components of the Royal Residence

It can be inferred from an account of the Scottish king's household compiled during the late thirteenth century that the principal elements of the royal residence were the hall, the chamber and the chapel of the king (Bateson 1904, 31–43) and this evidently continued to be the case during the period that we are now considering. To this inner core was added, as circumstances required, accommodation for the queen and other members of the royal family, as also for guests and for the various other departments of the household, such as the wardrobe, kitchen and stables, each staffed by its own complement of officials. Little information about the size of the household is available prior to the sixteenth century, but it has been estimated that during the 1530s the king's household contained at least 300 to 350 named officials. The household of Mary of Guise, if we are to judge from figures relating to the period shortly after her husband's death in 1542, numbered about 140, of which some three quarters were men (Marshall 1993, 139). These figures, although only approximate, can be compared with estimates of about 500 and 600 persons for the households of Henry VIII and Francis I respectively (Thomas 1995, 3; Williams 1971, 34; Knecht 1994, 122–123).

That no particular building type or layout was prescribed for the design of a royal residence is demonstrated by the fact that the king's great hall could function as effectively in a tent, as when he was on campaign (*TA*, i, 346), as in a purpose-built structure such as that provided within the palace of Linlithgow. Likewise, the ecclesiastical (as opposed to the chancery) functions of the royal chapel could if necessary be accommodated within an oratory opening off one of the principal chambers, as at Doune Castle and perhaps also at Dunfermline, Newark and Ravenscraig, where no separate chapel is known to have existed.

It is noticeable that the buildings of the lesser residences were, in general, more loosely grouped than those of the palaces, although always contained within an enclosing wall. At Dundonald and Rothesay the chapel and ancillary buildings lay scattered across the courtyard and Newark and Ravenscraig may have presented a similar appearance. At Dunfermline and Doune, however, there were linked ranges round the perimeter of the courtyard and in some of the later palaces, such as Linlithgow and Stirling, there was clearly a deliberate attempt to achieve a regular quadrilateral layout with direct communication throughout. So far as can be established, the hall and other principal chambers were almost invariably placed at first-, or upper-, floor level, Scottish custom in this respect being more akin to Continental than to English practice, although the late fourteenth century saw something of a revival of the first-floor hall in England (Thompson 1995, 152–153).

THE HALL

In the royal residences the principal hall, often referred to as the great hall, was the focus of the public and ceremonial life of the court. During the thirteenth century, if we are to believe the account of the royal household already referred to, the king himself regularly took his two main meals of the day there, dining in considerable state and in accordance with strict rules of etiquette (Bateson 1904, 39–40). By the period that we are now dealing with, however, it is probable that the king usually ate in his own quarters, dining in the hall only on great feast days and other special occasions. The greater part of the household continued to eat daily in hall, however, although the lowest ranks, such as kitchen and stables servants, probably ate in their places of work. When the hall was not being used for this purpose it would function as a place for important meetings, for receptions and entertainment and, when necessary, as a court room. During the latter part of James V's reign the hall had an establishment of some three dozen officials, directed by the steward and principal marshal and including keepers of the silver and pewter vessels, of the cuphouse and of napery and ewery, as well as an usher of the hall door who doubled as a collier (responsible for supplying fuel for the fires) and a considerable number of table servants (Thomas 1995, 2; *TA*, vii, 125–127).

Our general understanding of the role played by the hall in the daily life of the court and household can be filled out by specific references to individual events and functions. We are told, for example, that in 1369 the proceedings of a parliament at Perth took place in the 'hall of our lord the king' (*aula domini nostri regis*), the building in question probably having been either the Dominican friary church, where a general council had met a few years previously, or the friars' refectory (Neilson 1900–01, 137–141; *APS*, i, 507–508; Simpson and Stevenson 1982, 2–3). Presumably this hall was also used for other royal functions, for the king's Perth residence lay within the precincts of the friary. When the castle of Newark was in the possession of the Earls of Douglas during the first half of the fifteenth century, their baronial courts were held in the great hall there and, following the forfeiture of the Douglases in 1455, the king's twice-yearly forest courts no doubt assembled in the same building (*Roxburghe MSS*, 25).

In 1457–58 repairs were made to the great hall of Edinburgh Castle in prepa-ration for a meeting of parliament (*ER*, vi, 385), while the fact that the great hall at Stirling was nicknamed the 'parliament hall' suggests that it was some-times used in a similar way, although it was more usual for parliament to be held in the local tolbooth. In 1585 parliament was held in the great hall of Linlithgow Palace (Moysie 1830, 55).

When Robert II received envoys from France and England at Dunfermline in 1389 it is likely that the great hall of the palace featured prominently in the handsome entertainment that was offered them (*ER*, iii, p. lxxi, 699–700) and this was certainly the case on a similar occasion at Linlithgow a century later, when payment was made for laying rushes in the hall at the time of the Spanish ambassadors' visit (*TA*, i, 118). Lindesay of Pitscottie's interesting, if somewhat highly coloured, account of the festivities that accompanied Bernard Stewart, Lord of Aubigny's, visit to the court in 1508 speaks of three days of banqueting at Holyroodhouse, accompanied by plays, dancing and conjuring tricks. The most spectacular of these involved the spiriting away of the mysterious black lady — a character who had already figured prominently in the accompanying tournament — into a cloud which appeared from beneath the roof of the hall (Pitscottie 1899–1911, i, 242–244; *TA*, iv, pp. lxxxiii–lxxxiv, 119). How this effect was achieved we do not know, but if the hall of Holyroodhouse, like those at Stirling and Edinburgh, had an open timber roof, it would presumably have been possible to have rigged up some appropriate type of theatrical apparatus.

Other activities that are known to have taken place in the great hall at Holyroodhouse include shooting matches (p. 204) and the use of all or part of the building as a joiners' shop during building operations elsewhere in the palace (*MW*, i, 69, 72). This last incident occurred in 1531–32 and the fact that the workmen were obliged to vacate the premises for Yule could indicate that by this time hall was kept only on high days and holidays. We have already seen that the great hall at Falkland drops out of the record at about this time and that the great hall at Edinburgh Castle was adapted for use as a workshop for at least part of the later sixteenth century. At Holyroodhouse itself the old great hall seems to have been abandoned by about the middle of the century. In England the king had effectively withdrawn from the great hall by the early sixteenth century and in the Eltham Ordinances of 1526 it was laid down that hall should be kept only in the greater royal houses. By the end of Henry VIII's reign the great hall in England was used only for court entertainments and as a communal dining-room for the lower members of the household. Senior officials dined closer to the king, either in the great chamber or elsewhere (Thurley 1993, 113–114, 120; Thompson 1995, 186).

If a similar situation prevailed in Scotland, as seems not unlikely, where, it may be asked, did the upper and middle ranks of the household take their meals? This is a question to which we shall return in Chapter 5, for there are indications in the record evidence that, on some occasions at least, senior officials dined in the outer chambers of the king's and queen's suites.

Some light is thrown on this subject by a reference to arrangements at Holyroodhouse, where the building accounts record that early in 1532 the queen's outer chamber on the first floor of the south range was remodelled to become the hall 'quhair now the houshald eittis' (*MW*, i, 75–76). Whether this was a temporary expedient linked to the appropriation of the great hall as a workshop at about the same time, or an attempt to make separate provision for certain members of the household is not clear. Certainly, however, the queen's chamber would have been a good deal smaller than the great hall and thus able to accommodate only part of the household at a sitting. In any event the arrangement cannot have lasted longer than about four years because in 1535–36 this particular chamber was again remodelled to become part of the new chapel (*MW*, i, 191).

We also hear of the construction of a room described as 'the lordis hall' within David's Tower at Edinburgh Castle in 1517 (*TA*, v, 120). This hall seems to have replaced what was originally the king's hall of the royal suite (p. 146) and would have been similar in size to the queen's outer chamber at Holyroodhouse. An inventory of 1561, in which it was described as 'Daviddis tour hall', shows that it then contained a dining table and two benches, together with a chest (Thomson 1815, 175). During the second half of the sixteenth century there are references to the court hall ('cowrthall') in the palace block at Stirling and to the court hall in the palace of Holyroodhouse (*MW*, i, 310; *TA*, xiii, 140). In these cases the court hall may be an alternative name for the outermost room of the royal suite or, less probably, a separate room elsewhere.

These references, scrappy and ambiguous though they are, would seem to indicate that during the first half of the sixteenth century arrangements were sometimes made for leading courtiers and the upper ranks of the household to dine in a separate hall of smaller size than the great hall, the aim presumably being to provide them with more comfort and greater privacy. If so, this might explain the existence in the royal palaces of certain well-appointed chambers for which no obvious function has been identified, for example the first-floor chambers usually described as anterooms which lie adjacent to the royal suites at Linlithgow and Falkland. To judge from the arrangements that are known to have prevailed during the latter part of the sixteenth century the food for these select members of the household would have been provided from the king's kitchen, rather than from the court kitchen. It would also have been apportioned along strictly hierarchical lines, the upper tables receiving their dishes directly from the kitchen, while those lower down the pecking order were expected to eat food already sampled by those above them. Entitlement to wine, as opposed to ale, would probably have been handled in a similar way (Gibson and Smout 1988, 33–39).

For those courtiers and officials lucky enough to have lodgings in or near the royal palaces, there was also the opportunity to follow royal example by dining in their own quarters. It is difficult to know, however, to what extent this practice prevailed during the period that we are now considering.

4.1 Doune Castle. Interior of great hall, as restored in 1883–86, showing central hearth and brazier.

4.2 Linlithgow
Palace. Interior of
great hall, as
remodelled by
James IV. The hall
rose to a lofty
timber roof, except
at the upper end,
where it was ceiled
with a barrel
vault.

Turning now to the design and furnishing of great halls it is not surprising to find considerable variations in size and layout. At Kindrochit and Dundonald, where the principal residential accommodation seems to have been contained beneath a single roof, the hall occupied virtually the whole of one floor of the building in question. At Kindrochit the original hall-house could have contained a hall up to about 30m in length, whereas the late fourteenth-century tower-house that replaced it would have been hard pressed to accommodate a hall half that size; in neither case, however, do we know what the precise arrangements were. In the larger royal residences the halls were very grand indeed, that at Stirling being larger that the English royal halls at Eltham and Hampton Court.

In some cases, such as Dunfermline, Doune and Linlithgow, the hall was fully integrated within the range or building of which it formed part, as was customary on the Continent, but less common in England (Thompson 1995, 9, 33, 74), although good examples of this arrangement are to be found in the northern castles of Bolton and Lumley. Only occasionally in Scotland, and noticeably in James IV's works at Stirling, Edinburgh and Falkland, was the great hall designed as an independent unit in the English manner. As already noted, the hall was invariably placed on the first floor, usually being set above a vaulted basement or undercroft. At Edinburgh and Stirling the great hall reads 4.5 as a ground-floor hall on the courtyard side because of the slope of the underlying rock, but neither there nor elsewhere do we find anything approaching the classic medieval English ground-floor hall with its uniform arrangement of service and chamber wings.

Regardless of their size and situation most halls conformed to a similar plan. One end was designed to accommodate a high table, being provided with a raised platform or dais lit by extra large windows. Presumably the high table was set transversely, facing the main body of the hall, within which rows of tables and benches would have been placed lengthways, as in a college hall today. At the lower end of the hall, where the principal entrance was usually situated, was a lobby screened off from the main dining area, but linked to the kitchen and other service departments. Heating was provided either by a central hearth venting through a louvre, as at Doune and perhaps originally at 4.1 Linlithgow, or by mural fireplaces, which had the advantage of taking up less space. The capacious interior of the great hall at Stirling required no less than 4.4 five fireplaces to heat it, one of these being so placed as to give extra warmth to the party on the dais. Indeed, dais fireplaces seem to have been especially popular in Scotland and there are also examples at Linlithgow (as remodelled 4.7 by James IV), Edinburgh and Falkland. The fire itself was kindled in an iron grate known as a chimney, which needed frequent maintenance; in 1461, for example, payment was made for the repair of the iron chimney in the hall of Falkland (*ER*, vii, 79). At Dundonald the hall seems to have been heated by

*Hall
and
Chapel*

❧

4.3 Stirling Castle.
Conjectural
reconstruction of
exterior of
James IV's great
hall by Geoffrey
Hay, 1963. The
hall was originally
separated from the
inner close by a
lean-to passage, the
principal entrance
being reached by a
bridge or forestair.

braziers vented by chimneys rising through the haunches of the vault. In the principal castles and palaces the great halls were lofty, well-lit structures covered with open timber roofs of which restored examples survive at Darnaway, Doune, Edinburgh and Stirling, this last being still under reconstruction at the time of writing. The vaulted space beneath the hall provided convenient space for storage of plate and other utensils.

Festivities in hall were invariably accompanied by music, for which the king could command the services of his own minstrels and singers. In the latter part of James IV's reign there were stands of French and Italian minstrels at court, while James V's household contained some two dozen minstrels, including trumpeters, drummers and string players, as well as two dwarfs and two fools (Shire 1996b, 120–126; Thomas 1995, 2; *TA*, v, 53–54). The minstrels seem generally to have been accommodated above the service area at the lower end of the hall, but at Linlithgow they could also have used the clearstorey passage on the west side of the hall, while at Stirling there was not only a trumpeters' loft at the lower end of the hall (*MW*, ii, 162), but also a small, upper chamber overlooking the central area. Perhaps this was sometimes used as a royal box and also as a place from which to make announcements, as when the royal heralds of arms performed their ceremonial duties at Christmas and Easter (*TA*, iv, 91, 112, 400, 407). When the court was at Stirling the players were provided with their own living quarters, described in an inventory of 1584 as 'the violers'

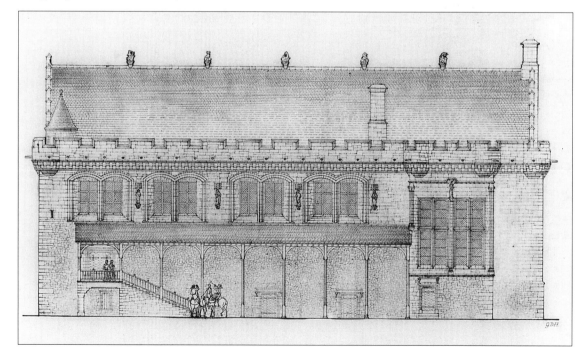

chamber beside the great hall'. At that time the chamber is said to have been equipped with tables and benches, three freestanding beds and an old chest, as well as a table in an adjoining building, so it looks as if there was space for them to practise their latest pieces as well as to sleep between times (*Elphinstone MSS*, 192–193).

4.4 *Stirling Castle. Conjectural reconstruction of interior of great hall by John Knight, 1978. The dais was lit by lofty bay windows on either side.*

115

4.5 Edinburgh Castle. North elevation of James IV's great hall as restored in 1887–91. Like the near contemporary hall at Stirling, the building seems originally to have had a lean-to passage along the courtyard side.

Another chamber sometimes found associated with the great hall was the chamber of dais, which — in this context, at least, — seems to have been a private room to which the high table party could withdraw for refreshment and social conversation.[1] At Linlithgow a mid seventeenth-century building account enables us to tentatively identify the chamber of dais as the little, second-floor room behind the hall chimney (*MW*, ii, 342); it was approached from the upper end of the hall by means of the south-east newel stair. Beneath this chamber lay another, smaller one entered directly from the rear of the dais. There were also chambers of dais at Stirling and Dumbarton, the former associated with a building described as the 'wester auld hall' (*MW*, i, 350) and the latter with the great hall in the nether bailey (MacPhail 1979, 40).

Other structures occasionally mentioned in the accounts and which are probably to be associated with the hall were the silver-vessel house, the court-vessel house, the court cup-house and the napery house. These were probably used for the storage of the more valuable items of table ware employed in hall, the great majority of utensils in daily use there no doubt having been

of pottery and wood. Plate used in the king's chamber was stored separately (pp. 177–179).

The fact that separate officials of the hall were responsible for silver and non-silver (pewter) vessels suggests that these items were housed separately (*TA*, vii, 125–126, 332–333) and the accounts, scrappy though they are, tend to confirm this. In the building accounts of 1531–32 for Holyroodhouse, for example, mention is made both of a silver-vessel house with a lockable aumbry and of a court vessel-house, which may be the one afterwards described simply as a vessel-house (*MW*, i, 73, 98, 226). In 1539 a new silver-vessel house was constructed at Linlithgow Palace (*TA*, vii, 195). At about the same time reference is made to a court cup-house at Holyroodhouse and to a 'cophous' at Falkland Palace (*MW*, i, 73, 257). There is also a reference to a napery-house at Holyroodhouse in 1537–38 (*MW*, i, 226).

There is little indication as to the location of any of these structures, apart from the cup-house at Falkland, which seems to have occupied the basement of the east range. In most cases, however, the most convenient location for the vessel- and cup-houses would seem to have been the cellarage beneath the great hall. At Stirling, for example, the small cellars at the upper end of the hall may have served this purpose. At Holyroodhouse, there is mention of a vessel-house situated alongside the court-kitchen, but this may have housed kitchen vessels (*MW*, i, 101).

The principal method of decorating the interior of the hall was to line the walls with hangings of tapestry or other woven material, which also helped to keep out draughts. All but the simplest hangings travelled with the royal baggage train and were installed only when the king actually arrived, and rooms were provided with fixed metal hooks for this purpose. For example, we hear of the great hall at Stirling being equipped with six dozen hooks on its completion *c.*1503 (*TA*, ii, 408), while ten years later there is record of payment for 'the hynging of the arres clathis in the Hall of Striveling' (*TA*, iv, 407). On special occasions a cloth of state (a richly decorated canopy suspended above the king's seat) might be erected in the hall, as at Stirling at Easter 1498[2] (*TA*, i, 387).

In the grandest halls, including that of Stirling, the exposed wall-surfaces above the hangings (and possibly also the area behind the hangings) were lined with plaster, an expensive material whose application — at least in the early sixteenth century — required the services of foreign craftsmen (*TA*, ii, 381); whitewash provided a cheaper substitute, as at Holyroodhouse in 1535–36 (*MW*, i, 191). It is likely that these broad expanses of plaster were used as a field for painted decoration and that carved work in stone and timber, such as chimney-pieces and roof-trusses, was likewise enriched by painting and gilding, but we have no detailed knowledge of the way in which decorative painting

was used in great halls during the period that we are now considering.[3] It is worth remembering, however, that traces of colouring have been found on the carved figures of the late fourteenth-century open timber roof at Darnaway Castle (Stell and Baillie 1993, 172). The floor was sometimes paved, as at Stirling, where recent investigation has revealed a floor of cut stone slabs apparently arranged in accordance with the different functional divisions of the hall. At Linlithgow there is some evidence to suggest that during the first half of the sixteenth century the floor of the great hall was paved, at least in part, with green-glazed tiles (Caldwell and Lewis 1996, 837).

At the beginning of our period glass was still a scarce commodity and it is not surprising to hear that the windows of the great hall at Edinburgh Castle were repaired with canvas in 1458 (*ER*, vi, 385). By the first half of the sixteenth century, however, glass was in more general use and in 1535–36 there is record of the partial glazing of the great hall at Linlithgow, using both white and painted (i.e. coloured) glass[4] (*MW*, i, 128). Nevertheless, we find a special kind of French canvas being purchased for the window-frames ('casis') of the

4.7 Linlithgow Palace. Great hall chimneypiece, probably installed during the 1490s. Restored in 1906. This magnificent triple fireplace may draw its inspiration from France, where such designs were considered suitable for palaces of the first rank.

4.8 Stirling Castle.
One of the original
great hall
fireplaces, probably
installed c.1500.
Restored in 1973.
The dressed
stonework of the
jambs and arched
lintel would
probably have been
enhanced by
painted decoration.

great hall of Edinburgh Castle in 1517 (*TA*, v, 120) and canvas being fitted to the hall windows at Holyroodhouse at Yule during the 1520s (*TA*, v, 261, 325). Possibly in these instances the canvas formed part of a timber frame filling part of the window and capable of being removed in summer weather.

Chambers in medieval houses contained little solid furniture, for domestic arrangements were flexible and furnishings were moved from one room or house to another as and when required (Thompson 1995, 115, 152). Great halls were no exception to this rule and in 1510 the hall at Dumbarton Castle seems to have contained only four tables, together with their benches (Fraser 1858, 293), while in 1561 the great hall of Edinburgh Castle held two dining tables with benches and 'ane dressour for setting of stouppis' (a cupboard for the display of drinking vessels) (Thomson 1815, 174). The late sixteenth-century inventory of Stirling Castle already quoted (p. 114) records the contents of the great hall there as a great high dais of fir boards, a long, old dining-table with a long form, a locked chest for clothing and a great ladder. Dining-tables (known as boards) were mounted on trestles so that they could be easily disassembled and stacked against the walls after meals if space was required for other purposes (*MW*, i, 128, 194; *TA*, iv, 526). The standing tables ('standand burdis') supplied for the halls of Holyroodhouse, Stirling and Falkland in 1535–36, however, were probably solid pieces, perhaps intended for the display of vessels or plate (*MW*, i, 182; Warrack 1920, 16–17).

THE CHAPEL

Although the king's personal devotions could be performed in the privacy of his own closet, there was also a need for a place of corporate worship where the daily round of religious services could be maintained for the spiritual benefit both of the royal family, living and deceased, and of the court and household. The chapel was therefore a major department of the household and, in spatial terms, an integral component of the royal residence. In the larger palaces, at least, the chapel was invariably a prominent building of considerable architectural distinction.

At Edinburgh there were two, if not three, chapels within the castle, as well as one built under the south wall to serve the tilting field that was located in that vicinity (p. 203). Stirling, too, contained an early chapel as well as James IV's splendid new chapel royal, while at Falkland an earlier chapel, perhaps the one mentioned in 1454 in association with the castle (*ER*, v, 687), remained in use for a time following the erection of another one to serve James IV's new palace (*MW*, i, 111, 217, 280). Linlithgow Palace is likely to have had its own chapel from the beginning, although none appears to be recorded prior to the erection of the present one by James IV. Possibly, in the temporary absence of a separate chapel, space was found within the adjacent parish church of St.

Michael, which James I had at one time hoped to erect into a collegiate foundation[5] (Cowan 1967, 113). At Dunfermline the royal residence stood adjacent to the abbey church (itself a royal foundation) and is not known to have had its own chapel, but at Holyroodhouse, in similar circumstances, a separate chapel was provided as part of James IV's new palace. At Doune Castle space was left for additional accommodation, probably including a chapel, to be built on the south side of the courtyard, but it is not clear to what extent this intention was, in fact, fulfilled and the only identifiable space for religious worship is the alcove opening off the duchess's hall (afterwards the queen's). This alcove, which may have been designed as a combined closet and oratory, is equipped with a credence and piscina, with space for an altar close by.

We do not know, in those cases where a royal residence contained more than one chapel, what differentiation of function, if any, there was between them. It is possible, however, that in some cases one chapel was set apart for the private use of the king or queen, as frequently happened in France and occasionally in England.[6] As we have already seen, James IV was a particularly ardent chapel builder, providing new or refurbished chapels at Edinburgh Castle, Stirling (two), Falkland, Linlithgow and Holyroodhouse and it may be that his efforts in that respect, like some of his other religious activities, were prompted by a desire to atone for his part in his father's death (Macdougall 1989, 52–53).

So far as the other royal residences are concerned, we find a sixteenth-century chapel at Rothesay Castle — perhaps a replacement of an earlier one —, while at Dundonald there are footings of what may have been a small chapel in the immediate vicinity of the tower-house. There are no identifiable remains of chapels at the castles of Kindrochit, Newark and Ravenscraig.

In the main these chapels were served by clergy who travelled with the king from one residence to another, the plate and other ecclesiastical furnishings being transported at the same time. In 1490, for example, payment was made for carrying the 'chapell grayth' from Edinburgh to Linlithgow before Yule and back again to Edinburgh after Yule (*TA*, i, 174). In July 1494 £6 13s 4d was paid 'to the chapell, to thare expensis' when the king was at Tarbert Castle in Kintyre (*TA*, i, 237), and when James IV made a pilgrimage to the Isle of May in June 1504 a boat was chartered to carry 'the clerkis of the Kingis chapell to Maii to sing the mes (mass) thare' (*TA*, ii, 437).

There were also chapels royal of a collegiate character (i.e. comprising a body of clergy attached to a particular church) at St Mary on the Rock at St Andrews and, for a time during the latter part of the fifteenth century, at Coldingham and Restalrig, while James IV, as we have seen, erected the principal chapel within Stirling Castle into a highly prestigious foundation of this type. As constituted in 1501, the chapel royal of Stirling comprised a dean — who also assumed responsibility for the itinerant clergy serving the court —, a subdean, a sacrist, sixteen canons and six boy clerics or songsters. In the mid 1530s the establishment of the king's chapel is estimated to have comprised some 27 chaplains at court, under the master almoner, in addition to the clergy of the chapel royal at Stirling (Watt 1969, 333–335; Rogers 1882, pp. xxxi–xxxii; Thomas 1995, 2–3 and pers. comm.).

It is impossible to say how frequently the king and other members of the royal family themselves worshipped in chapel and no doubt practice varied. Certainly, however, there were occasions on which those seeking audience of the king found that he could be met with in chapel and was prepared to conduct business there. During the course of his three-week mission to James IV in 1513 the English ambassador, Nicholas West, twice encountered the king in the chapel at Holyroodhouse. On the first occasion the king was hearing mass, but found time to converse with West, while on the second, after West had waited for some time in the chapel, the king came in and at once began to discuss affairs with him (Mackie 1953, 320–324). When Sir Ralph Sadler, another English ambassador, came to visit James V at Holyroodhouse in 1540 their first meeting took place in the chapel, where the king was hearing mass in the company of a large body of nobility, gentlemen and clergy. Subsequent meetings were held in greater privacy elsewhere, but Sadler also mentions a meeting with the queen in chapel, where she was hearing a sermon in French (Clifford 1809, i, 19–22, 40). Sadler, of course, would have been familiar with this way of doing business, for it was the practice of Henry VIII to show himself daily in chapel, where he would attend to correspondence, conduct interviews and receive supplications and petitions (Thurley 1993, 198–199).

At Holyroodhouse, where the adjacent abbey church offered a more elaborate and spacious setting for major public events, these were normally held there rather than in the king's chapel. When James IV received the gift of a hat and sword from the papal legate on Easter Day 1507 the ceremony took place during high mass in the abbey church, although the king also made an Easter offering in the chapel (*TA*, iii, 289, 378–380; Lesley 1830, 75). The abbey church was also the setting for the investiture of James V with the order of the Golden Fleece by the Imperial ambassador, Sir Peter de Rosimboz, in 1532. (*MW*, i, 99). The wedding of James IV and Margaret Tudor was likewise celebrated in the abbey and James V's second wife, Mary of Guise, was crowned there (*Diurnal of Occurrents*, 23).

The only royal chapels of late medieval date to survive today are those at Linlithgow, Falkland and Rothesay. The main features of James V's chapel at Holyroodhouse can be deduced from Mylne's plan of 1663 (Mylne 1893, opp. 148) and the slightly earlier drawing by James Gordon of Rothiemay, but of the celebrated chapel royal at Stirling Castle, almost certainly the finest building of its kind in all the royal residences, there remains little but foundations and

2.13
2.12

some records of its furnishings. It is possible however, that a fragment of a chapel of somewhat earlier date survives at Stirling, although the plan of this has still to be established.

The chapels exhibit a number of similarities in their location and planning. Apart from the chapel royal at Stirling, which seems to have been at ground level, and James V's chapel at Falkland, which was on the second floor, all were situated at first-floor level. In the major palaces and castles, where a quadrangular

4.9 Linlithgow Palace. Interior of James IV's chapel, probably completed in the early 1490s. The windows contained a mixture of plain and coloured glass and between each bay stood a carved statue. Behind the high altar at the far end a door opened into the vestry.

layout was usually preferred, the chapel occupied all, or the greater part, of one side of the courtyard. At Linlithgow, Falkland and James V's palace of Holyrood the chapel stood on the south side, while at Edinburgh, Stirling and James IV's Holyroodhouse it stood on the north. Either of these positions allowed the chapel to be correctly orientated and in fairly close proximity to the royal lodging, which in many cases was aligned north and south, where it could command maximum light (p. 152). At Rothesay, where the courtyard was circular, the chapel was largely freestanding, the space behind the east gable being occupied by a staircase leading to the wall-walk.

Most of these chapels were of simple, oblong plan, their internal dimensions varying from about 24.1 x 7.3m at Falkland to 12.5 x 6.0m at Rothesay. However, St Mary's Chapel at Edinburgh Castle and the chapel royal at Stirling were probably larger than any of these, and the latter may, in fact, have been aisled, although their exact dimensions are not known. At Falkland and at James V's chapel at Holyroodhouse there was a vestibule at the west end with a loft above, and the same arrangement was probably found at Linlithgow, where the corbels that supported the loft can still be seen. The first two of these also incorporated a vestry at the east end and the little chamber opening off the passage behind the high altar at Linlithgow probably served the same purpose. The chapel royal at Stirling also had a vestry (*Elphinstone MSS*, 192–193). Mylne's plan of James V's chapel at Holyroodhouse shows a small south outshot, but this may have been added to serve the pulpit that seems to have been installed during the 1580s (*MW*, i, 312). There is also mention in the accounts of a 'sangstaris (i.e. choristers') chalmer' at Holyroodhouse (*MW*, i, 103), possibly one of the two chambers afterwards described as lying above the new vestry (*MW*, i, 193).

4.9

2.13

Convenience of access from the royal lodging was evidently high on the designers' list of priorities, although at James V's chapel at Holyroodhouse there was also a forestair from the courtyard; at Rothesay there was a forestair only. At Stirling a bridge may have provided a direct link between the King's Old Building and a loft at the west end of the chapel royal, while James IV's chapel at Holyroodhouse also seems to have communicated directly with the royal lodging. At Falkland and Linlithgow the royal lodging and chapel were linked by corridors, while at James V's palace of Holyrood the king and queen had only to walk through the reception rooms in the west range to reach the west end of the chapel. It would seem from Mylne's plan of this area that the royal seat, for which a carpet and cushions were provided in 1541 (Mylne 1893, opp. 148; *TA*, vii, 468), occupied a loft directly above the vestibule. Although the particular arrangement shown by Mylne probably dated mainly from the early seventeenth century, the fact that one of the corridors at Linlithgow also led directly into a loft at the west end of the chapel suggests that this may have been the usual position of the royal pew. At Falkland, however, the access arrangements for the loft above the vestibule seem awkward, so perhaps this was the organ loft, of which mention is made in the accounts (*MW*, i, 284), the king's seat having been in the main body of the chapel.

Organs, in fact, played an important role in the worship of the royal chapels and were among their most costly furnishings. An inventory of the contents of the chapel royal at Stirling includes three pairs of organs, of which one was of timber and the other two of pewter and lead (Rogers 1882, pp. xliv–xlix). Considerable sums were laid out by James IV on the installation of organs at Linlithgow, payments being made to a French craftsman called Gilyem (William) 'that maid the organis' as well as to James Carver and his assistants, presumably for their work on the organ case (*TA*, i, pp. ccxxxiii–ccxxxiv; iv, 275, 523, 525;). In 1541 John Drummond, the king's master-wright, made an organ loft for the chapel at Holyroodhouse, following which a pair of organs was installed at a cost of £60 (*TA*, viii, 55, 121). As already noted, there was also an organ loft at Falkland.

Except when the king was in residence, most chapels are likely to have been scantily furnished. An inventory of the contents of St Patrick's Chapel at Dumbarton Castle made in 1510 turned up only a chalice and cruet, a few vestments and 'ane auld mess book of parchment' (MacPhail 1979, 45). A very different picture is revealed, however, by the inventory of the munificently endowed chapel royal of Stirling drawn up in November 1505, just two or three days after the king had left the castle for Edinburgh carrying what was described as the 'hale chapell graith' (also 'certane kirk graith') with him (*TA*, iii, 169; Rogers 1882, pp. xliv–xlix). Presumably, therefore, the items listed were considered to belong to the permanent furnishings of the chapel.

They included costly hangings of velvet and damask for the high altar, brass candlesticks, three large bells brought from London, a clock and the three organs mentioned above, as well as many rich vestments, and a large quantity of jewels, plate and books. Among the more substantial fittings were two large desks of wood standing in the choir and a table carrying what seems to have been a triptych depicting the Virgin Mary and the Christ Child between two angels. Many of these items were probably acquired during the programme of improvements to the building undertaken in the run-up to the formal establishment of the chapel royal in 1501. Particular mention is made in the accounts of the contribution of David Pratt, painter, and David Kervour, wright and carver, who was afterwards awarded a bounty of £15 in recognition of 'all his werkis done to the King, and specialie of the loftis in the chapel of Strivelin' (*TA*, i, 228, 238, 331, 357, 370; ii, 61–69, 429). This programme may also have included the construction of the choir stalls whose canopies were specified as models for those installed in Glasgow Cathedral in 1506 (Fawcett 1995, 46; 1997, 31).

At about the same time work was under way on James IV's new chapel at Holyroodhouse, for which the Treasurer's accounts of 1505 record payments for the purchase of boards 'to the said chapell siling' (*TA*, ii, 280) — a word then used to describe the process of lining roofs and/or walls with timber boards. Possibly in this case it was the ceiling that was close boarded, like the contemporary wagon ceiling of the chapel of King's College, Aberdeen, which is decorated with false ribs. Similar ceilings of earlier date can be found elsewhere in Scotland and they were also common in the Low Countries (Fawcett 1994, 161–162).

4.10 Falkland Palace. Interior of James V's chapel, completed in 1540–41. Refurbished in 1633 and restored in 1893. The timber ceiling is probably original and the timber screen and loft at the west end may also date from the 16th century. The painted decoration belongs mainly to the 1630s.

The accounts also show that considerable sums were expended on the decoration and fitting out of the new chapels erected at Holyroodhouse and Falkland during the 1530s. At Holyroodhouse oak timber was used in the construction of the chapel desks and 'chancelry wall' (perhaps a timber screen dividing off the inner part of the chapel), the ceiling was decorated with turned 'knoppis' (pendants) and the king's arms were prominently displayed, all the carved work being richly painted and gilded by Thomas Angus (*MW*, i, 184, 190–191). As part of the funeral ceremonies of Queen Madeleine in 1537 hangings of Milanese fustian were installed in the chapel (*TA*, vi, 352). At Falkland, where Richard Stewart was responsible for all the woodwork of the chapel and loft (*TA*, vii, 219–220, 274; *MW*, i, 281), we again hear of the desk and chancellary wall, as well as of the ceiling and the carved work of the main east wall of the chapel.

4.10 Happily, the ceiling is still in place, being among the few fittings that survive to illustrate the original internal appearance of the royal chapels of this period. The ceiling, which is of oak, is of simple geometric design, being divided into boarded compartments by moulded ribs; the existing painted decoration is of 1633. The ceiling of the Holyroodhouse chapel was probably similar, but with pendants at the intersections of the ribs and perhaps also in the compartments, as in some English ceilings of the period. The oak screen and loft at the west end of the Falkland chapel (Small 1878, Pls.96–100) and the much restored panelled screen at the east end are also in keeping with what is known of the original design, although they may, in fact, be of somewhat later date. At Linlithgow the chapel ceiling was refurbished or renewed in the mid 1530s, when payment was made to the painter, John Ross, 'for the payntting of the lyning of the chapell syloring with fyne asur and xii ballis under the chapell loffit' (*MW*, i, 123–124, 128).

Another fitting sometimes found in the royal chapel was the traverse (sometimes trevis or tryvis), a small space partially screened off for greater privacy, in which the king could hear mass or receive important visitors. When James V received the Emperor's ambassador in the abbey church of Holyroodhouse in 1532 he did so from a seat and traverse — in this case a timber screen lined with hangings — which had been specially installed for the occasion (*MW*, i, 99). Occasionally the king occupied neither the royal pew — perhaps used mainly during the great festivals — nor a traverse, but simply knelt under a cloth of state, as a James V was doing when Sir Ralph Sadler found him hearing mass in the chapel at Holyroodhouse (Clifford 1809, i, 19). Some thirty years previously an earlier English ambassador, Dr Nicholas West, thought it worthy of remark that James IV had heard mass in chapel 'without any traverse' (Mackie 1953, 321).

Like the hall and chamber, the chapel usually had a paved or tiled floor. In 1468–69 220 squared stones were shipped from Dundee to Stirling to pave and adorn the chapel there (*ER*, vii, 660). The floor of James IV's chapel at

4.11 Falkland
Palace. Chapel
doorway of c.1540.
Finely-cut
mouldings
displaying a roll
and hollow profile,
elaborated by
quirks and fillets,
are found through-
out James V's
work at Falkland.

129

Linlithgow was covered, or partly covered, with what have been identified as imported Flemish tiles (Norton 1994, 151, 153) and these may date from 1506, when the chapel is known to have been paved[7] (*TA*, iii, 297–298). James V's chapel at Holyroodhouse was partly paved in stone (*MW*, i, 194).

4.9   If the chapels of Linlithgow and Holyroodhouse were typical of those in the major royal residences, we can assume that these were normally glazed with a mixture of plain and coloured glass. At Linlithgow in 1534–35 Thomas Peebles installed what was described in the accounts as an image of painted work — perhaps the figure of a saint — in each of the five principal windows of the south wall (*MW*, i, 128), while at Holyroodhouse a year or two later the coloured glass provided for the chapel was of the same character and quality as that installed in the reception rooms of the west quarter (*MW*, i, 190).

NOTES

1   Subsequently the term came to be applied to the parlour or principal bedroom of a castle or mansion (Warrack 1920, 28–30).

2   The keeping of this cloth of estate was entrusted to James Dog, a wardrobe official subsequently commemorated in two of William Dunbar's poems (*TA*, i, 387; Mackenzie 1932, 61–63).

3   The early seventeenth-century scheme for repainting the great hall at Stirling is well documented. At that time (1628–29) it was specified that the upper parts of the walls were to be painted white and the lower parts blue grey. The chimneypieces were to be marbled and decorated with 'crownells' (garlanded crowns?), while the trumpeters' loft was to be 'weill paintit and set af with housingis and pilleris' (*MW*, ii, 257).

4   This assumes that the 'Lyon chalmer' mentioned in the accounts is an alternative name for the great hall.

5   William Lang, one of James I's chaplains, celebrated at the altar of St. James within the parish church (*ER*, iv, 485).

6   The château of Saint-Germain, as reconstructed in the 1540s, had no less than seven chapels, including those of the king and queen. Both the king and queen had their own private chapels at the palace of Westminster (Chatenet 1988, 21–23; Thurley 1993, 195–196).

7   The fact that the floor was laid by masons does not preclude the use of tile and the term 'paviour' can apply to either tile or stone (Cherry 1991, 192 n.11).

Chapter 5

CHAMBER AND WARDROBE

The Role of the Chamber

While the great hall was the main focus of the public life of the court and household, the chamber had a mixed role, part public and part private. In the late thirteenth-century account of the Scottish royal household already quoted the chamber is described in terms which could suggest that it was a particular room to which the king retired after eating in hall and in which he generally lived and slept. (Bateson 1904, 39–40). This may have been so in the smallest residences, but such early records as we have suggest that elsewhere the king might be provided with two or more rooms, as we know had long been the case in England and France (*ER*, i, 389–390; Colvin 1963–73, i, 121–122; Thurley 1993, 4; Mesqui 1991–93, ii, 128). Certainly by the period that we are now considering the chamber invariably comprised a suite of rooms and in contemporary documents the word is used to describe both the suite as a whole, as the physical setting of this particular department of the household, and also the individual chambers within it. The outer room, or rooms, were used for public business and entertainment and were open to at least the higher ranks of those resident at court, while the inner rooms, to which access was strictly controlled, comprised the king's private retreat. The queen and other members of the royal family had their own separately staffed chambers which operated in a similar way.

During the 1530s the staff of the king's chamber numbered just over two dozen, under the direction of the chamberlain and principal carver. They included stewards (sewers), carvers, cupbearers, ushers of the outer and inner chamber doors, yeomen, grooms and a barber, as well as someone to clean and lay fires (Thomas 1995, 2; *TA*, vii, pp. xxxi–xxxv). A similar, but perhaps smaller, complement of chamber servants is known to have existed during the previous reign (*TA*, i, pp. clxxxix–cxci) and some offices can be traced at an earlier period.

The most detailed account to come down to us of the way in which the royal suites functioned on great occasions of state is John Young's eye-witness description of the royal wedding festivities at Holyroodhouse in 1503 (Leland 1770). Since he also provides a very useful account of the furnishing of the

2.9

various rooms, which can be supplemented by entries in the Treasurer's accounts, it is worth quoting at some length here.

As explained in Chapter 2, the royal lodgings were probably grouped round the inner quadrangle of James IV's palace, the king's rooms being situated on the west side and the queen's occupying the south-west corner and part of the south side. Young's account suggests that each suite comprised three main rooms, which he names as hall, great chamber and second chamber or chamber. The only other room that he specifically mentions is the queen's wardrobe and it is probably safe to assume that he did not enter the innermost rooms of either suite. On the royal wedding day, so Young tells us, a large number of the Scottish party dined in the king's hall, the bishops and abbots sitting at a high table and the lords, knights and gentlemen occupying another three tables according to rank. He describes the occasion as a 'double Dynner', which may suggest that two sittings were required to accommodate the large numbers involved. The hall was lit by six large wax candles and decorated with tapestry hangings; there was also a rich dresser for the display of plate. The queen's company, dining in the queen's hall, had to make do with used candles, but there was 'a riche Dressor, good chere and good Wyn'. Since it was only the 8th August the specific mention of candles 'for to lyght at Even' indicates that proceedings continued well into the evening. The hall was hung with tapestries, one piece of which seems to have been bought from an Edinburgh merchant in a job lot shortly before the wedding (Leland 1770, 295–296; *TA*, ii, 214).

The principal receptions were held in the king's and queen's great chambers. On the wedding morning the king received the English delegation, including the Archbishop of York and the Earl of Surrey, standing in his great chamber, bonnet in hand. Thereafter the king sat in a chair of crimson velvet, with the assembled company siting on forms before him, while speeches were delivered by learned divines from each nation. Above the king's chair, and signifying his sovereign rank, hung his cloth of state, which was of blue velvet figured with gold. After the wedding the great chamber served as a dining room for the chamberlain, the steward and other officers of the king's household and we are told that on this occasion, as presumably also during the morning session, it was hung with history tapestries (Leland 1770, 292, 295–296).

The queen's great chamber, too, was hung with tapestries and the windows incorporated panels of painted glass. On the day before the wedding the queen, escorted by her future husband, received the wives of the Scottish lords in her great chamber, the introductions being performed by the Bishop of Moray. After the wedding the ladies of the queen's household, with other English ladies of the highest rank, dined at a table in the queen's great chamber. At another table sat the queen's chamberlain, with many nobles and knights, while a third table accommodated ladies and gentlewomen and a fourth gentlemen alone. On

C.1 Linlithgow Palace. Aerial view from south east showing parish church of St Michael and south and east entrances to the palace. The flying buttresses linking the 'bulwark' to the east range provided structural support.

C.2 Linlithgow Palace. Detail of outer gateway of c.1535 incorporating insignia of the four orders of chivalry to which James V belonged. They are (left to right) the Garter (England), the Thistle (Scotland), the Golden Fleece (Burgundy) and St Michael (France).

C.3 Linlithgow Palace. East entrance. The canopied niches on either side formerly contained statues. The vertical slots flanking the royal achievement housed the gaffs and chains of the drawbridge.

C.4 Linlithgow Palace. Interior of east entrance. The three niches above the transe formerly contained statues. In the centre was a figure of the pope flanked on one side by a knight and on the other by a labourer.

C.5 Linlithgow Palace. View from south west showing (left to right) west range (royal lodging) and south-west tower, south entrance, chapel and stump of south-east tower.

C.6 Linlithgow Palace. View from north west showing (left to right) kitchen tower, north range, north-west tower and west range (royal lodging). The oriel windows lit the closets of the king's inner chamber.

C.7 Falkland Palace. Aerial view from south east showing the shell of the royal lodging in the east range and the footings of the great hall on the north side of the courtyard.

C.8 Falkland Palace. View from north west showing gatehouse and south courtyard range. The water-course serving the palace flowed through the orchard shown in the foreground.

C.9 Falkland Palace. View of gatehouse of c. 1537–41 from south west, as restored during the 1890s. The keeper's lodging occupied the first and second floors.

C.10 Stirling Castle. Aerial view from south showing the 18th-century defences fronting James IV's forework and gatehouse. Beyond lie the palace and other residential buildings grouped round the upper square.

C.11 Stirling Castle. View of James V's palace from south east. The queen's chambers occupied the south range (left), overlooking a terrace behind the forework. The king's chambers occupied part of the east range (right) and most of the north range.

C.12. Holyrood Palace. Aerial view from north west. The late 17th-century palace stands on the site of the earlier one, now represented only by James V's great tower at the north-west corner. The forecourt and stables (foreground) also occupy their earlier positions.

C.13. Edinburgh Castle. Aerial view from north east showing Half Moon Battery (enclosing the stump of David's Tower) and beyond it the principal residential buildings grouped round Crown Square.

C.14 Edinburgh Castle. Interior of Queen's Bedchamber. This little room was originally a chamber or closet within James IV's lodging. James VI was born here in 1566 and in 1617 the chamber was refurbished to commemorate that event. The panelling was added during a more recent refurbishment.

C.15. Edinburgh Castle. Aedicule on Portcullis Gate of c. 1577. The coat of arms, renewed in 1887, is that of the King of Scots, while the heraldic insignia on the frieze above commemorate the Earl of Morton, Regent of Scotland at the time the gateway was built.

C.16. Edinburgh Castle. Heraldic panel incorporated in north façade of James IV's great hall during restoration of 1887–91. It displays the full armorial achievement of the King of Scots.

C.17. *Doune Castle. Aerial view from south east. The design would have been more compact had buildings been erected along the west and south sides of the courtyard as originally intended.*

C.18. *Doune Castle. View from west showing (left to right) gate tower, great hall and chamber (kitchen tower).*

certain other days the king joined the queen in her great chamber after supper for dancing or to watch a play. Indeed, this room may have been particularly favoured for such occasions, and one of William Dunbar's poems on court life is entitled 'Of a dance in the quenis chalmer' (Leland 1770, 291, 295, 299; Mackenzie 1932, 60–61).

The third room of the suite was what Young called the second chamber and which in other contexts was often described as the inner chamber. This functioned as a private sitting room and, depending on the number of rooms available, perhaps also as a bedroom. Throughout the festivities the king and queen seem to have dined and supped separately in their inner chambers, accompanied by a few select guests. On the day of the wedding the king dined with the Archbishops of St Andrews and York (the former being his own brother), the Bishop of Durham and the Earl of Surrey, while the queen entertained the Archbishop of Glasgow. The royal dinner was a formal affair in which high ranking officers of the two households had specific personal duties to perform at table. There was no shortage of gilt and silver plate, for substantial sums had recently been spent on replenishing the king's vessel house. The king's chamber was furnished with red and blue hangings and contained a canopy of state made of cloth of gold. There was also a bed of estate and a rich cupboard of plate. The queen's chamber had hangings of red and purple blue velvet which had cost some £369 and her bed of estate was covered with cloth of gold (Leland 1770, 294–295; *TA*, ii, 213, 241).

Another contemporary description of the way in which state affairs were conducted at Holyroodhouse is provided by an account of James V's reception of the English ambassador, Sir Ralph Sadler, in 1540 (Clifford 1809, i, 17–42). By that date the palace had been equipped with a new set of public rooms in the west range linked to the king's private lodging in the great tower. According to Sadler, his first meeting with the king took place in the chapel. Sadler then sought a more private audience and over the next couple of days further meetings took place in what Sadler describes as the king's privy chamber — a term then unknown in Scotland but which in England was applied to a room, or rooms, situated between the public and private chambers of the royal suite, which accommodated a variety of social and business functions (Thurley 1993, 135–139).

During one of Sadler's audiences with the king the master of the household arrived to tell James that his dinner was on the table. The king thereupon retired to his own quarters to eat, leaving Cardinal Beaton to escort Sadler to a room which he describes as a chamber where the lords used to dine. Here he was entertained by a distinguished company which included the chancellor (the Archbishop of Glasgow), the constable (the Earl of Errol) and the king's nephew, the Earl of Huntly. The whereabouts of this chamber is not specifically stated, but the context suggests that it was either the outer or middle chamber of the reception suite in the west range of the palace.

The account offers a number of clues to the location of the room described by Sadler as the privy chamber. During one of their meetings the king moved from the 'privy chamber' to another room, 'where out of a window he looked into a fair court' where some horses — a present from the ambassador — were paraded for his benefit. It was from this second room that the king was called away for dinner, presumably a solitary repast taken in his own quarters in the 2.9 great tower. Looking at the plan of Holyroodhouse in the light of this account, it seems likely that the 'privy chamber' was the innermost of the three rooms in the west quarter and that the room overlooking the courtyard (i.e. the inner court) was either the north chamber or the mid chamber of the west range.[1] Be that as it may, the episode is of interest in throwing at least a little light on the way in which the chamber functioned on such occasions.

We have already seen how the chamber might be used for organised recreation and entertainment on great occasions of state and it is clear from the records that less formal activities of a similar kind were an integral part of court life. In 1448, for example, we hear of Christmas festivities taking place in the king's chamber at Stirling (ER, v, 318), while the early sixteenth-century Treasurer's accounts include payments to singers and other musicians, including an English cornet player, performing in the king's and queen's chambers (TA, ii, 398; iii, 162, 369). We also hear of the king playing chess and, more frequently, cards there, this latter pastime sometimes being undertaken in the queen's chamber — perhaps her inner chamber —rather than in his own (TA, ii, 388; vi, 464). When James II murdered the Earl of Douglas at Stirling Castle in 1452 the event is said to have taken place in the king's inner chamber, where James was entertaining his friends after supper (McGladdery 1990, 165 quoting Auchinleck Chronicle). We are not told that the company actually supped there although it seems likely that they did. A reference to the 'kingis awine eting chalmeris' at Holyroodhouse c.1530 again suggests that by that time the king probably took most of his meals in an inner room, although a contemporary reference to the 'kingis grace grete chalmeris quhair he eittis' — in this case at Stirling —suggests that there were also occasions on which he dined in one or other of the outer rooms (MW, i, 21, 104). There is some evidence to suggest that towards the end of the sixteenth century the king and queen normally ate either together in the king's chamber, but at separate tables, or separately in their own chambers (Gibson and Smout 1988, 34).

Sleeping habits are equally hard to pin down. We have already seen that at the time of the royal wedding in 1503 the inner chambers of the king's and queen's suites at Holyroodhouse each contained a richly furnished bed of estate. Such beds were designed more for symbolic and ceremonial, than for everyday, use, however, and it is likely that the royal couple normally slept elsewhere. Indeed, we know that at Holyroodhouse the queen had a separate, and more simply furnished, bed in her closet and it was no doubt there that she slept most of the time (*TA*, ii, 213). The great bed that stood in the king's great chamber at Stirling Castle at about the same time was also probably a bed of estate (*TA*, ii, 410) and it likely that he actually slept in one of the inner rooms of his suite in a smaller and less elaborate bed that was transported in the royal baggage train; there are numerous references in the accounts to the carriage of the king's and queen's beds from one palace to another at this period (*TA*, ii, 142; iii, 135, 157; iv, 75, 129, 356).

Indeed, the only persons who are likely to have slept in the outer rooms of the chamber on a regular basis are the chamber servants. In one of the earliest volumes of the Treasurer's accounts to have survived there is an entry recording the purchase in 1473 of 10 ells of canvas 'to mak Nikky and Bell a bed to ly on in the Kingis chalmire' (*TA*, i, 16). Evidently these were two of what are described elsewhere as the children or little boys (i.e. grooms) of the chamber (*TA*, i, 68; ii, 412). Other references suggest that up to half a dozen or so servants might sleep in the chamber at any one time[2] (*TA*, iii, 149, 151; iv, 202).

When the king happened to be a minor, different arrangements had to be made, although these were still governed by carefully considered rules of protocol. An ordinance drawn up in 1522 for the keeping of the ten-year old King James at Stirling Castle under the guardianship of Lord Erskine laid it down that the king's schoolmaster, together with his usher and valets, were to sleep in the king's chamber. Outside the chamber twenty footmen, under the captain of the guard and his lieutenant, were to keep guard throughout the night in watches of four. So far as eating arrangements, were concerned, the king was to dine alone at his own table, Lord Erskine and a few senior members of the household were to dine simultaneously but at a separate table, while other officials were to eat in another building (*Mar and Kellie MSS*, i, 11–12).

The most private room of the suite was usually described as a closet, but occasionally as a study or oratory and in most cases it is probably a mistake to try to distinguish between these three designations in terms of physical space. Among the activities more particularly associated with this innermost room, or rooms, the most important was private devotion. Although the king might frequently hear mass in the palace chapel, as James V was doing when Sadler was first presented to him in 1540 (p. 123), he also worshipped daily in his own closet or oratory. The closet was invariably furnished with an altar and the appropriate plate and vestments — even the closet of the five-week old Prince James had its own altar at Holyroodhouse in 1507 — and the clerks of the closet often served as private chaplains to the various members of the royal family (*TA*, i, 19; ii, 293; iii, 285–286, 288, 403; iv, 268, 441). There is mention of what seems to have been a separate closet and oratory in the king's suite at Holyroodhouse in 1504 and of a separate study and oratory there in 1531–32 (*TA*, ii, 417, 419; *MW*, i, 103). Possibly in these cases the space round the altar was partitioned off to form what in the English royal closet of the period was described as a kneeling-place (Thurley 1993, 126–127).

The closet was also a convenient place in which to transact legal and business matters. In July 1513, for example, James IV received payment of a sum of money from John Gordon of Lochinvar 'in his closet' (*TA*, iv, 419). During the same reign there is record of certain legal transactions concerning the abbey and palace of Holyroodhouse being conducted at various locations there, including the king's chamber, the king's inner chamber and the king's closet (*Prot. Bk. Young*, Nos. 63, 267, 503, 790, 879, 947, 1361, 1422). In 1470 James III gave sasine of the royal castle of Ravenscraig to William, Earl of Caithness, within the royal chamber at Edinburgh Castle in the presence of various bishops and nobles (*Scots Peerage*, ii, 333). In that case, however, proceedings presumably took place in one of the outer rooms of the royal suite and the same was probably true of the 'sises' (assizes) held in the queen's chamber at Stirling Castle in 1504 (*TA*, ii, 441).

Finally, we may note that the closet also provided the most convenient setting for personal hygiene and ablutions — it is no coincidence that the word 'closet' was also used at this period to describe what was otherwise known as a stool of ease or latrine (DOST, closet). The closet was likewise used for bathing, which at that time was usually performed in a wooden tub filled with hot water carried up to the royal suite. In 1504 a tub was provided for the king's closet at Stirling at a cost of 12d; it seems to have been well used for a replacement was required only three years later (*TA*, ii, 429; iv, 77). The queen, too, no doubt bathed in her closet, or in one of the other inner rooms of her suite. Since the closet did duty as a bathroom it was important to keep it warm and there are occasional references to the supply of chimneys (i.e. grates) for he king's and queen's closets (*TA*, i, 22, 36). The more general aspects of hygiene in the royal residences are discussed in Chapter 6.

THE PLANNING OF THE CHAMBER

Turning now to the layout of the chamber it will be helpful to look at surviving examples of royal lodgings in the light of the available documentary evidence. Since all pose problems of interpretation it seems sensible to start with those palaces and castles that are sufficiently well preserved or well documented to enable at least the main elements of the plan to be discerned and then to move on to consider those for which the evidence is largely or wholly tentative.

At Linlithgow the west range contains substantial remains of James IV's lodging, probably completed during the 1490s, while the south range incorporates elusive traces of a previous lodging dating from the reign of James III or earlier. Of this last little can be said other than that it seems to have occupied the space between the south end of the great hall and the chamber tower at the south-west corner of the palace; indeed, the first-floor suite may have extended into the chamber tower. There seem to have been three good-sized chambers at first-floor level with a similar range on the floor above. A latrine shaft visible at the base of the external south wall of the south range confirms that the middle chambers, at least, were residential, while a handsome, canopied fireplace now built into one of the cellars beneath may originally have adorned one of the principal rooms. Presumably the lodging was entered from the upper end of the great hall, where the existing chambers at the south-east corner of the palace could replace an earlier king's hall or great chamber in this position,

1.4

Chamber and Wardrobe

5.1 Linlithgow Palace. King's hall with queen's hall above. The canopied chimey-pieces with elaborately moulded jambs are characteristic of James IV's work in the royal palaces.

while the innermost chambers would have communicated with the original south-west turnpike stair.

James IV's lodging, on the other hand, remains largely intact although it has been roofless since the palace was burnt out in 1746. The king's suite, approached from the contemporary south-west, or King's, turnpike, occupied three main chambers of diminishing size together with a number of smaller rooms. In the building accounts of the 1620s the three larger rooms are identified as king's hall, presence chamber and bedchamber (*MW*, ii, 259–274), although in James IV's day they would probably have been termed hall, great chamber and chamber, or inner chamber. The hall and great chamber both communicated with a timber balcony which straddled the partition between them and provided fine views looking westwards over the loch. The blocked doorways to this and other former balconies and galleries can be seen in the exposed masonry of the internal and external walls. These balconies had evidently disappeared by the time that Slezer's drawings were made in about 1690, but a similar one can be seen in his drawing of the north-east tower (Slezer 1693).

The inner chamber at the north end of the suite could also be entered from the north-west, or Queen's, turnpike, which presumably functioned mainly as a private stair. It gave access not only to the main courtyard of the palace, but also, via a ground-floor corridor, to a little doorway leading into the palace garden on the north. The inner chamber, too, was originally provided with west-facing balcony, as also with several closets, including a group of richly decorated mural chambers in the north gable, one of which was lit by an oriel window. Two of the closets of this group had fireplaces, while the one in the oriel also communicated directly with the north-west turnpike by means of a corridor. Opening off the south end of the chamber was a purpose-built latrine and a strong-room equipped with mural cupboards.

The whereabouts of the queen's suite is not certain and the present writer has previously suggested that it was situated on the first floor of the north range and was thus largely destroyed when that part of the palace was rebuilt *c*.1620 (Dunbar 1984, 21). On further consideration, however, it may be suggested that the balance of the evidence favours a location directly above the king's rooms, where there is an almost identical suite, although there is nothing in the documents to associate these chambers with the queen. It also has to be said that these rooms are less well appointed and less conveniently laid out than those below. Neither the great chamber nor the inner chamber had any west-facing window or balcony, and although there seems originally to have been a balcony opening off the corridor at the south end of the hall, this was not conveniently placed for the queen's use. Nor was the queen's inner chamber as well provided with closets as its counterpart, there being only two corridor-like rooms, together with a latrine. Possibly the queen was expected to ascend the

5.2 *Linlithgow Palace. Closet off king's (inner) chamber. This was one of several small, richly decorated compartments in the innermost part of the king's suite. Here he could say his prayers, transact business and relax with his familiars.*

139

5.2

north-west turnpike to the little chamber known as Queen Margaret's Bower, which is perched at the stair-head. Alternatively she could have descended to the king's floor, where there are traces of what seems to have been a second oriel chamber formerly approached from the corridor running along the side of the king's inner chamber. The better preserved of the two oriels is traditionally known as Queen Margaret's Oratory, and may be the one mentioned in a document of 1513 (*TA*, iv, 524), but it is possible that this name in fact applies to its neighbour.

2.5

At Stirling Castle the shell of James IV's lodging of *c.*1496–97 survives within the fabric of the King's Old Building, while its successor of *c.*1538–42 remains almost intact, although lacking its original fittings and interior decoration, within James V's adjacent palace block. Investigations undertaken by Dr Fawcett during the conversion of the King's Old Building into a regimental museum during the 1970s and 1980s showed that the first floor originally comprised a suite of three principal rooms, two of them contained in the main block and the third, which was ceiled at a lower level, within a wing set at right angles to the north end of the building. A fourth chamber at the south end was identified as a probable kitchen, its oblique alignment suggesting that it incorporated part of an earlier building (Fawcett 1990b; 1995, 35–39). The suite was entered from a turnpike stair at the south end, while traces of a second stair, possibly of secondary construction, were found in the re-entrant angle of main block and wing. The east end of the wing may have communicated directly with the adjacent chapel royal, thus allowing the king private access to a loft or gallery overlooking the main body of the chapel.

The planning of this suite and the overall dimensions of the individual rooms are so similar to those at Linlithgow that we can be fairly confident in identifying the three principal rooms as hall, great chamber or outer chamber, and chamber or inner chamber. Some are named in the documents, which include references (in 1531–32) to 'the turgreis (turnpike stair) that passis up to the kingis chalmer', 'the kingis grace grete chalmeris quhair he eittis', the king's outer chamber and the 'cros chalmer' —perhaps the chamber in the wing (*MW*, i, 103–111). There is also mention of the king's closet and the king's wardrobe (*TA*, iv, 77; *MW*, i, 105), both of which may have been contained within what seems to have been a timber-framed lean-to building at the north end of the main block; there was also a latrine at the north-west corner (Fawcett 1990b, 177). This timber outshot may be the timber gallery built in 1497 (p. 41).

Unlike James IV's lodging at Linlithgow, the Stirling lodging seems not to have incorporated a comparable second-floor suite. The king was, of course, a bachelor when the lodging was built, but there was certainly a queen's suite elsewhere in the castle because there are numerous references to it in the documents (*ER*, vii, 59; *TA*, ii, 441; iii, 151; *MW*, i, 105–111).

James V evidently found these arrangements unsatisfactory and when he came to build his new palace he was careful to commission twin suites for himself and his queen. As we saw in Chapter 2, these were set out, all at one level, round three sides of a hollow square. The king and queen each occupied three principal rooms named in the late 1550s as hall, outer or mid chamber and chamber (*MW*, i, 294–297), together with a group of closets. Each suite was entered independently from a corridor, or gallery on the west, which also contained, at its north end, the principal entrance to the lodging from the inner close. About midway along the corridor another door opened into a balcony, or staircase (now the latter) overlooking the Lions' Den, which may have functioned mainly as a garden and outdoor theatre. The king's outer chamber also communicated directly with the dais end of the adjacent great hall by means of a bridge, while the two chambers (i.e. inner chambers) were placed back to back with intercommunicating doors. The king's chamber had its own strongroom, concealed in the thickness of the north wall.

5.8

The queen's closets have disappeared, but an early eighteenth-century plan (RCAHMS 1963, i, Pl.59) shows that they comprised three intercommunicating rooms opening off her inner chamber. The west one also gave access to a terrace commanding fine views of the adjacent burgh and the Vale of Forth, while between the other two rooms there seems to have been a little private stair leading down to the Lower Square. The king's closets opened off the west side of his inner chamber, being contained within a narrow lean-to building overlooking the Lions' Den. Again there were three small rooms, the north one, which had its own doorway, evidently having been a latrine. The south room had an eastward-facing extension which could well have housed an altar, while the central one also communicated with a private stair leading up to the second floor. From there the king would presumably have followed a rather roundabout route to a stair which seems to have stood at or near the north-west corner of the palace.

With the building of James V's new palace the earlier royal lodgings at Stirling seem to have been demolished or, in the case of the King's Old Building, converted to other uses and there is no indication that any attempt was made to retain one of them as a separate suite, as seems to have been done in similar circumstances at Falkland. When additional accommodation eventually came to be required for another member of the royal family it was contrived within the early sixteenth-century tower adjacent to the queen's hall, long known as the Prince's Tower.[3]

Both James IV and his son erected new lodgings at Holyroodhouse, but only James V's private chambers in the great tower survive, our knowledge of the remaining rooms of that period, as of James IV's lodging in its entirety, being largely dependant upon documentary and graphic sources. As we saw in

Chapter 2, James IV's lodging probably occupied two sides of a quadrangle standing in the same position as the present main court of the palace. We know from later building accounts that the queen's rooms lay mainly on the south side, with her great chamber at the south-west corner of the courtyard (*MW*, i, 189, 191; *TA*, v, 220). The accounts also make it clear that the north side of the quadrangle was occupied by the chapel, which itself seems to have abutted the king's chamber (*MW*, i, 188; *TA*, v, 219). We can also infer from a passage in John Young's report of the royal wedding celebrations of 1503 that the king's and queen's suites communicated directly with each other. In this passage he mentions an incident which occurred on the last day of the festivities, after the weather had broken down. When James IV came to escort Queen Margaret back to her own quarters from the abbey church, so Young tells us, he did not lead her across the courtyard, but 'for Cause that it renned (rained), she passed thorough the Kings Chamber for to go in hyr awne (her own)'[4] (Leland 1770, 300). On this showing, the king's rooms would seem to have occupied all or part of the west side of the courtyard.

Putting these various scraps of information together and bearing in mind that Young also describes and names the principal rooms of each suite (p. 132), we can construct the conjectural first-floor sketch-plan shown on p. 60. The dimensions of the individual chambers — only the principal ones are shown — are based on those found in James IV's lodgings at Linlithgow and Stirling. There would, of course, also have been closets, and perhaps other smallish rooms, either occupying part of the same space or contained within the outshots or galleries whose existence is known from the building accounts. Likewise we must allow for two or more stairs giving access from the courtyard below and perhaps also continuing upwards to an attic floor, but the location of these is uncertain. These rooms remained in use until at least the late 1520s and if the plan is broadly correct in showing twin suites placed end to end on the same level it can be seen as a possible model for James V's lodging at Stirling.

With James V's lodging we are on firmer ground, because not only do the chambers in the great tower itself survive, but the layout of the adjacent rooms in the west quarter is recorded in a first-floor plan prepared by John Mylne in 1663 (Mylne 1893, opp. 148)). As we saw in Chapter 2, James V's lodging was built in two stages, the great tower having been completed in 1528–32 and the west range in 1535–36. The great tower incorporated twin suites on the first and second floors, each suite containing two main rooms named in the building accounts as outer and inner chambers (*MW*, i, 93–95). The two inner chambers were also equipped with pairs of closets contrived within the west angle-turrets of the tower. We know from the accounts that the windows of the outer and inner chambers on the first floor were fitted with painted glass roundels bearing the king's arms and later sources confirm that these were, indeed, the king's

2.9

2.13

own rooms, the queen's suite being placed directly overhead (*MW*, i, 94; Dunbar 1984, 18). The principal entrance was by means of a forestair leading up to a doorway in the east wall of the king's outer chamber on the first floor. There was also a spacious spiral stair in the north-east angle-turret serving all floors and, at some levels, at least, a lesser stair in the south-east angle.[5] In addition, a private stair in the north wall led up from the king's inner chamber to the queen's rooms above.

Part of the former king's suite had already been demolished to make way for the great tower, so James probably moved into his new rooms as soon as they were finished. The queen's new suite, however, is likely to have remained empty until the king's first wife, Madeleine de Valois, arrived at Holyroodhouse five years later. Nor was the former queen's suite in the south quarter retained as an entity for her great chamber was converted into a hall for the household in 1531–2 (*MW*, i, 76). All this must have left the palace rather short of good-sized public rooms and in view of the fact that Holyroodhouse was by now firmly established as the premier Scottish royal residence it is scarcely surprising that James lost little time in supplementing the fairly modest accommodation in the great tower by the construction of a new reception suite.

This comprised two principal rooms described in the building accounts as outer and mid chamber and named in drawings of *c.*1670 as guard hall and presence chamber (*MW*, i, 186, 189–191; Mylne 1893, opp. 168). The outer chamber was approached by an elaborate forestair, while the inner end of the mid chamber opened into the third room of the suite, less than half the size of the other two, which is described in the accounts as a wardrobe or inner chamber and named in seventeenth-century drawings as a lobby (*MW*, i, 186, 190–191; Mylne 1893, opp. 148 and 168). As Mylne's plan shows, this originally provided the only direct means of communication between the reception rooms and the king's private suite in the great tower.[6] A fourth room, described in the accounts as 'the north chalmer nixt the toure' and named in the seventeenth century as the privy chamber (*MW*, i, 186; Mylne 1893, opp. 168) may have formed part of the reception suite (p. 134). Mylne's plan shows an extruded spiral stair in the angle between this chamber and the mid chamber of the west range, but this was probably a seventeenth-century addition. The two small stairs shown at diagonally opposite corners of the inner chamber were no doubt original features.

At Falkland, too, both James IV and his son constructed new royal lodgings and some remains of these survive on the upper floors of the east quarter of the palace. However, the fragmentary state of this range, coupled with the elusive nature of the documentary evidence, makes it difficult to draw firm conclusions about the layout of the royal suites.

Of James IV's lodging of *c.*1501–1512 we can be fairly sure that the principal

2.13

rooms occupied the first floor of the range (p. 27). The building accounts are unhelpful, making mention of the great chamber of Falkland and the queen's chamber, but giving no indication of their whereabouts (*TA*, iv, 283; vi, 215). The spacing of the windows in the west wall and the traces of internal partitions suggest, however, that there were four main rooms, of which the two middle ones communicated with the centrally-placed cross-house. The overall dimensions of the two outer chambers at the north end correspond closely to those of the two outer rooms of James IV's suites at Linlithgow and Stirling, while the chamber in the cross-house, whose position recalls that of the wing at Stirling, was similar in size to the inner chambers of those suites. The dimensions of the two rooms at the south end of the range don't present quite such a close match, but again a possible interpretation would identify these as the hall and outer chamber of the queen's suite, with the inner chamber being situated above the king's inner chamber in the cross-house. Moreover, there is structural evidence to show that the chambers in the cross-house were provided with latrines, which would have suited their proposed role as inner chambers. There must also have been closets, perhaps contained within lean-to buildings opening off the cross-house, as at Stirling.

The king's suite, if that is what it was, would have been approached both directly from the dais end of the great hall, as in James V's suite at Stirling, and by means of a stair occupying the position of the present one of 1537–41 at the north-west corner of the east quarter. Likewise, the queen's suite would have been entered from a stair at the junction of the east and south quarters. Both suites would have used the spiral stair in the cross-house as a private stair to the garden on the east side of the palace, which seems to have been laid out during James IV's reign.

The layout of James V's lodging is even more problematic than that of his father's. Various rooms are mentioned in the accounts, including the queen's inner chamber, the king's closet and, during the 1620s, the presence chamber, but with no indication of their locations (*MW*, i, 214, 218; ii, 291). More helpful are references, in 1583, to 'the corshows (cross-house) nixt the kingis grace chalmur (chamber)' in a context which suggests that the king's rooms lay immediately beneath the roof and, in 1616, to the re-roofing of the king's and queen's galleries, earlier termed the north and south galleries (*MW*, i, 313; *RPC*, x, 517–518).

Certainly there would seem to have been important rooms at this level, because in contrast with the (blocked) second-floor windows of *c.* 1501–12, which are only big enough to have lit an attic, the existing windows of *c.* 1537–42 are good-sized openings which, as depicted by Slezer (1693), originally rose well above eaves level. Internally, the first floor seems to have been divided very much as in James IV's day and one, at least, of the partitions rose through the second floor, where, however, the other divisions are less obvious. The big difference was, of course, that James V's lodgings incorporated corridor-galleries on either side of the cross-house at both first- and second-floor levels.[7] Since the footings of their outer walls incorporate a number of latrine chutes, it is likely that these galleries also accommodated various small rooms.

A possible explanation of these features is that the first floor housed a series of reception rooms, while the king and queen occupied twin private suites on the floor above. The new spiral stair at the south-east corner of the courtyard would have provided the principal means of access to the reception suite, its upper flight serving the queen's rooms above. The king's suite, probably situated on the north side of the cross-house, would have been served by the other new stair at the north-east corner of the courtyard. Each suite would have had its own corridor-gallery — some of the space probably being allocated to closets — and each would have had direct access to the cross-house and garden stair. Such an arrangement, with a clear division between public and private space, would have been broadly similar to the one that we know had actually been introduced at Holyroodhouse a few years earlier. At Falkland, as at Holyroodhouse, there may have been three, rather than four, principal reception rooms, the large chamber at the south end of the range possibly having been utilised primarily as a lords' hall (p. 110). Likewise there would have been space at either end of the private suites for two or three ancillary rooms, such as wardrobes. An alternative interpretation, postulating stacked lodgings for the king and queen, as at Linlithgow, fits the available evidence less well but cannot be ruled out (Dunbar 1984, 22–23).

Turning now to Edinburgh Castle we have already seen in Chapter 3 that fragments of what appears to be the earliest identifiable royal lodging in Scotland survive within David's Tower of c.1368–72, while the shell of James IV's new lodging of the late 1490s can be identified within the adjacent palace block. Only the lowest portion of David's Tower is preserved, but the original L-plan structure seems likely to have contained a stack of chambers within the main block, together with an associated series of closets in the wing. Probably within a century or so of the tower's construction, the re-entrant angle was filled in to form a third room at each level (RCAHMS 1951, 18). The precise layout cannot be established, but a possible arrangement, anticipating that of James V's tower at Holyroodhouse, would place the king's hall (or outer chamber), chamber and closet on the first floor with perhaps a similar suite for the queen on the floor above. The Treasurer's accounts give us a partial glimpse of the interior of the royal suite, for we learn that when the 'cloissat of Daudis Toure' was searched for treasure in 1488 it was found to contain a somewhat mixed bag of artefacts, including a silver vessel for holy water, an empty casket, a glass vessel containing rose water and, surprisingly, 'King Robert Brucis serk (shirt)' (TA, i, 83).

3.5

During the 1430s we hear of the construction of a new great chamber, which appears to have been situated immediately south west of David's Tower and would thus have communicated directly with the king's suite therein. The structural evidence is difficult to interpret, but part of this great chamber may subsequently have been incorporated in James IV's new lodging, which was itself afterwards absorbed within the early seventeenth-century palace that now occupies the site. James IV's lodging was laid out horizontally, its principal floor (above a basement) containing what seems to have been a three-room suite comprising two good-sized chambers with a much smaller one at the south end. To judge from their size and position, the two north chambers were originally designed as a pair of reception rooms — probably hall and great chamber — to supplement the existing rooms in David's Tower. At its north end the hall is likely to have communicated not only with the tower, but also with the kitchens that seem to have stood in this vicinity since the late fourteenth century.[8] The requirement for separate reception rooms evidently did not continue (this was the period when state occasions were increasingly held at Holyroodhouse), for in 1517 the old royal suite in David's Tower was abandoned (TA, v, 120–122) and James IV's hall and great chamber, with the smaller room to the south, seem to have become the principal royal suite of the castle.

So far as we know, James IV's lodging did not contain a parallel suite for the queen on the first floor, but no doubt there was other accommodation, perhaps including the schoolroom in which the infant James V was taught during his childhood years at the castle (ER, xiv, 350; TA, v, 129). The ground-floor apartment continued to be used from time to time until the building of the new palace in 1615–17 (when it again became a reception suite) and the future James VI was born in the little south chamber in 1566.

3.5   At Dunfermline the original fourteenth- and fifteenth-century layout has been obscured both by later alterations and by the loss of the north-west side of the upper court. If we are correct in identifying the very large first-floor chamber at the centre of the south-west range as a great hall, however, then the adjacent chamber at the north-west end is likely to have been a reception room — presumably the king's hall or great chamber — linking the great hall to the more private rooms of the royal suite, which we must assume to have been located in the missing north-east wing and adjacent courtyard range. Such an arrangement would resemble the one proposed for Linlithgow prior to the construction of James IV's new royal lodging in the west range there. In the middle of the seventeenth century the king's lodging at Dunfermline seems to have comprised a three-piece reception suite (guardhall, drawing-room and dining-room), together with his own chamber and bedchamber (SRO GD 28/1705), but it is impossible to say to what extent this arrangement reflected that of the later middle ages.

When we turn to residences of middle and lesser rank documentary evidence that might help to identify the names and functions of the various rooms becomes even scarcer and in most cases interpretation has to be based on comparison with buildings about which rather more is known. This is certainly the case at Doune Castle where, as we have seen in Chapter 3, the royal lodging (originally the duke's) was contained within a massive frontal block situated immediately adjacent to the great hall. On the first floor is a large, well-appointed chamber entered both from the courtyard by means of a forestair and directly from the adjacent great hall via a doorway in the mutual partition. Two spiral stairs lead up to a similar chamber above, the wider one also giving access to a series of small chambers placed at intermediate levels in the north-east drum-tower. Most, but not all, of these lesser chambers were heated and had latrines, either *en suite* or opening off the adjacent stair. The arrangement on the third floor is similar, except that the main floor-area appears to have been subdivided to contain two or more chambers.

5.3 Doune Castle. Duke's (king's) hall, as restored in 1883–86. The double chimney-piece proclaims the occupant's high status and beside it a stair leads to the adjacent chambers in the drum tower.

Current opinion varies as to the way in which these rooms functioned
(Pringle 1987, 18–21, 30; Fawcett 1994, 10), but reading back from later royal
residences such as James IV's lodging at Linlithgow and James V's private lodging
at Holyroodhouse it seems most likely that the two lower floors contained superimposed suites for the duke and duchess (later occupied by the king and queen),
each comprising a hall or great chamber and one, if not two, lesser chambers
in the drum-tower, where there are five chambers in all. In addition, each hall
had a closet opening off the south side, the one on the second floor evidently

*5.4 Dundonald
Castle. Conjectural
reconstruction of
upper hall by
David MacGibbon
and Thomas Ross,
1887. This was
probably the king's
hall. The door at
the far end gave
access to what may
have been a closet
on one side and a
latrine on the
other.*

functioning as an oratory. As Denys Pringle has pointed out, however, the keeper of the castle had also to be accommodated, the most likely position for his lodging also being the frontal block straddling the principal gateway below. Possibly the third-floor chambers were his, or perhaps the planning arrangements were flexible so that when, for example, the castle was being used chiefly as a royal dower-house, as for much of the late fifteenth and early sixteenth centuries, the queen-mother would reside in the second-floor suite, leaving the king's rooms below to be occupied by the keeper.

We know nothing of the arrangements at Kindrochit (p. 95), while at Dundonald (p. 97) only the king's hall appears to have survived. At Ravenscraig (p. 103) the hall in the central block could originally have been designed either as a separate great hall (for which it seems rather small) or as the outermost chamber of the presumed royal suite in the adjacent west tower. The tower itself contained three superimposed chambers (there was also a garret), each provided with one or more closets and a latrine, so, depending on whether or not there was a separate great hall, the royal lodging could have comprised either a pair of suites, each of two main chambers or, as Douglas Simpson argued (Simpson 1938b, 20–21), a single three-roomed suite stacked vertically in the tower.

3.15

The very grand tower-house of Newark (p. 101) contained no fewer than seven floors, of which the three middle ones probably accommodated the royal lodging. On the first floor, and approached directly from the courtyard by means of a forestair, was the king's hall, together with a rather cramped kitchen; opening off the hall were three mural chambers or closets. From the upper end of the hall a private stair rose to what were probably the king's outer and inner chambers, each provided with its own closet and latrine. Above was a similar pair of chambers presumably available for the queen, should she choose to join the royal hunting expeditions to Ettrick Forest. The principal stair in the north-west angle of the tower seems latterly to have served all floors, but the doorway leading into the king's inner chamber is awkwardly placed, suggesting that the king's own rooms may originally have been accessible only from the private stair.

3.15

Finally, the upper floors of the forework of Rothesay Castle contain the fragmentary remains of the lodging begun by James IV *c.*1512 and completed by his son some 30 years later (p. 97). Interpretation is made difficult by the loss of most of the original south and east walls of the building and by its subsequent reconstruction for the 3rd Marquess of Bute in 1900, but the first floor evidently contained a well-appointed chamber having its own latrine housed in an adjacent turret on the west side. Access was obtained both internally via a mural stair leading up from the entrance passage below and externally by means of a forestair from the courtyard. This last opened into a little chamber at the south end of the forework, which seems to have served both as a lobby, or anteroom, and as a place from which to operate the portcullis mechanism associated with the passage below (Hewison 1893–95, ii, 114–121; Simpson 1937–40, 174–79; Pringle 1995).

The principal first-floor chamber is probably to be identified as the king's hall and its overall dimensions correspond closely with those of the corresponding rooms in James IV's suites at Stirling and Linlithgow. The two upper floors were approached by a spiral stair opening off the lower end of the hall. Each also communicated with the latrine turret, while on the second floor there are traces of what may have been a vaulted closet or oratory immediately to the south of the stair. The positions of the dividing partitions are not entirely clear, but the arrangement may have been similar to that proposed for Newark, with the king's outer and inner chambers on the second floor and a similar suite for the queen above. Alternatively, the queen may have been accommodated within one of the two adjacent drum-towers which communicated with the lodging by means of the earlier wall-walk. The wall-walk and towers seem to have been heightened at the time of the construction of the forework.

As is all too obvious from this review of the planning arrangements of the individual residences, the available evidence is patchy and often ambiguous. It would therefore be foolish to construct neat conclusions and try to discern clear patterns of development. Some tentative generalisations may, however, be attempted.

As we have seen, the Scottish royal chamber normally comprised either two or three main rooms, together with one or more lesser ones. In fact, it is difficult to find convincing evidence of the two-room suite, except in private lodgings such as James V's great tower at Holyroodhouse. Thus, the two first-floor rooms in David's Tower at Edinburgh Castle that have been tentatively identified as the king's hall and chamber may from the beginning have been linked to an adjacent great chamber, the one built during the 1430s quite possibly having been a direct replacement for the great chamber that is known to have been constructed during Edward III's occupation of the castle (*Cal. Doc. Scot.*, iii, No. 1186). Likewise the king's suite (originally the duke's) at Doune Castle, which seems at first sight to have comprised only a hall and chamber, could well have included two of the stacked chambers in the north-east drum-tower, although only one of these has a built-in fireplace. Certainly, by the reign of James IV, which is the earliest period for which there is sufficient information for us to speak with some degree of confidence, the three-room suite, plus closets, had become the norm and this continued to be the case during the following reign.

The terminology of these rooms, as recorded in contemporary documents, is inconsistent, perhaps in part reflecting a flexible approach to planning. The outermost room was generally known as the hall, but occasionally as the outer chamber; subsequently it became the guardhall (*MW*, ii, 256). This was the most public room of the suite and was probably used mainly as an assembly room, where those awaiting access to the inner rooms would gather under the eyes of the ushers and yeomen. It was also used as a dining room for senior members of the household. The middle chamber was sometimes described simply as such, but more often as the great chamber or outer chamber; in 1584 we find it named (at Stirling) as 'our awin hall' (*Elphinstone MSS*, 192–193), while in the early seventeenth century is was sometimes known as the presence chamber (*MW*, ii, 267). The great chamber was the principal room of public reception and, like the hall, also served as a dining-room for courtiers and selected members of the household. The third room was generally known as the inner chamber, or chamber, but occasionally as the second chamber or the wardrobe; subsequently it became the bedchamber (*MW*, ii, 267). This functioned as a private sitting-room and sometimes also as a bedroom. Beyond the principal chambers lay the most intimate space of the suite, comprising one or more smaller rooms described as closets, studies or oratories. Here the king could perform his personal devotions, conduct private business, relax with intimates and, on most days, also eat and sleep.

It is interesting to find that these room divisions do not correspond precisely with what we know of the contemporary staffing divisions of the chamber which, at least during the late 1530s, distinguish only between ushers of the outer and inner chamber doors (*TA*, vii, p. xxxiv; Thomas 1995, 1–2). Possibly these arrangements reflected an earlier, two-fold division of space which had become obsolete by the sixteenth century in all but the smallest royal houses. Elsewhere, it would seem likely that the ushers of the outer chamber controlled access both to the king's hall and great chamber, while the ushers of the inner chamber had responsibility for all the inner rooms. Payments made for livery clothes show that the ushers of the inner chamber door ranked higher than their colleagues of the outer chamber door, receiving in the late 1530s £20 per annum as against £13 6s 8d (*TA*, vii, 125; 331–333). Similar payments made during the late 1520s suggest that at that time the ushers of the outer chamber were known as ushers of the high chamber or great chamber (*TA*, v, 307–310; 382–384; 431–432; vi, 203–205).

Although the Scottish chamber developed independently and its planning shows a number of distinctive features, the sequence of rooms described above is broadly comparable to that found in France and England. In France the arrangement during the reign of Francis I usually comprised an assembly room (*salle*), a principal reception room which doubled as a bed-sitting room (*chambre*) and one or more private rooms (*cabinets, garderobes* etc.). This, in turn, had grown out of an earlier system again involving three (originally two) main rooms

(Prinz and Kecks 1985, 129–148; Mesqui 1991–93, ii, 127–134; 1996, 58–59; Boudon and Chatenet 1994; Baillie 1967, 182–93).

In England there was greater differentiation of space, the Early Tudor palace normally containing a sequence of four main rooms — great chamber or guard chamber, presence chamber, privy chamber and bedchamber, in addition to which, in the larger palaces at least, there were usually a number of smaller and more intimate rooms. Previously the English royal suite, too, had comprised three main rooms and the privy chamber, introduced by Henry VII to safeguard the monarch's personal privacy, became both an additional room and a separate department of the household. Subsequently Henry VIII expanded the inner chambers of the suite still further, leading to a multiplication of rooms for which there is no parallel in Scotland and France (Colvin 1963–73, iv, part ii, 11–14; Thurley 1993, 120–143; Starkey 1987). Although, as we have seen (p. 133), the English ambassador to the court of James V recorded a meeting with the king in his privy chamber at Holyroodhouse in 1540, there is, in fact, no evidence of the existence of the Scottish privy chamber as an administrative entity prior to the reign of James VI, while in architectural terms it seems to appear only in the 1630s (SRO, E 34/35, fol.5^r; *Marriage Papers*, Appendix III, 23–38; Balfour 1824–25, ii, 198).

Although the Scottish chamber had an established sequence of rooms, the actual planning arrangements varied in accordance with the size and layout of the individual residence. With the erection of David's Tower at Edinburgh Castle in the late 1360s and the adoption of the tower-house as a favourite royal and seigneurial building-type it is not surprising that a number of later royal lodgings also took this form. Indeed, all the smaller castles and houses that we have discussed incorporated tower-residences, as also did Doune Castle and James V's palace of Holyroodhouse. We know that in the great tower at Holyroodhouse the queen's rooms were placed directly above the king's and this makes it likely that the same arrangement was followed in other stacked lodgings. A similar system seems to have prevailed in France, although with some notable exceptions, such as Charles V's Louvre, whereas in England during the short period that stacked lodgings were fashionable, it has been suggested that the king's rooms usually occupied the higher position (Mesqui 1991–93, ii, 29, 122–123; Thurley, 1993, 18, 31, 41–43; Meirion-Jones *et. al.* 1993, 179).

In the larger palaces the suites were usually laid out horizontally, the royal lodgings being placed along one or more sides of a courtyard. They might comprise single suites, like James IV's lodging at Stirling, or twin suites placed either at the same level, as in James V's palace at Stirling and perhaps James IV's palace at Holyrood, or one above the other as probably at Linlithgow. With the chapel necessarily laid out on an east-west axis, it was often found convenient to align the royal lodging north-south, a position which, in a northern latitude, gave the occupants the benefit of both morning and evening light. This arrangement is found in James IV's lodgings at Stirling, Linlithgow and Edinburgh, as also at Falkland and, in part, at Holyroodhouse and James V's lodging at Stirling.

Whatever the precise planning arrangements adopted, the rooms were always placed in diminishing order of size and increasing order of intimacy. Although it is not feasible to make precise comparisons, it looks as if room sizes were to some extent standardised. For example, the outermost room (i.e. the hall) of the king's suite in a number of palaces falls within a range between about 14.0 x 6.0m and 15.1 x 6.7m, with an average proportion of about 1:2.1, while the middle room (i.e. the great chamber or outer chamber) falls within a range between about 10.0 x 7.0m and 11.7 x 7.0m, with an average proportion of about 1:1.6.[9]

Except where the external ground level was high enough to permit direct entry, as in James IV's lodging at Edinburgh and James V's lodging at Stirling, access was by staircase. In the larger residences there were usually at least two staircases, the principal, or ceremonial, one leading directly up to the outermost room of the suite and a private one giving separate access to the inner chamber and closets. At Linlithgow, in James III's day, the principal stair, composed of a straight flight of steps, led up to the great hall, while a spiral stair at the SW corner of the courtyard gave direct access to the royal lodging, an arrangement which recalls that often found in fourteenth and fifteenth-century France, where different stair types were used to distinguish public and private means of access to the royal suite (Whitely 1996, 73). At Doune, and at James V's Holyroodhouse, the principal stair was an open forestair leading to the first floor only, but elsewhere there was usually an external spiral staircase serving all the main floors very much like the *grande vis* in France (Mesqui, ii, 93–96, 165–167).

The suites were usually of single-room width, the individual chambers opening directly into one another and often being lit from two sides. The exception was the east quarter of Falkland Palace as remodelled in the late 1530s. There the building was divided longitudinally into two unequal parts by a spine   1.12
wall, on one side of which there seem to have been suites of principal rooms overlooking the courtyard, while on the other there were smaller rooms and galleries overlooking the gardens below. As the present writer has pointed out at greater length elsewhere (Dunbar 1991, 6–7), the main elements of the Falkland plan appear to be paralleled in the Francis I wing of c.1515–24 in the royal château of Blois, although there, as at Falkland, the detailed room arrangements are uncertain (Boudon and Chatenet 1994, 72). We know that James V and his future wife, Madeleine de Valois, and probably also the master-mason Moses Martin, stayed with Francis I at Blois on two occasions during the autumn of

1536 (Bentley-Cranch 1986, 88), immediately prior to the commencement of building operations at Falkland, and while the initial construction of the galleries there had probably taken place a few years previously, it may well be that the ensuing remodelling of the royal lodging owed something to the planning at Blois.

Only in one or two of the largest and most important residences did the king and queen enjoy the luxury of a separate private lodging. At Holyroodhouse, which by the beginning of the sixteenth century had become the principal seat of the court, there is evidence to suggest that James IV had additional private accommodation in the south tower (p. 59), while his son took care to build himself a separate private lodging in the great tower before going on to create a new reception suite nearby. At Edinburgh Castle David's Tower may have functioned as a private lodging for a short time during the reign of James IV (p. 146), while at Falkland, if the interpretation proposed above is correct, James V constructed twin private suites for himself and the queen on the second floor of the east quarter.

THE FITTINGS AND FURNISHINGS OF THE CHAMBER

Although something has already been said about the interior decoration of the king's and queen's chambers at Holyroodhouse at the time of the royal wedding there in 1503 (p. 132), it may be useful to say a little more about the fittings and furnishings of the royal chamber in general. As we might expect, only a very few artefacts of the period now under review have survived the vicissitudes of more recent centuries and, although our knowledge of the royal interior can be filled out to some extent from contemporary sources such as the Treasurer's accounts and the accounts of the masters of works, these do not supply much in the way of detailed information before about 1500.

4.11 Among the most durable internal fittings were the dressed stone surrounds of doorways, fireplaces and other openings. These were usually treated quite plainly, featuring either a simple, chamfered arris or some variant of the ubiquitous roll and hollow moulding. The private lodgings of the king and queen within James V's tower at Holyroodhouse provide a good example of the unostentatious, but seemly, effect achieved by this sort of approach. For the outer and more public rooms of the royal suite, however, a greater element of display was often considered appropriate and this is well seen in the prominent and boldly-

5.3
5.6 modelled chimneypieces that were installed in the duke's hall at Doune Castle
5.7 and in James IV's lodgings at Edinburgh Castle and Linlithgow. The most elaborate items of this kind to have survived are the exotic Renaissance chimney-pieces in the royal suite of James V's palace at Stirling, whose ornate capitals were probably originally set off by painted decoration on the simply modelled jambs and lintels. Almost certainly carved by French masons, and reflecting the

5.5 Stirling Castle.
Ground-floor
doorway of James
V's palace of
c.1538–42. Quirked
edge-roll mouldings
of this kind are
found throughout
the palace. Such
mouldings were
carved from timber
templates.

155

5.6 Edinburgh
Castle. Chimney-
piece probably
installed during the
1490s in what was
then the hall of
James IV's lodging
(now the laich
hall).

sort of work that James must have seen during his recent travels in France, for example at Blois and Bury, these chimneypieces cannot fail to have impressed upon the king's visitors that they were entering the presence of a well-travelled monarch, fully abreast of the latest fashions in Western European architecture and decoration.[10] Another innovative feature of the palace of Stirling was the use of broad edge-roll mouldings to frame doorway- and window-openings, a device which soon became popular in baronial architecture throughout Scotland.

So far as the surrounding wall surfaces were concerned, these were usually lined, or partly lined, with hangings, the exposed areas being plastered and painted. During the reign of James V, and perhaps earlier, some rooms were also fitted with timber linings in the form of close boarding or framed panels

5.7 Stirling Castle. Chimneypiece of c.1540 in king's chamber of James V's palace. The effect of the carving was probably heightened by gilding and painting.

157

5.8 Stirling Castle. Detail of chimney-piece of c.1540 in king's outer chamber of James V's palace. The eagle capital is likely to have been carved by a French mason. To the right is a cupboard or strongroom.

covering at least the lower parts of the walls. Hangings varied both in kind and quality, the finest and most costly items, such as cloth of gold (i.e. silk containing a high proportion of gold thread) and tapestry woven with metallic thread, invariably being imported. Most of the subjects depicted in tapestries were drawn either from the Bible or from classical mythology, but non-narrative tapestries known as 'verdures', which featured flowers and foliage intertwined with exotic beasts, were also popular and armorial subjects were purchased from time to time (*ER*, iv, 680).

Although there are numerous references in the Treasurers' accounts to the purchase and transport of hangings for the royal chamber, these seldom reveal the precise disposition of the articles in question. In any case, hangings, like other furnishings, were often moved around or taken from one residence to another. We learn, however, that in 1501 the king's inner chamber at Stirling Castle was hung with scarlet, lined with Breton cloth and bordered with velvet; there were matching bed hangings (*TA*, ii, 23). Scarlet cloth was also used for the hangings of the queen's closet at Holyroodhouse in 1503 (*TA*, ii, 213). James V seems to have had similar tastes for in 1532 his closet at Stirling was hung with scarlet, bordered with black velvet, this time with a matching cover for the table (*TA*, vi, 25). In addition to mural hangings and bed hangings, window curtains were also provided, for example of sey (serge) for the queen's windows in 1507 (*TA*, iii, 397), as well as cloths of state, which were usually constructed of the most expensive materials.

Scottish kings had for long been accustomed to lay out money on the purchase of tapestries from the great manufacturing and trading centres of northern Europe (*ER*, iv, 678, 680), but so far as we can judge James V was more active than most in this respect. At about the time of his two French marriages, in particular, he made several significant purchases in Flanders and in Paris, including tapestries showing the *Story of the Triumphant Dames*, the *New and Old Stories*, the *Creation of the World* and the *Histories of the Gods*, of which these last alone may have cost as much as £1174 (*TA*, vi, 151; vii, 17, 28, 39, 43–44, 51, 257, 290; Thomson 1815, 31–54). A further purchase in 1541 'to complete ane chalmer of the antique historie' may refer to the same set of tapestries (*TA*, vii, 471).

An inventory of James V's wardrobe drawn up in 1539 lists over 100 fine tapestry hangings, some recently purchased but others evidently far from new, and most of them depicting scenes from the Old Testament and ancient history. There were also a dozen pieces of cloth of gold and cloth of silver with several pales of the same (Thomson 1815, 49–51). So far as is known, none of these pieces is extant today, although some may have survived long enough to be taken south in 1603. The inventory does not reveal the whereabouts of these items and little precise information is available on this subject. It is clear from

Young's account of the wedding celebrations at Holyroodhouse in 1503, however, that great care was taken in the selection of chamber hangings on ceremonial occasions (Leland 1770, 290–300; *TA*, ii, 213). If Young's report is accurate, only the two outer rooms of each suite were hung with tapestry, the king's hall with the *History of Old Troy* and the queen's hall with the *History of Hercules*. The same subjects were displayed in the two great chambers, but in the reverse order i.e. *Troy* on the queen's side and *Hercules* on the king's side. Possibly this choice of subject matter carried an allusion to the principal characters at the wedding, with the king in the role of the valiant but art-loving Hercules and his bride in that of the lovely Helen. Either at this time, or on some similar occasion, the court festivities must have included an open-air enactment of the siege of Troy, for a charter of 1582 mentions the existence of a garden in the abbey precincts '*vocatum the Sege of Troy*' (*RMS*, v, No. 456). The king's and queen's inner chambers were apparently furnished with velvet hangings and their beds of state and cloths of state were covered with cloth of gold. It seems likely that this arrangement was designed to achieve a progressive build up in magnificence from one room to another, although the absence of tapestry from the inner chambers is surprising. It may be noted that schemes of interior decoration in Tudor England seem usually to have been organised along hierarchical lines (Campbell 1996, 115; Thurley 1993, 222).

Although textile hangings were the most usual form of wall covering throughout the period under review, timber linings, employed either with or without hangings, became increasingly fashionable from the early sixteenth century onwards. As well as providing a field for carved and painted decoration, timber cladding was valued for its insulating qualities and its ability to keep out draughts. The earliest dateable examples of mural panelling of a secular character to have survived in Scotland, the celebrated Montrose panels, were apparently installed (possibly in the hall of a hospital founded by Abbot Panter of Cambuskenneth at Montrose) *c.*1516–19 (*Angels*, 108) and are evidence that the technique was already well established by that time. If so, the royal houses and castles are likely to have led the way, although clear evidence of the use of timber linings becomes available only in the 1530s.[11]

The building accounts for James V's tower at Holyroodhouse show that the walls of the royal chambers on the first and second floors were lined with 'estland burd' (Baltic fir). The work was carried out by a highly skilled team of wrights and carvers and some of it was evidently of a decorative character for we hear of 'certane pannalis and wyndo breddis' (shutters), 'mullaris and fillatis' (mouldings and fillets) and 'certane fyalis upon schorne verk' (certain finials upon carved work) (*MW*, i, 76–77, 87, 89–91). The reception rooms in the west range of the palace may also have been lined or panelled,[12] as were some of the royal chambers at Falkland (*MW*, i, 214, 281). A report on the condition of the east quarter at Falkland, drawn up in 1583, specifically states that the north and south galleries and the cross-house had originally been 'syllowrit perfytlie with wanescott' (*MW*, i, 313), probably indicating the use of oak in this instance and the building accounts of the 1530s do, in fact, contain several

5.9 *Stirling Castle. Mid sixteenth-century oak panel possibly originally installed in one of the royal chambers of the palace. Several of James V's palaces contained excellent examples of Renaissance design.*

161

references to the purchase of oak timber (*MW*, i, 73, 219, 261–263, 285–287). As in certain other cases, however, it is difficult to know whether the cladding was applied both to wall and ceiling or to one or other of these alone.

5.9
None of this work survives and, apart from a panel of about 1540 from Linlithgow Palace which could, in fact, come from a piece of furniture (Pringle 1989, 22), the only extant fragments of chamber linings of this period appear to be the series of oak panels with medallion heads said to have formed part of the wainscoting at Stirling Castle (Richardson 1925–26, 402–404; RCAHMS 1963, ii, 400; *Renaissance Arts*, no. 50). Prior to their purchase for museum purposes in 1876 these panels were still in their frames, apparently arranged in four rows having a total height of about 2.0m. Their original location is not known, but in his description of the king's and queen's chambers in the palace compiled *c.*1720 John Macky specifically commented on 'the Fineness of the Carv'd Work, in Wainscot and on the Cieling, there's no Apartment in *Windsor* or *Hampton-Court* that comes near it' (Macky, 1723, 187). As it happens, evidence for the former existence of timber linings in the queen's inner chamber has recently come to light in the form of 'dook holes' extending from the floor to about the height of the door lintels.[13]

There seem to be too many panels for these to have formed part of a cupboard or other article of furniture and it appears probable that they were, indeed, employed as wall linings for one of the royal chambers in the palace, although their precise disposition can only be guessed at.[14] The panels probably date from the early 1540s, when the palace was being fitted out, and among the various names that have been suggested in connection with their authorship (p. 52), the most likely would seem to be that of the French carver and wright, Andrew Mansioun, who is known to have been particularly skilled in the execution of fine detail. The panels are of exceptionally high quality, superior to that found in the associated chimneypieces, and Mansioun, as a young craftsman recently arrived from France, is more likely than most to have been conversant with the fashionable Renaissance style so confidently displayed in the carvings.[15]

5.3

5.4
Ceilings, too, were generally of timber, although some of the earlier castles had stone ones, the most notable examples being the lofty barrel-vault of the duke's hall at Doune Castle and the pointed vault spanning the king's hall at Dundonald, of which only the springers now survive. This last was decorated with planted ribs imitating the structural ribs of a genuine quadripartite vault. Of timber ceilings we know little prior to the turn of the fifteenth and sixteenth centuries and the few surviving examples belong to this, or to a slightly later period. To judge from the scanty evidence that remains, James IV's chambers in the west quarter of Linlithgow Palace were covered with flat ceilings comprising a horizontal framework of joists clad on the under side with boards (and perhaps ribs), like the surviving ceiling of St. Machar's Cathedral, Aberdeen.

*5.10 Holyrood
Palace. Detail of
timber ceiling of
queen's outer
chamber in great
tower. The ceiling
probably dates
from the 1530s, but
it was refurbished
in 1558–59 and
again in 1617. The
initials are those of
James V, his
daughter Mary,
Queen of Scots,
and her first
husband Francis,
the dauphin of
France.*

163

C.14

5.10

5.11 Holyrood Palace. Ceiling of queen's inner chamber in great tower. The ceiling probably dates from the 1530s, but was refurbished in 1617 and again later.

The south chamber of James IV's suite at Edinburgh Castle retains a ceiling of this type, which may have originated in the late 1490s, although it owes its present construction to a refurbishment carried out for James VI's homecoming in 1617. The contemporary royal lodging at Stirling seems to have had no upper floor and eighteenth-century drawings suggest that the principal rooms rose into the roof space, the ceilings being of polygonal cross-section, perhaps creating the appearance of a wagon vault (Fawcett, 1995, 37).

Although the building accounts for the fitting out of James V's great tower at Holyroodhouse in the early 1530s are not particularly informative (*MW*, i, 56–105), it is likely that the existing, flat, timber ceilings of the queen's rooms on the second floor were installed either at that time or later in the same decade. They are divided into geometrical-shaped panels by moulded ribs, the boarded panels containing carved and painted insignia which in their present form evidently date mainly from 1558–59 and 1617 (Laing 1866–68; RCAHMS 1951, 151; Fawcett 1988, 34–35). Like the similar ceiling in the chapel of Falkland Palace, the design and construction resemble that found in contemporary English and French ceilings, e.g. at Whitehall and Plessis Bourré (Thurley 1993, figs. 281–282; Babelon 1986, 175) and in the slightly earlier ceiling at St. Machar's Cathedral. The ceilings of the reception rooms in the west range at Holyroodhouse do not survive, but it would seem from the painter's account of 1535–36 that they were of similar type, but with 'gret hingand knoppis' (large pendants) at the intersection of the ribs (*MW*, i, 191), as in the ceiling of the great watching chamber at Hampton Court (Thurley 1993, 122, 232).

The finest ceilings of this kind in any of the royal houses, however, were almost certainly those covering the king's and queen's rooms in James V's palace of Stirling (Dunbar 1975; Shire 1996a, 84–96). How many there were is uncertain, but the surviving fragments — a series of oak medallions known as the Stirling Heads — formed part of what was probably the most elaborate of these ceilings, that of the king's outer chamber (afterwards the presence chamber).

5.12 Stirling Castle. Conjectural reconstruction of king's outer chamber of James V's palace by Geoffrey Hay, 1963. Medallion heads and figures of classical inspiration, here used to decorate the ceiling, were a characteristic feature of Renaissance design.

5.13 Stirling Castle. One of the oak medallions of c.1540 known as the Stirling Heads, which originally formed part of the ceiling illustrated in figure 5.12. It may represent Apollo.

The large size of the medallions (0.74m in diameter on average) and the bold relief of the carving, coupled with the fact that many of the heads are likely to represent well-known figures at James V's court, make this a work of outstanding artistic and social interest. Based ultimately upon Italian models, but possibly derived more directly from a French source, such as the coffered stone ceiling of the principal staircase at the château of Azay-le-Rideau,[16] the ceiling is evidently the product of two or more carvers and in style and subject matter shows links both with the stone carvings of the palace and with the contemporary wainscot panels already described. Some of the medallions show traces of colouring and it is likely that the whole ceiling was originally painted.

Floors were generally of timber strewn with coarse grass (bent) and rushes mixed with sweet-smelling herbs such as bog-myrtle (gall) and the accounts contain numerous references to the provision of these materials for the royal chambers (*ER*, iv, 615; *TA*, ii, 428, 450; iii, 150–151, 154, 163). During the reign of James

*5.14 Linlithgow
Palace. Glazed
floor tile from
king's great
chamber. The
initials are those of
either James IV
and Margaret
Tudor or James V
and Mary of
Guise.*

IV there are records of the carriage of grass from East Lothian, where the sand dunes in the vicinity of Dunbar and Dirleton seem to have provided an abundance of suitable materials (*TA*, ii, 111, 113, 117, 139, 383, 407, 418, 428). These particular consignments were probably destined for the royal suites at Edinburgh Castle and Holyroodhouse and storage facilities for bent were maintained in Edinburgh by staff of the wardrobe (p. 177).

Some floors, however, were paved with stone or tile, the best known example being that of the king's great chamber at Linlithgow Palace, now represented by a simplified modern copy. In its original state this comprised stone quarries combined with green-glazed tiles, the whole forming a decorative, geometric pattern; the central area incorporated a number of tiles stamped with the intertwined initials IM (Kerr 1880–81; Norton 1994, 50–4). This floor is usually assigned to the period 1503–13 on the grounds that the initials are those of James IV and Margaret Tudor, but the associated chimneypiece belongs to the same series as those in James V's suite at Stirling Castle and probably dates from c.1540. It is possible, therefore, that the floor was laid, or re-laid, at that time and that the initials are those of James V and Mary of Guise.[17]

The Linlithgow tiles are thought to be mostly local products, but there is evidence of the sporadic importation of Flemish floor tiles into Scotland from the late fourteenth century to the mid sixteenth century (Norton 1994, 153) and those purchased for Holyroodhouse in 1503 were probably of this kind (*TA*, ii, 271); the fact that they cost £3 per 1000 suggests that they were of good quality though probably not patterned. The plain, green-glazed tiles of which fragments have been discovered in the king's rooms in James IV's lodging at Stirling (Fawcett 1995, 37) may also have been imported from the Low Countries. James V's reception rooms in the west quarter of Holyroodhouse may have had floors similar to that at Linlithgow for there is record of the laying of mixed pavement stone and tile at the palace in 1536 (*MW*, i, 136). Later in the same year 8000 plain tiles were imported for use at Holyroodhouse, together with five chests of what were probably patterned tiles (*MW*, i, 184). These were presumably intended for use either in the royal chambers or in the chapel. The red, buff and black floor-tiles in the Duke's hall at Doune Castle are said to be based upon fragments recovered during the restoration of the 1880s, but it is not known whether or not these dated from the foundation of the castle c.1400 (Simpson 1982, 30).

It is possible that a few of the finest floors were composed of plaster, while some of the most intimate chambers, as also those in which the king held state, would have been provided with carpets. In 1503 James IV purchased 'ane gret liar of set werk of worsait' (a large carpet of wrought worsted work) for £40, while during his visit to Lyon in the autumn of 1536 James V bought two large Turkey work carpets for £190 the pair (*TA*, ii, 214; vi, 314). James V had four large carpets of this kind — each possibly measuring abut 5 x 10m — in his wardrobe, as well as fifteen smaller ones, some of which were probably used as table covers (Thomson 1815, 49–51; Thurley 1993, 230).

Plaster was probably employed as a cladding material, especially as a covering for stone walls, throughout the Middle Ages, although evidence of its use in secular buildings is scanty prior to the reign of James IV. At that time the plaster used in the royal residences seems to have been either imported directly from France or manufactured locally from alabaster stone brought from England, and the plasterers themselves were either French or English[18] (*TA*, ii, 274, 381, 389; iv, 284). In 1504, for example, 20 tons of plaster costing 50s per ton were purchased from a French merchant for use at Stirling and Holyroodhouse and later in the same year clothing was supplied to 'the Franch plaistirman' in his capacity as a royal employee (*TA*, ii, 277, 324, 450, 469, 473). All this suggests that plasterwork was then seen as an expensive and highly specialised craft and

5.3

therefore one to be employed sparingly in places where it would achieve the greatest effect. However, the documents give little indication as to where and how plaster was applied, although it seems likely that it was employed not only for internal but also for external use. The plaster purchased for the turrets of the gatehouse at Holyroodhouse in 1503, for example, was probably for external application (*TA*, ii, 273–274).

The building accounts of James V's reign are a little more informative. From these we learn that plaster was still being imported, probably mainly from France, and that there was at least one French pargeoner (the term usually employed at that time) in the service of the royal works, as well as several Scots (*MW*, i, 184, 213, 280). One of the pargeoners at Linlithgow was described as 'bayth slatar' and 'perjonar' (*MW*, i, 129). Their work, described as pargeoning, harling and whitewashing, seems mainly to have involved the plastering of internal and external walls and specific reference is made to the pargeoning of the queen mother's oratory at Holyroodhouse by Hector Beato, Frenchman, in 1538 (*MW*, i, 93, 106, 109, 191, 213, 224, 257, 280). It is impossible to draw a clear line between harling and pargeoning, but in one case the former is specifically stated to be external work and the latter internal work (*MW*, i, 280). There is no evidence of the use of ornamental or modelled plasterwork, but a reference to 'layand the plaster in the kingis chalmeris' at Holyroodhouse in 1535 may refer to the installation of plaster floors of the kind sometimes found in Tudor palaces (*MW*, i, 191; Thurley 1993, 230).

Painted decoration, applied to stone, timber and plaster, is likely to have been a familiar feature of the royal interior from an early date although little specific information is available prior to the sixteenth century. In 1328, for example, verdigris and olive oil were used for painting the king's chamber at Cardross, while the building accounts for Linlithgow Palace in 1433–34 record the expenditure of the considerable sum of £37 16s on the purchase of colours for Matthew, the king's painter (*ER*, i, 118; iv, 579). Surviving work of a date earlier than 1500, virtually all of it in ecclesiastical buildings, shows a fondness for simple geometric patterns and conventional foliage, together with figure painting of a religious nature, but such schemes can provide only the very roughest of guides to the likely character of the interior decoration of the medieval royal chamber (Apted 1966, 1–3).

Even when we turn to the period after 1500 information about decorative painting is extremely scrappy. We learn from the building accounts of 1531–32 for Holyroodhouse that the walls of the king's outer chamber and closet — probably located in the south tower — were freshened up in preparation for a royal visit by colouring them above the hangings, which suggests the application of a single primary colour to the exposed plasterwork (*MW*, i, 99). A few years later the painter Thomas Angus was paid for gilding the ornate timber ceilings of the reception rooms in the west quarter and for colouring the mould-ings in the same rooms with azure (*MW*, i, 191).

At Falkland Palace Angus and his colleagues were responsible for much of the external and internal paintwork of the palace, including 'sylingis' (timber ceilings and wall linings), using azure, gold, vermilion, rose of Paris and var-ious other colours, but no details are given of the individual colour schemes (*MW*, i, 215). At Linlithgow, in the mid 1530s, an extensive programme of painting was carried out by John Ross (*MW*, i, 128). Nothing is said about work in the royal suite, but the chimneypiece in the king's great chamber, which was probably installed in about 1540 is known to have borne traces of painted decoration in orange, red and black until about a century ago (Kerr 1880–81, 197). This seems to be the only recorded example of royal chamber decoration of the period now under review, but the somewhat later scheme of mural painting at Kinneil House, West Lothian, which incorporates scenes from the Parable of the Good Samaritan probably derived from tapestry cartoons, may give some indication of the general character of such work (Apted 1966, 69).

Although glass windows were provided for the royal chamber at Cardross as early as 1328–29 (*ER*, i, 125), glass was an expensive commodity and did not come into general use in the royal residences until about the beginning of the sixteenth century. By that time there was enough glass about to justify the employment of a glazier to maintain the glass in the principal royal palaces on a contractual basis (p. 235). So far as we know, all glass used in Scotland at this period, both plain and coloured, had to be imported either from the Continent, where the finest glass was made, or from England. There is as yet little evidence as to what extent glass painting was carried on in Scotland and, if so, whether by foreign or native craftsmen. The actual fabrication and fitting of windows, however, was undertaken by Scottish glazing-wrights who had their own workshops either in the royal residences or in a neighbouring town[19] (*TA*, iv, 278; Graves 1994; Marks 1991). Thomas Peebles, who was king's glazier for much of the first half of the sixteenth century, seems to have had a workshop at Holyroodhouse, where the abbey also provided him with a house (p. 198).

During the reign of James II the king's chamber at Stirling Castle was fitted with glass windows, whereas those of the queen's hall and chamber were covered with linen cloth (*ER*, v, 274; vi, 415). By the end of the fifteenth century the chambers comprising the royal suite seem normally to have been supplied with plain glass and we begin to hear of the use of coloured glass in certain rooms, e.g. in the queen's oratory at Holyroodhouse in 1512 (*ER*, vii, 75; *TA*, i, 46; iii, 297; iv, 375). In that case payment was made for the installation of 'vii payntit roundis with chaiplatis', a description which suggests the employment of wreathed or garlanded medallions of Renaissance character. We know, too, that the windows of the queen's great chamber nearby incorporated painted glass, including a design featuring the impaled royal arms of Scotland and England with a thistle and a rose interlaced (Leland 1770, 295). What were probably similar rounds and panels ('squair pecis'), some of them incorporating the king's coat of arms, were installed in the royal chambers in the great tower at Holyroodhouse in 1531–32, while the glass provided for the reception rooms in the west quarter, as also for the chapel, a few years later included 'Flanderis roundis and squair antik peces' and 'paintit glas in bordouris and antik faces' (*MW*, i, 94–95, 190). Some of these rounds were purchased from the Edinburgh merchant, William Anderson, which suggests that they were imported ready made (*MW*, i, 95; *TA*, iv, 292).

Although glass was plentiful during the sixteenth century — the king's kitchen at Stirling Castle was glazed by the 1530s (*MW*, i, 107) —, it is clear, as we saw when discussing the glazing of the great hall, that some use was still made of canvas. In the late 1550s, for example, it would seem that the upper parts of the windows of the royal chamber in the palace of Stirling were filled with glass set in lead cames, while the lower parts of the opening may have contained outer frames covered with canvas with shutters behind. (*MW*, i, 295–296). This may explain the term 'double cases' used with reference to the windows of the king's chamber at Edinburgh Castle in 1517 (*TA*, v, 120), the purpose being to admit light in inclement weather while allowing the outer frames to be removed or dismantled during the summer season. Alternatively the canvas may have been used as a decorative cover and additional draft proofing for the shutters.

Although little, if any, glass from the royal palaces now survives, some idea of the glasswork that adorned James V's suite at Holyroodhouse is provided by the medallions set in the windows of the Magdalen Chapel, Edinburgh. Here, too, there are roundels with chaplets, some bearing the royal arms, others incorporating fragments of arabesque borders in the Italian taste. They probably date from the mid 1540s and have been judged to be of high quality and craftsmanship by European standards (Graves 1994, 131–132; Seton 1886–87, Pl. ix).

Scottish furniture of the late medieval and early Renaissance periods is a large, but under-researched topic and one that is not central to the architecture of the royal residences. All that is attempted here, therefore, is to say a little about some of the principal articles of furniture that were characteristic of the royal chamber. The majority of these, as we shall see when we come to consider the work of the wardrobe department, had no fixed location, but were transported from one residence to another in accordance with the king's progress. As in the case of fittings, it is only with the survival of the Treasurers' accounts from the reign of James IV onwards that any significant quantity of information becomes available.

Perhaps the most important, and certainly the most substantial, items were the king's and queen's beds of state, which were usually located in either the outer or inner chambers of the royal suite. While these for the most part probably had plain, timber frames of local manufacture (some, however, may have been carved), their furnishings were invariably made up from imported materials of great splendour. In 1503, for example, no less than £386 was spent on hangings of cloth of gold for the queen's 'gret bed of stait', with further outlay for linings, silk fringes and strings (*TA*, ii, 213, 215). These beds were intended mainly for ceremonial use, however, and no doubt the royal couple usually slept elsewhere in more simply furnished and perhaps more comfortable beds (p. 135). We also hear of various *lits-de-camp* belonging to the king, including one made of oak and ash and another of walnut, with very costly hangings, which last was used by James V during his travels in France (*TA*, ii, 134; vii, 5–6, 11–12; 43, 55; *MW*, i, 42). The royal infants had their own cradles and the one provided for Prince James in 1540 was evidently fairly elaborate, having been carved by Andrew Mansioun at cost of £42 (*TA*, i, 39–42; iii, 272–279; vii, 307). What could be one of the few surviving pieces of early chamber furniture, although probably at least half a century later in date than that carved by Mansioun, is the inlaid and decorated cradle reputed to have been James VI's (Hill 1953, 235).

Two other important articles were the king's cloth of state and his chair of state with its associated dais, cushions and carpets, which marked out a clearly identifiable zone of royal authority, reserved for the person of the sovereign alone. The king occupied his chair of state on formal occasions, such as audiences and receptions, a cloth of state being suspended immediately overhead in the form of a canopy. It would seem that the chair was usually located in the king's outer chamber (afterwards known as the presence chamber), but chairs and/or cloths of state were also used outside the royal suite, as for example, when the king was dining in hall or worshipping in chapel (*TA*, i, 387; viii, 43; *MW*, i, 99).

At about the time of the royal wedding in 1503 James IV purchased five chairs of state and their furnishings from Jerome di Frescobald, a Lombard merchant operating in Flanders. One chair was covered with cloth of gold, three with green velvet and the fifth, perhaps intended for use during periods of court mourning, with black velvet. The chairs were decorated with balls of gilded metal as well as fringes and braid ribbons. The frames, which may have been of a type widely used in northern Europe, known as the X-frame, seem to have been made in Bruges (*TA*, ii, 227–228, 241; Thurley 1993, 238–239). Whether all of these chairs were for the king's exclusive use is not clear, but a chair of state for the queen was covered in scarlet cloth a few years later (*TA*, iv, 31). Cloths of state, too, were made of the finest materials and since they usually incorporated both a canopy and a backcloth they could be extremely expensive; a cloth of estate made from cloth of gold for James IV in 1503 cost £219 (*TA*, ii, 213).

What other seat furniture there was seems to have been quite simple. In 1469, for example, three tables, with stools (*tripodes*) and forms, were provided for the king's chambers at Falkland (*ER*, vii, 654), while the five stools made for the queen's chamber in 1506 cost only 3s each (*TA*, iii, 267). When James IV received the English lords in his great chamber at Holyroodhouse in August 1503 the king occupied his chair of state while the assembled company sat upon a form, or forms, facing him (Leland 1770, 292). In 1537 payment was made to a goldsmith 'to gilt the knoppis of the Kingis gracis stule', but this must have been an unusually elaborate piece, perhaps even a chair of state (*TA*, vi, 299). We also hear of folding chairs, used for outdoor events, although it is not clear whether or not these should be regarded as chamber furniture (*MW*, i, 227).

As we have just seen, the furniture of James III's suite at Falkland included several tables. James IV's oratory at Holyroodhouse was also provided with a table, while Queen Margaret had what was described as a 'round burd' in her chamber there (*TA*, ii, 417; iv, 378). These items, and others like them, were probably fairly plain, all-purpose tables of local manufacture that could easily be dismantled for carriage between one house and another. One or two of them, however, seem to have been of better quality, like the table and chair of cypress wood made or purchased for use at Holyroodhouse in 1502 at a cost of £2 14s (*TA*, ii, 33). We also hear of the acquisition of more specialised items, many of them probably imported. These included chess tables, provided with chess men for the king's chamber (*TA*, vi, 464), and counter boards (sometimes known simply as 'comptars'), of which no fewer than 20, of different sizes, were purchased at the time of the royal wedding in 1503 at a cost of between £1 and £2 each (*TA*, ii, 216). As its name suggests, the counter board was in origin a table designed for making up accounts. It was built on fixed legs to keep it steady and the top was marked out in squares to facilitate calculations, which were made with disc-shaped counters (Warrack 1920, 22–26). By the early sixteenth century, however, the counter board seems to have been in demand for more general domestic use, the top sometimes being covered with a cloth (*TA*, viii, 173). Some of the larger ones may actually have been regarded as fixtures, for an entry in the Treasurer's accounts for 1502 refers to 'ane double countour bocht to the King to the bos window of the chamir in the Abbay' (*TA*, ii, 33).

One of the most prestigious items of royal furniture was the king's cupboard of plate. Silver and gold plate and jewellery were established indicators of wealth and status and their conspicuous display was a prominent feature of the royal interior. Both James IV and James V purchased considerable quantities of plate and it was also widely used for presentation purposes (*TA*, i, 351; ii, 160; vii, 34–36). In 1512, for example, James IV made a present of several pieces from his cupboard to two English ambassadors, while in 1526 the fourteen-year old James V received 'ane copburd of silver' from the lord of Campvere (*TA*, iv, 348; v, 307).

The 'board' on which the cups and other articles were displayed could be simply a table, or something more elaborate, with a backboard and fitted shelves; eventually it developed into a cupboard with opening doors of the kind still used today (Warrack 1920, 23–24, 52). We don't know exactly what early sixteenth-century cupboards looked like, but in his account of the wedding festivities at Holyroodhouse John Young, an Englishman, describes one of the cupboards (he calls them dressers) that he saw there as being 'after the Guyse of the Countre', a phrase which suggests that Scottish cupboards had a distinctive national identity (Leland 1770, 295). On that occasion he noted the presence of cupboards in the king's inner chamber and in the king's and queen's halls, but there may well have been others elsewhere. An inventory of furnishings in the royal lodging at St Andrews Priory, drawn up in 1565, when it was occupied by the Earl and Countess of Moray, shows that the two great chambers each contained an oak cupboard. In the great chamber of the old lodging, which stood nearby, there was 'ane copeburd of thre staige of Aisland burd' (a three-tiered cupboard of Baltic fir) (Fleming 1910, 608–612).

Other articles of furniture that are mentioned from time to time include chests, used to store and transport jewellery and other precious items, and a kind of reading desk known as a latron, which was usually to be found in the king's closet or study. In September 1497, for example, payment was made 'to haf the Kingis quhit bandit kist (white, banded chest) out of the Kingis chamir of the Halyrudhous to Leith, in a cart, to send to Strivelin' (*TA*, i, 355), while a few years later there is a similar payment 'for ane lok to the Kingis latron that standis in the Kingis studee', evidently at Holyroodhouse (*TA*, iv, 100).

The mention of locks reminds us that, in order to maintain the security and privacy of the royal chamber, keys and locks were provided to the doors of the various rooms, as well as to certain articles of furniture. It is clear from the master of works' accounts that locks in the king's houses were changed with considerable frequency, particularly when a royal visit was anticipated (*MW*, i, 218). Most, if not all, of these locks seem to have been regarded as fixtures and they were usually made by one of the royal smiths attached to the house in question; sometimes, however, they were bought locally. (*MW*, i, 217, 260; *TA*, iii, 348). There is little evidence of the use of ornamental locks, but in 1541 'twa antik lokis at the kingis grace command' were purchased for Falkland Palace from a lorimer in Leith. They cost £2 each and must have been quite elaborate pieces, perhaps decorated with Renaissance ornament (*MW*, i, 284). Presumably the keys giving access to the royal suite were issued on a restricted basis, but there is no mention in the accounts of privy locks or pass keys until after 1600 (*MW*, ii, 76, 202, 290–291 330, 333; Thurley 1993, 83).

Considerable importance was also attached to chimney furniture and there are several references in the accounts to the provision of iron chimneys (grates) for the king's and queen's chambers (*TA*, i, 22, 36; ii, 406). Firedogs of iron (*le landirnys*) were supplied for the queen's chamber at Falkland in 1461 (*ER*, vii, 79). In 1533 a local smith made a sconce (screen?) for the chimney of the king's chamber at Stirling Castle using 20 plates of white iron supplied for that purpose (*TA*, vi, 84; cf. also ii, 441). Cast-iron firebacks were probably in use by this time and it is possible that some of these were manufactured in Scotland. Part of a cast-iron fireback of probable late sixteenth-century date bearing the royal arms of Scotland is preserved in the Victoria and Albert Museum, London, but its provenance is unknown (Gloag and Bridgewater 1948, 24).

While candlesticks no doubt provided the normal means of lighting for the royal chamber, chandeliers were also in use. In 1513 Thomas Peebles, the king's glazing wright, constructed 'ane gret lantern of glass for to hyng in the palice of the abbay of Halyrudhous to hald lycht thairin' (*TA*, v, 41). We do not know exactly where this lantern was placed, but some, at least, of the dozen or so silver and silver gilt chandeliers purchased by James V in France in the late 1530s are likely to have been destined for the royal chamber (*TA*, vii, 34–35).

The same is probably true of the few clocks mentioned in the accounts. In 1502 Sir James Petegrew was paid for his expenses in going to Stirling 'to divis ane knok' (*TA*, ii, 159). Another clock (*orlage*) of local manufacture was the one made for Falkland Palace by Alexander Lindsay, one of the ushers of the queen's chamber, in 1540 (*MW*, i, 275; *TA*, vii, 182, 206, 477), but the one previously sent to James IV by the French ambassador was no doubt of Continental manufacture (*TA*, iv, 324). Finally, in this short list of luxury furnishings, mention should be made of 'certane fyne picturis of Flandris' bought for James V at a cost of £17 in 1535 (*TA*, vi, 250).

THE WARDROBE

The wardrobe was an important department of the household, responsible for the safe custody and repair not only of the king's wearing apparel, but also of the royal jewels, the plate and vestments of the royal chapel and the hangings and other furnishings of the king's houses and castles (*TA*, i, pp. cci, ccvii–ccviii). The wardrobe also housed the king's hunting weapons, saddles and harness gear and was likewise a repository for spices — especially those valued for their medicinal properties — wax and drugs (*ER*, i, pp. cxiv–cxvi; ii, 213; *TA*, i, 282; v, 436; vi, 443; vii, 178, 292; Bateson 1904, 41; Thomson 1815, 31–106). In the mid and late 1530s the king's wardrobe had a staff of about three dozen, including tailors, shoemakers, furriers, embroiderers, tapissiers (two of them French), goldsmiths, seamstresses and laundresses, as well as yeomen, grooms and carters (Thomas 1995, 2 and pers. comm.).

When there happened to be a queen consort there was, of course, also a separate queen's wardrobe organised along similar lines and likewise for other members of the royal family. For example, when Queen Margaret Tudor came to Scotland in 1503 she brought with her a sizeable household establishment, including her own master of the wardrobe, two grooms, a tailor and a furrier (*TA*, ii, 225, 238, 336, 405, 461; iii, pp. xciv–cii), while her first-born son, Prince James, who lived for only a year, also had his own wardrobe, complete with two cradles (*TA*, iii, 272–279). The senior officials of the wardrobe were prominent figures at court and their duties brought them into close contact with the royal family. Something of this intimacy is conveyed by William Dunbar's pen-portrait of James Dog, who became keeper of the queen's wardrobe towards the end of James IV's reign (having previously occupied a post in the king's wardrobe) and continued to serve her in her widowhood (Mackenzie 1932, 61–2, 210).

The great majority of wardrobe items required for the king's daily use travelled with him as he moved from one location to another. The principal exceptions seem to have been heavy furniture, such as tables, forms and standing beds and perhaps also some of the more bulky or more precious hangings. Beds and tables were, however, transported on some occasions (*TA*, vi, 421; vii, 165). Although the wardrobe had its own allocation of carters, transport arrangements often involved local carriers (*TA*, ii, 349–350, 392; iv, 348, 356; vi, 420; vii, 266). Sometimes the king travelled light, with a minimum of furnishings, as when the nineteen-year-old James V made a short hunting expedition to the Forest of Ettrick in August 1531. On that occasion, with the party evidently living under canvas, seven horses seem to have been sufficient 'to turs the graith of the wardrob to the huntis in Megetland' (*TA*, v, 422–423, 436). When the same king went to greet his second wife, Mary of Guise, upon her arrival at Crail seven years later, however, the return trip to Edinburgh through Fife and Lothian became a major operation involving the hire of some three dozen carts at various locations, as well as several boats, including a ferry boat at Queensferry (*TA*, vi, 419–423). The considerable strain placed upon officials by the frequent movements of the household from one residence to another is reflected in an entry in the Treasurer's accounts for 1539 recording payment to one of the grooms of the wardrobe 'for small expensis debursit be him upoun the gardrop in sindry placis and chengeing thairof fra ane chalmer to ane uthir' (*TA*, vii, 158).

Precautions were taken to safeguard valuable items both in transit and *in situ*. We hear, for example, of the use of coffers and gardeviars (strong boxes) to carry plate and other valuables and of 'grete bawhuvis' (?large wicker baskets) for the transport of cloth of gold and small pieces of tapestry (*TA*, i, 82, 99; vi, 420; vii, 57, 267). Upon arrival hangings were carefully placed in position by the tailors of the wardrobe, using the hooks already installed for that purpose, and canvas was hung between the tapestries and the underlying wall surface as a protection against damp (*TA*, ii, 408; vii, 458). Sometimes nails were used instead of hooks and eyes, the tapestries presumably being nailed to wooden battens embedded in the walls (*TA*, vii, 94). The wardrobe chambers themselves were provided with aumbries for the storage of valuables — the little strongroom opening off the king's bedchamber at Linlithgow is perhaps the best surviving example — and lockfast cupboards known as 'wairstalls', within which the king's robes were hung in canvas covers to protect them against dust and dirt (*ER*, vi, 387; *TA*, ii, 399; iv, 111; vi, 256). Arrangements were also made for clothes to be washed regularly, the finer garments being either brushed or sponged by hand (*TA*, ii, 27, 471; vi, 304).

Every royal residence was provided with at least one wardrobe chamber and the larger houses had several. If there was insufficient space within the residence itself, as sometimes happened when the king was staying in a religious house or private lodging, a separate house or houses would be rented for the use of the wardrobe, as at Perth on various occasions during the late fourteenth and early fifteenth centuries (*ER*, ii, 509, 582; iv, 90). It was the responsibility of the wardrobe to supply grass (bent) to cover the floors of the royal suite in the various castles and palaces (p. 167). In 1473–74, for example, Andrew Balfour, a wardrobe official, received an annual fee of £13 6s 8d 'for his bent to the chalmiris' (*TA*, i, 65), while during the early 1500s payments were made for the hire of a bent-house at Edinburgh in which to store materials brought in from the surrounding countryside (*TA*, ii, 381, 436, 467).

None of these houses survive and the royal castles and palaces contain very few chambers that can confidently be identified as late medieval wardrobes. This is probably due in part to the accidents of survival, but also to the fact that, unlike the hall, the chapel and the chamber, the wardrobe, when empty and unfurnished, has few distinctive characteristics.

At James IV's palace of Holyroodhouse, the king's accommodation in the south tower evidently included a wardrobe, while there was another, presumably for his consort, above the queen's gallery (*MW*, i, 27, 103). There was also a treasure house, used for storing plate and, presumably from time to time, the crown jewels (*TA*, iii, 363, 390). Repairs to jewels seem to have been carried out in a separate establishment known as the lapidary's house (*TA*, v, 221). Thomas Wallace, James IV's lapidary and goldsmith, received an annual fee of £10 (*RSS*, i, No. 1108; *TA*, iv, 309).

So far as James V's palace is concerned, the northernmost chamber of the

2.13

west range is referred to in the building accounts both as a wardrobe and as an inner chamber (*MW*, i, 186, 190–191). This was a small room linking the two principal reception rooms with the king's private suite in the great tower. As a wardrobe, it would probably have housed only the king's wearing apparel and bed hangings, leaving the bulkier items, perhaps those described elsewhere as the 'great wardrobe' (*TA*, vii, 158), to be stored in some other part of the palace. Mylne's plan of 1663 (Mylne 1893, opp. 148) suggests that the chamber had a large built-in cupboard on one side, but its most prominent feature was a spacious bay-window overlooking the palace forecourt and this would have increased its attractions for use as an intimate reception room. It has already been suggested that this chamber may have been the venue for Sir Ralph Sadler's private meetings with James V in 1540 (p. 134) and it is interesting to find that the king's wardrobe was used in a similar way in France at about the same time (Boudon and Chatenet 1994, 68, n.17). Another reference in the accounts indicates that there was a second wardrobe on the uppermost floor of the great tower (*MW*, i, 94, 331; ii, 399). There was a separate vessel-house for the storage of the king's plate (*MW*, i, 30), while during the closing years of James V's reign the tapissier also had his own house within the palace precincts, apparently occupying part of the outer gatehouse (*MW*, i, 222, 226–227, 290; *ER*, xvii, 283).

At James V's palace of Falkland there seem to have been two wardrobes in the east quarter, their proximity to the royal chamber suggesting that these were the king's and queen's wardrobes of the robes and beds (i.e. bed hangings). As at Holyroodhouse, the bulkier items, together with any permanent furnishings put into store when the court moved on, were probably housed in a more remote part of the palace. So far as can be deduced from the building accounts the wardrobes were situated on the second floor, perhaps being placed at either end of the range and communicating directly with the king's and queen's private suites (*MW*, i, 257, 260, 285). Another possibility is that all or part of the first-floor chamber at the south end of the range, tentatively identified as a lords' hall (p. 110), may have functioned as a wardrobe.

We know little about the location of wardrobes at Linlithgow Palace, although the most convenient position for the king's and queen's wardrobes would seem to have been the west end of the north quarter, respectively at first- and second-floor levels. Wardrobes in these positions would have communicated readily with the innermost chambers of the two royal suites, as also with the north-west turnpike stair. The presumed strongroom opening off the king's bedchamber has already been mentioned. There are references in the documents to the existence of several wardrobes at Stirling Castle, but their whereabouts remain uncertain (*ER*, vii, 59; *MW*, i, 105; ii, 246; *Elphinstone MSS*, 192–193). We may speculate, however, that James IV's lodging incorporated a wardrobe at the north end of the main block and that James V's palace included wardrobe accommodation either in the west quarter or directly above the king's and queen's suites. Locating wardrobes directly beneath the royal suites, as was often done in Tudor England (Thurley 1993, 75, 138–139) would have involved storage in vaulted, and usually unheated, cellars and this practice seems seldom to have been followed in Scotland. There was also a vessel-house for the king's plate, possibly located, prior to the erection of James V's palace, in one of the cellars of the King's Old Building (*MW*, i, 110).

At Edinburgh Castle there is a casual reference to King James I taking personal delivery of coin in his wardrobe in the castle in 1435 (*ER*, iv, 663). This may be the wardrobe with cupboards (*garderoba et ammoriolis ejusdem*) that was refurbished in 1458 (*ER*, vi, 387) and which is also perhaps to be identified with the treasure house mentioned in later fifteenth-century records (*ER*, vii, 424; *TA*, i, 110, 268). It was there, following the sudden death of James III in violent circumstances, that search was made for the late king's treasure on 17th June 1488. According to a list prepared on that occasion the treasure, contained in several coffers, a box and a casket, comprised large quantities of coin and jewels, together with important items of plate (*TA*, i, 79–83). The crown jewels seem not have been stored within the treasure house on that occasion, but this was, presumably, their usual repository. The location of this treasure house is uncertain, but it has been suggested that it was accommodated within the vaulted basement of David's Tower (MacIvor, 1993, 37).

NOTES

1 Drawings of *c.*1670 (Mylne 1893, opp. 168) show that by that time the north chamber had become the privy chamber. The innermost chamber of the west range overlooked the palace forecourt, but had no view of the inner court.

2 In 1578 William Murray, valet in the king's chamber, was paid for furnishing two beds for the king's servants to lie on in the chamber, as also a bed for grooms in the outer chamber (*TA*, xiii, 229–230).

3 The name may have originated through the use of the tower by Prince Henry, eldest son of James VI (*MW*, i, 349–350; ii, 233, 239; RCAHMS 1963, i, 193, n.2).

4 The most convenient undercover route would have run from the west end of the church, via the chapel and the king's suite, to the inner end of the queen's suite.

5 Above second-floor level the south-east angle may have sprouted an angle-turret similar to those on the other three corners (*MW*, i, 42, 85, 93).

Hollar's view of 1670 (reproduced in Fawcett 1988, 9) shows a south-east angle-turret rising from the ground floor.

6 The north gallery on the north side of the north range was not built until 1576–78 (*TA*, xiii, 150–151, 162).

7 These galleries are shown on Kierincx's view of *c*.1640, but Slezer's view of *c*.1680 suggests that the second-floor galleries had by then disappeared. Both views are reproduced in Puttfarken *et. al.*, 4, 32–33.

8 The kitchens of the seventeenth-century palace occupied a similar position (RCAHMS 1951, 22).

9 A number of factors make it impossible to ascertain precise measurements, but the following list of approximate overall dimensions, as recorded in the standard published accounts, is suggestive. *King's Hall* Linlithgow 15.1 x 6.7m; Stirling, King's Old Building 14.5 x 7.0m, Palace 14.9 x 7.0m; Holyroodhouse, west quarter 14.0 x 6.7m; Falkland, (north chamber, first floor) 14.9 x 7.0; Rothesay 14.5 x 6.7m. *Great Chamber* Linlithgow 10.7 x 6.4m; Stirling, King's Old Building 10.0 x 7.0m, Palace 11.4 x 7.0m; Holyroodhouse, west quarter 11.4 x 6.7m; Falkland, (second chamber from north, first floor) 11.7 x 7.0m. Cf. also Charles McKean's remarks on room proportions in certain early sixteenth-century buildings in McKean 1995, 1078, 1088.

10 Cf., for example, the dolphin capital from the courtyard arcade of the Louis XII wing at the château of Blois and the eagle console from the parish church of Bury illustrated in Prinz and Kecks 1985, figs. 342d and 345b. The king's itinerary in France during 1536–37 is shown in outline in Cameron 1996 and described in detail in Bentley-Cranch 1986, 88.

11 The building accounts for the royal palaces in James IV's reign contain numerous references to the purchase of timber boards (mainly of Scandinavian origin), some of which could have been used for this purpose (*TA*, ii, 86, 274, 277, 279).

12 A painter's account of 1535–36 included work 'for the haill cullering of the millouris (mouldings) of the inner, myd and uter (outer) chalmeris', but this could refer to the ceilings (*MW*, i, 191).

13 Information from Dr Richard Fawcett.

14 Cf. the arrangement of the panelling of the Waltham Abbey Room of *c*.1530 and other English examples (Smith 1924, 11).

15 Mansioun's employment in the Royal Works seems to have spanned the

period November 1535, when he probably appears in the Holyroodhouse labour force as 'Andreis Francheman' to August 1579, when he was replaced by Frances Mansioun, probably a son (*MW*, i, 172; *TA*, xiii, 283). For his intervening career see Dunbar 1975, 23 and Caldwell 1994, 182.

16 The existing medallions at Azay-le-Rideau may be nineteenth-century replicas.

17 Although there are similarities between the initials IM and those found in the Book of Hours of James IV and Margaret Tudor, the letter forms are by no means identical and Roman letters similar to those on the tile floor occur in inscriptions of James V's reign. Cf. also Macfarlane 1960 and Campbell 1994, 17, n.28.

18 The main sources of supply in France were the gypsum beds of Montmartre, near Paris (Salzman 1967, 155).

19 In 1559 Adam Symmeris, glazing wright, prepared glass for Falkland Palace 'in his awin bwth (booth) in Edinburgh' (*MW*, i, 297).

Chapter 6

OFFICES, LODGINGS AND RECREATIONAL BUILDINGS

THE KITCHEN

This was one of the largest departments of the household, having a complement during the 1530s of about 60 persons under the direction of the king's 'catour' (caterer or purveyor), a highly responsible job usually held by a cleric (*TA*, vii, 125–127, 331–334; Thomas, A., pers. comm.). Wine and other exotic items were imported and some produce was obtained from the royal estates, but the bulk of the food consumed in the royal residences was purchased locally on a day-to-day basis. About half the staff worked in the kitchen proper and the remainder in the other offices, which included the bakehouse, the bread-house, the pantry (for the storage of bread and certain other items, such as saltfatts (salt containers) and chandeliers, Thomson 1815, 73–75), the wine- and ale-cellar (or buttery), the larder (where meat and other perishable foods were stored), the pastry-house, the spice-house (for the storage of non-medicinal spices), the scullery (where table and kitchen vessels[1] were washed and the latter also stored) and the coal-house. Among other offices which may have existed at this period, at least in the larger residences, but which appear not to be mentioned until the early seventeenth century, were the boiling-house (for boiling meat, poultry and fish and for making stock) and the timber-house (for storing firewood) (*MW*, ii, 206–207, 266–267, 442).

Several of these offices were duplicated in a way which reflected the division between hall and chamber and, at least in the larger residences, the respective functions seem to have been carried out in separate buildings or rooms. Thus, there were separate caterers for the great hall and the king's chamber and likewise separate court and king's kitchens, each with its own master cook and staff of cooks, yeomen, grooms and 'turnbrochis' (to turn the revolving spits upon which meat was roasted). The bakehouse, pantry, ale-cellar and larder were organised in the same way (Thomas 1995, 2–3, *TA*, vii, 125–127, 331–334). How far back this division of function went is hard to say, for no detailed documentation is available prior to the sixteenth century. Some elements certainly seem to have been of long standing, however, for there is evidence of the existence of a separate king's kitchen at Edinburgh Castle as early as the reign of James I (*ER*, iv, 627; v, 274).

The queen and other leading members of the royal family also had their own kitchens. For example, the young Duke of Rothesay had a separate kitchen in Edinburgh Castle in 1434 (*ER*, iv, 603), while in 1541 the infant Prince of Scotland had a kitchen staff of five, including his own master cook, foreman and patissier (*TA*, vii, 477–478). The household of Mary of Guise operated along French lines, under which the *cuisine de bouche* fed the queen and her principal courtiers and officials, while the *cuisine de commun* supplied everyone else who was entitled to be fed at her expense (Marshall 1993, 139).

Allied to the kitchen, but usually occupying separate premises, was the brew-house, which had its own staff headed by the king's master-brewer (*ER*, xv, 232; *TA*, v, 383). The finest ale, such as was supplied for the king's table, was mostly imported from Germany (*ER*, vi, 114, 118; *TA*, i, p. ccxii), but by the second half of the fifteenth century most of the larger royal residences were equipped with their own brew-houses for the supply of ale to the household.

Among the major castles and palaces the best preserved examples of kitchens and associated offices are to be found at Linlithgow and Stirling. At Linlithgow the principal kitchens were from the beginning located at the lower end of the great hall, occupying what eventually became known as the kitchen tower (*MW*, ii, 145) at the north-east corner of the palace. It is clear both from the building accounts and from the evidence of the structures themselves that the kitchens were remodelled on several occasions, for example in 1464–65, 1470–71 and 1539 (*ER*, vii, 320; viii, 65; *TA*, vii, 195), and the arrangements visible today probably date mainly from the late fifteenth and sixteenth centuries.

The main kitchen premises were approached from the east entry transe of the palace and comprised three main working levels linked by a complex series of stairs and passages. Not all the chambers can be satisfactorily identified, but the big first-floor kitchen adjacent to the great hall was presumably the court kitchen (*MW*, ii, 343), while the cross passage connecting it to the hall was evidently a servery. On either side of the great hall itself are mural chambers (one opening into a passage), which are probably the pantries mentioned in the building accounts (*MW*, i, 127; ii, 341); these may have been used to distribute bread during meals in hall. The court kitchen was originally rib-vaulted as a precaution against fire and may have been vented by some kind of central flue, as at Holyroodhouse; however, the thrust of the vault seems to have displaced the north-east corner of the palace and the vault was subsequently removed. The upper floors of the kitchen tower and the adjacent space to the west probably served as sleeping quarters for kitchen staff.

1.4

*6.1 Linlithgow
Palace. Laich (low)
kitchen showing
fireplace and well.*

To the west of the court kitchen is a smaller chamber, one of a series placed at intermediate levels in this position; most were probably larders and bread-houses, but one may have been a spice-house (*TA*, iv, 524). Beneath the court kitchen and extending into the east range lie what may be another two larders, both vaulted, and beneath these again is a basement containing two more chambers, each equipped with a large fireplace. The north one, which also contains a well, was probably the laich kitchen (*MW*, ii, 343), worked in tandem with the court kitchen above. The adjacent chamber to the south is usually identified as a brew-house, perhaps the one mentioned in an inventory of 1648, which lists various items of brewing equipment (Ferguson 1910, 381–383). A brew-house within the palace was repaired in 1495 and another was built in 1512 (*ER*, x, 495; *TA*, iv, 379). Neither of these, however, was necessarily situated within the principal courtyard and the one erected in 1512, which seems to have had wattle partitions and a heather-thatched roof, almost certainly stood in the outer court. The main bakehouse, too, may have been situated outside the palace proper.

The location of the king's kitchen, also referred to in the accounts (*TA*, vii, 195) is uncertain. Prior to the reconstruction of the north range *c.*1620 it could have been situated in that quarter, close to the inner rooms of the king's suite, but a reference of 1628–29 indicates that the king's kitchen of that date had a large window looking north and another looking east (*MW*, ii, 273). This suggests that it was situated in the main north-east, or kitchen, tower and it is possible that the king's food was prepared in an annex of the court kitchen, whose windows seem to match those mentioned in the accounts. This could explain a reference in Mary of Guise's household accounts to a banquet held at Linlithgow in 1543, when one wall of the *cuisine de commun* (presumably the court kitchen) was temporarily pulled down to provide more working space and then built up again. Some of the cooking on that occasion, however, may have been done in tents brought out from Edinburgh (Marshall 1993, 142–143).

The cellars beneath the south end of the great hall were possibly used for storing the court vessels, as well as ale, wine and perhaps coal (*TA*, vii, 195). Ale and wine for the king's and queen's personal use, on the other hand, were more probably stored in the cellars beneath the royal suites in the west quarter. A makeshift kitchen located in one of the cellars opening off the south entrance transe that was built during the 1530s may have been provided for the convenience of the porters and palace guards.

At Stirling Castle, where space was less restricted, the kitchens and offices were more widely dispersed. James IV's great hall was served mainly by a kitchen which had been constructed within the north gatehouse some time during the fifteenth century — possibly in 1458 (*ER*, vi, 415) — and then remodelled and linked to the north-east corner of the hall by what may have been a combined

1.2

service lobby and dressory (where food was dressed and garnished before being brought to table) in 1511–12 (*TA*, iv, 281). From this kitchen, probably to be identified as the court kitchen, food was passed through hatches to the lobby (now demolished) and thence carried up to the servery at the lower end of the hall via the stairs and corridors provided for that purpose.

Immediately to the south of the court kitchen is a range of vaulted offices apparently constructed soon after the completion of the great hall. Rediscovered in the 1920s after being buried beneath an artillery battery since the late seventeenth century, this seems originally to have contained, at the north end a bakehouse with adjacent larder or bread-house, and at the south end a supplementary kitchen together with what may have been a dressory. The working area opens through a series of hatches into a corridor which emerges opposite the main east turnpike stair of the hall, where, however, there is no direct access to the interior. Probably the corridor originally extended further north to link with the service lobby at the north end of the hall. Within the hall the pair of cellars at the lower end, with connecting stairs to the servery above, may have functioned as buttery and pantry, while the cellars at the upper end, also with a connecting stair, were probably used as wine- or ale-cellars for the high table and for the storage of vessels and napery.

The king usually ate not in hall, however, but in his own chamber and at Stirling, in contrast to Linlithgow, separate cooking facilities were provided adjacent to the royal suite. In James IV's lodging the kitchen, probably the one described in 1531–32 as the king's kitchen and dressory (*MW*, i, 105–108), occupied the south end of the building, communicating directly with the king's hall (Fawcett 1990b, 180). Mention is also made in the accounts of the petty larder, the pantry and the wine-cellar, all probably situated, like the king's vessel-house, in the cellars beneath the royal suite (*MW*, i, 105, 109–110).

2.5

Two new kitchens were built in 1542 to serve James V's palace, and it seems likely that these were intended to provide separate facilities for the king and queen (*TA*, viii, 72, 84). They may have occupied the space between the north-west corner of the palace and the south end of the King's Old Building, possibly replacing an earlier chapel in this position (p. 41). By the early eighteenth century this space was occupied by the governor's kitchen and an adjacent yard (Fawcett 1995, 99). The early sixteenth-century Elphinstone Tower, probably used at one time as the lodging of the keeper of the castle, also had its own kitchen (RCAHMS 1963, i, 196). There was also a brew-house within the castle (*ER*, vi, 415), but its location is not known.

So far as Falkland Palace is concerned, we know almost nothing about the arrangements for storing and cooking the food served in the great hall. The ground-floor kitchen at the north end of the adjacent east quarter could have communicated directly with the upper end of the hall and might perhaps have supplied the high table. But it was not well placed to serve as a court kitchen and it seems likely that this occupied a separate building on the north side of the hall, within the precincts of the earlier castle. A kitchen, bakehouse and brew-house, all possibly situated thereabouts, are on record during the 1450s and there are also references to the storage of salted marts there (*ER*, vi, 253, 254, 417, 565). The kitchens at the south end of the east quarter, with the adjacent kitchen or bakehouse at the east end of the south quarter, probably include the king's kitchen referred to in the building accounts of the 1530s, which also mention a petty larder, dressories and a bakehouse, all apparently situated in that vicinity (*MW*, i, 218, 257–260). Unless there was any direct means of communication with the little stair that commences above the bakehouse oven, however, access from the kitchen to the royal suite above would have been intrusive. The keeper's lodging in the gatehouse had its own kitchen situated on the first floor of the south quarter. Of particular importance to the smooth operation of the palace kitchens and offices was the provision of an ample supply of fresh water and considerable efforts were made to achieve this (p. 194).

At Dunfermline Palace the great hall of the royal lodging was evidently served from the well-preserved first-floor kitchen situated at its lower end. The kitchen, probably in its present form mainly of late fifteenth-century date, also supplied the monastic refectory. The undercroft of the chamber at the upper end of the hall seems also to have been adapted for use as a kitchen at some stage and could perhaps have served either the high table of the hall or the royal suite in the adjacent north-west range.

The sixteenth-century palace of Holyrood must have possessed the most extensive series of kitchens and offices of any of the royal castles and palaces. Among the structures mentioned in the building accounts are the court kitchen and its dressory (*TA*, iv, 529; *MW*, i, 99–101, 290), the king's kitchen and dressory (*MW*, i, 98–99, 290), the little kitchen (*MW*, i, 290), the bakehouse (*MW*, i, 100), the king's bakehouse (*TA*, v, 325), the king's breadhouse (*MW*, i, 8), the court pantry (*TA*, v, 325), the ale-cellar (*MW*, i, 98), the king's ale-cellar (*MW*, i, 96), the larder (*TA*, v, 325), the petty larder (*TA*, v, 325), the queen's larder (*MW*, i, 226), the kellis house (probably a larder for dry fish) (*MW*, i, 226) and the spicehouse (*TA*, iv, 529; *MW*, i, 30, 103), as well as the brew-house and 'gilehous' (a steeping-house) (*MW*, i, 7–8, 10, 73, 226).

The court kitchen that was repaired in 1531–32 had 'ane aiphous in the heid of the samen for the mair went' (a beehive-shaped louvre on top of the roof to assist ventilation) (*MW*, i, 99–100). A new kitchen was built a few years later (*MW*, i, 193). So far as we can judge, the main kitchen premises were situated immediately to the south east of the inner court of the palace and some elements may still be identifiable on Mylne's plan of 1663 (Mylne 1893, opp.

3.5

3.12

2.13

❧

*6.2 Doune Castle.
Kitchen servery.
Food was passed
through these
hatches from the
kitchen within and
thence through the
servery to the lower
end of the great
hall.*

148). Possibly, as at Dunfermline, the kitchen was originally sited to serve the monastic refectory and subsequently adapted — and at Holyroodhouse greatly expanded — to meet the needs of the royal palace. The king's kitchen and its ancillary offices may have been located beneath the royal suites in the west quarter and great tower, but there is no firm evidence of this. As at Falkland, the kitchens had their own supply of running water (p. 193), while Mylne's plan also shows that two of the lesser courts on the south side of the palace contained wells.

We have little reliable information about the kitchen arrangements at Edinburgh Castle. There were separate kitchens for the king, the Duke of Rothesay and the captain of the castle during the 1430s; the king's meals were seasoned with herbs from the king's own herb garden within the castle (*ER*, iv, 603, 623, 627). The king's kitchen, built or re-built in 1409–10 and probably located in the vicinity of David's Tower, was repaired in 1447 and again in 1517 (*ER*, iii, 89; iv, 116; v, 274; *TA*, v, 121–122). At the same time the great arched fireplace of the new court kitchen was rebuilt (*TA*, v, 121). The location

of the court kitchen is not stated, but if it had been built to serve James IV's great hall, as seems likely, it may have been situated near the lower end of the hall. The castle also had a brew-house and a bakehouse (*ER*, v, 619; xiv, 108).

At Doune Castle the main kitchen was well placed to supply the needs of the household, being equipped with a servery opening directly into the lower end of the great hall. But unless the royal meals were prepared in one of the chambers opening off the private hall, or in a courtyard building that has since disappeared, there seem to have been no separate cooking facilities for the duke. A brew-house was erected in 1466–67 (*ER*, vii, 488).

A similar scaling down of facilities is found in some of the lesser royal residences, where the king's visits tended to be shorter, with only a small number of the household in residence. In most cases, however, our information is too scanty to allow firm conclusions to be drawn. At Dundonald and Rothesay the kitchens have still to be identified, although it is likely that they were contained within detached buildings standing in the courtyard. At Ravenscraig the kitchen and offices occupied the rear portion of the courtyard and there is nothing to suggest that separate cooking facilities were provided for either of the residential towers. The tower-house at Newark, however, was equipped with its own kitchen, which presumably catered for the king and any other occupants of the royal lodging. There is also some evidence to suggest that a second kitchen stood in the courtyard (RCAHMS 1957, 62) and this may have served the great hall that is on record in the fifteenth century.

3.15

3.15

THE STABLE

This was another sizeable department of the household, having a complement of more than 50 on the king's side during the 1530s. At its head was the king's master of the stable, who was assisted by an esquire, four keepers of horses and various yeomen, henchmen, grooms and sumptermen (who handled pack-horses), as well as an unknown number of junior officials. There was also a master of the avery (responsible for the supply of fodder), with two yeomen, together with a saddler, a lorimer (for the supply of stirrups, spurs and bits) and a farrier, or shoe smith. The stable was responsible for the upkeep of the royal riding establishment, including the king's sporting and military needs; it also furnished mounts for senior officials of the household and supplied some of the more general transport needs of the court. The queen had her own, somewhat smaller, establishment (Thomas 1995, 2 and pers. comm.; *TA*, i, p. clxxxix; vii, pp. xli–xlii).

To satisfy the king's enthusiasm for field sports there was also a master falconer, with up to ten assistants, and several kennel staff to handle the royal hunting dogs. The king invariably took a keen personal interest in the royal kennel and in James V's day 'the Kingis auld hound callit Bagsche' was commemorated in a poem by Sir David Lindsay of the Mount (*TA*, vii, 96; Murray 1965, 21, n.2).

As we might expect, stable buildings, averyhouses and kennels were invariably situated within the outer confines of the residence, so the chances of survival up to the present day are small. Only at Falkland Palace have any significant physical remains been recorded and even here the identification remains doubtful.

The king's and queen's stables at Falkland were repaired in 1458–59 and again in 1467–68, when an averyhouse was also re-roofed and repaired (*ER*, vi, 566; vii, 570). In 1531–32 structures described in the building accounts as 'the auld stabill' and 'the auld hay yard' were taken down and a new stable and averyhouse erected, probably on or near the site of the old ones (*MW*, i, 112–114). This new stable has sometimes been identified with the building running alongside the west side of the cachepell, or tennis-court, erected in 1539–41 (p. 208), which stands about 100m north east of the palace, a little beyond the site of the medieval castle (RCAHMS 1933, 141; Gifford 1988, 217). This building has

1.14 an internal length of 29.8m and a width of 4.6m and so could have accommodated about 18 horses in individual stalls separated by trevices (*MW*, i, 313); the space above could have served as a hay-loft. The structural evidence suggests, however, that the stable was, in fact, built after the cachepell, probably in the mid or late sixteenth century. Moreover, although the building may at some time have been used as a stable, its position and general character suggest that it was originally designed as an adjunct to the tennis-court.

At Holyroodhouse, during the reign of James V, we hear of the king's and queen's stables (*TA*, ii, 278; *MW*, i, 96, 225), as well as of what seem to have been separate stables for the king's mules and geldings (*TA*, viii, 94; *MW*, i, 7, 242, 289–290). There were also one or more averyhouses and a stable for the cart-horses employed on building operations at the palace, which were part of the masters of works' establishment (*MW*, i, 8, 96). The main focus of these activities was probably the west side of the outer court of the palace, where Mylne's plan of 1663 shows two adjacent stable-courts, together with what may have been a lodging for departmental officials (Mylne 1893, opp. 148). It is not possible to say whether any of the buildings depicted by Mylne went back to the sixteenth century, but continuity of occupation from that period is likely.

C.12 Indeed, the palace stables occupy the same site today. Falconry could be practised in the adjacent royal park and it was probably at Holyroodhouse that 'ane gallory for halkis' — perhaps a large, timber-framed cage — was erected in 1507 (*TA*, iii, 384). Presumably the partridges that were kept in the palace gardens (p. 209) were destined to provide sport for the hawks of the royal mews.

At Edinburgh Castle the stables were situated outside the defences, occupying a stretch of level ground beneath the south wall of the castle (*ER*, v,

397) in the vicinity of the present King's Stables Road. There were stone-built dog-kennels at the castle as early as Robert II's reign (*ER*, iii, 2). At Stirling, too, the stables lay outside the castle. Originally, it would seem, they were situated beneath the west side of the castle rock, adjacent to the King's Park. Direct access from the castle, for pedestrians only, was possible by means of a postern gateway in the nether bailey. New, and more conveniently situated, stables, were erected in or before 1633 in the vicinity of the present King's Stables Lane, off St. Mary's Wynd, where the ruin of a building similar in size and character to the supposed stable at Falkland was recorded at the end of the nineteenth century (*MW*, i, 56, 104; ii, 366–367, 370; Fleming 1898, 17–36). In 1534 a dog-house was built at Stirling, possibly in the nether bailey, where it was proposed to erect another in 1583 (*ER*, xvi, 585; *MW*, i, 311). The king's hawks, some brought from as far afield as Norway, were kept at Craig Forth, about 2km north west of Stirling (*ER*, xi, 142; *TA*, i, p. ccli, 332).

We know little about the stables at Linlithgow Palace, which are on record as early as the 1450s (*ER*, vi, 92). They seem to have been situated in, or adjacent to, the outer close of the palace and were enlarged, or rebuilt, in preparation for Charles I's visit in 1633 (*MW*, ii, 270–273, 348–349). The outer close, or court, as described by Macky (1723, 200), lay immediately to the south of the principal quadrangle, with the offices on the west side facing St. Michael's Church; other buildings may have occupied the area to the south and south east of the churchyard, which is accessible from Kirkgate. What may be the west wall of the outer court is depicted in Grose's view of 1791, which also shows the roof raggle of a two-storeyed building running south from the south-west tower of the palace (Grose 1797, ii, opp. 63). At Dunfermline, according to Macky (1723, 173), the stables, hawks and hounds were accommodated in the lower court of the palace along with the officers serving them (Macky 1723, 173).

WATER SUPPLY AND SANITATION

The provision of an adequate supply of fresh water was a fundamental requirement of all royal castles and palaces. In the case of the smaller and less frequently visited residences a modest permanent supply, supplemented by temporary imports, was sufficient, but for the major palaces, where the court might be in residences several times a year for days or weeks at a stretch, a substantial, dedicated supply was essential. Water was used primarily for the preparation and cooking of food, including brewing, but also for the sustenance of horses and other animals and for cleansing and sanitary purposes. Water was also required for certain domestic activities, such as gardening, and for various craft processes, including smithwork and building operations. It was not in much demand for the table, where wine and ale were the normal drink of the king and household. Little research has been done on the supply and drainage arrangements for the Scottish royal residences and the present state of knowledge leaves much to be desired. What follows is no more than a preliminary review of some of the more accessible evidence relating to the major royal castles and palaces.[2]

The most common means of supply was a well, which had to be deep enough to penetrate the underlying water table even after a prolonged period of drought. Alternatively, but less commonly, rainwater could be collected and stored in cisterns, as at Dundonald Castle, where the large, open tank — in fact, a natural pit enlarged by stone walls — within the outer courtyard is one of the few identifiable examples of its kind that fall within the period now under review (Ewart 1994, 170). Thirdly, running water could be led directly into the residence from an external source by means of a pipe or conduit, a method of operation that also afforded the opportunity, in favourable circumstances, of harnessing the outflow for the removal of sewage and other waste.

The method, or methods, of supply adopted in any particular case depended largely upon local topographical and geological conditions, as also on the degree of security that was considered necessary. Most of the major royal castles had been founded at a time when defence considerations were paramount and several, including Edinburgh, Stirling and Dumbarton, were sited on lofty rock outcrops. In such cases it was essential to have a reliable source of water located with the enclosed summit area and deep wells must have been sunk for this purpose at an early date.

At Edinburgh the carboniferous basalt rock upon which the castle stood proved less than satisfactory as a repository for ground water for, although the principal well had been excavated to a depth of nearly 28 m, it was apt to run dry if there was high demand during a period of drought. When the castle was dismantled by Robert I this well was deliberately blocked. During the ensuing years its whereabouts were evidently lost sight of, for in 1381 no less than £36 16s 6d was spent in relocating the well and restoring it to use. Meanwhile, supplies had been supplemented in 1361 by tapping a spring on the north side of the Castle Rock. This was shortly afterwards enclosed within a stone-built tower, known as the Well-House Tower, from which it was possible to raise water to the summit (*ER*, ii, 83, 113; iii, 81; Ruckley 1990, 18–19).

That internal water supplies at the castle were limited is demonstrated by the fact that is was often necessary to bring in additional quantities for use in building operations, presumably mainly to mix mortar and to clean tools. The evidence for this comes from the seventeenth century, when there is record of payments to watermen and 'burnleaders' for carrying water, or 'burne' into the castle — probably in carts —, but there is no reason to think that earlier practice was any different (*MW*, i, 363, 366–374; ii, 213–217, 222, 224, 379–380).

Corresponding payments were made during building operations at Stirling Castle, where similar conditions may have applied (*MW*, ii, 254).

The unsatisfactory nature of the water supply at Edinburgh Castle was no doubt one of the factors that prompted the Kings of Scots to make increasing residential use of Holyrood Abbey from the early fifteenth century onwards. When James IV's palace came to be built in the years after 1500 it was sited immediately alongside the abbey and so was presumably able to utilise or adapt the existing monastic water and drainage system. Almost nothing, however, is known about the workings of this system, although it seems likely that it harnessed the eastward flowing watercourse known as the Tummel Burn which, with its tributaries, skirted the north and south sides of the burgh of the Canongate, eventually flowing via Clock Mill and Restalrig to emerge into the Firth of Forth at Craigentinny (RCAHMS 1951, pp. xxxvi–xxxvii and Figs. 3–4; Harris 1996, 611).

By the time that the palace was built it is likely that the waters of the Tummel Burn had become too polluted to be used for culinary purposes and it may have been at this period that the spring known as St. Anthony's Well, situated on the north slopes of Arthur's Seat, was tapped and brought into the palace (Mylne 1893, 188). Holyroodhouse was also provided with a number of wells, three of which are depicted on mid seventeenth-century plans and drawings (Mylne 1893, opp. 148; Fawcett 1988, 8). Evidence that the palace incorporated a fairly extensive supply and disposal system by the time of James V is to be found in the accounts of the masters of works, which record payments 'for casting and clengand (cleaning) of the gret lang conduits fra the uter crofts to the abbay yairdis and closattis and inlykwys the conduitis within the place throch the lairdneris (larders) to the closattis byging (building) and flaging agane of the saidis connduttis' (*MW*, i, 222). The kitchens, too, were served by conduits (*MW*, i, 223, 242). That this system had been developed from the one originally installed by the Augustinian canons is suggested by the fact that the palace kitchens seem to have occupied roughly the same position as the monastic ones. Not far away, at the south end of the former east claustral range, was the site of the monastic reredorter, which was almost certainly connected to the original drainage system and it may well be that this continued to be used as a latrine during the early years of the palace.

Dunfermline Palace may also have been able to make use of an earlier monastic water supply, but little is known as to how this operated. At Linlithgow the large, freshwater loch lying immediately to the north of the palace afforded an abundant supply of water for general purposes, while a well situated within the basement of the kitchen tower provided a secure supply of known quality for culinary use. The palace seems also to have had a piped water-supply, brought from the neighbourhood of Poldrait, on the south side of the burgh.

2.12
2.13

6.1

This was discovered *c.*1818, when some of the pipes were damaged by workmen employed in the construction of the Union Canal (Ferguson 1910, 245). In all probability this was the supply that fed the fountain in the palace courtyard, as also the Cross-Well of the burgh, situated at the foot of the Kirkgate (Waldie 1829, 52; *MW*, ii, 204). If the report of the discovery of the fountain pipes beneath the surface of the Kirkgate in 1894 is correct, the supply is likely to have been installed in 1538, for one of the lead pipes is said to have been inscribed with that date (MacWilliam 1978, 297). There are a number of seventeenth-century references to the palace conduits and pipes, including specific mention of those serving the fountain and of others running from the cachepell in the outer court to the woman house within the palace (*MW*, ii, 130, 143, 204). This was presumably a pressurised system, with the fountain, which had its own lock (turn cock?), probably carrying off excess water, as in Henry VIII's fountains at Greenwich and Hampton Court (*MW*, ii, 341; Thurley 1993, 166–167). Some of these pipes are said to have been of lead, but those now on display at the palace, which may relate to an earlier system, are of fireclay (Laing 1968–69, 137).

The castle of Falkland is likely to have contained one or more wells, but their whereabouts are unknown. From at least as early as 1460 there was also a supply of running water in the form of a conduit flowing through the adjacent meadow (*aqueductus infra pratum de Faukland*). An annual payment of 11s was made to an official for the repair and maintenance of this conduit, which could have been either an underground, piped supply or an open water-course, similar to a mill-lade. From about the time of the completion of James IV's palace the wording of the entries for maintenance payments in the exchequer rolls seems to indicate that this supply also serviced the palace latrines (*pro sustentatione aqueductus de Falkland ad necessaria palatii ejusdem*). The precise line of the conduit is uncertain, but it seems likely to have been supplied by the Mespie Burn, which today skirts the north side of the burgh before flowing along the west boundary of the palace garden; presumably a dam was employed to raise the water to the required level (*ER*, vii, 77, 569 and later entries; xiv, 316).[3]

C.8

In 1538–39 a fountain was installed at the palace by Robert Murray, the king's plumber (*MW*, i, 261). Murray may also have been responsible for the contemporary fountain at Linlithgow and his remuneration included an annual fee for the maintenance of the lead roofs there and at Holyroodhouse (*TA*, vii, 199). It is not clear whether or not the Falkland fountain, the exact whereabouts of which is unknown, was supplied from the conduit already described. An alternative source would have been the springs on the lower slopes of East Lomond Hill, immediately to the south of the palace, from which a pressurised supply could have been led, as at Linlithgow, and it may be significant

6.3 Linlithgow
Palace. Courtyard
fountain probably
installed in 1538.
Restored during the
1930s. The design
combines Gothic
and Renaissance
elements.

that payments for the maintenance of the conduit cease after 1540 (*ER*, xvii, 325).

All the royal residences were supplied with sanitary facilities in the form of purpose-built latrines, sometimes known as closets and stools of ease. Since the king's houses invariably became overcrowded during court visits, however, it is doubtful whether, on these occasions at least, the permanent facilities were sufficient to serve any but the upper ranks of the household, important guests and those carrying out specific duties such as gate-keeping and sentry go. Possibly more rudimentary conveniences of a temporary nature were provided in the outer confines of the residence, but if so they have left no trace either in record or on the ground. Nor is there any evidence of the use of communal latrines, although it is possible that these existed, particularly at ex-monastic houses such as Holyroodhouse and Dunfermline.

Prior to the reign of James V purpose-built latrines usually took the form of a fixed seat located in a cubicle contained either in the thickness of a wall or in a projecting turret. Beneath the seat was a stone-built shaft, or open chute, through which the effluent descended to a pit or cistern at the base of the wall. Where the drainage system allowed, these pits were flushed by running water, as in the examples at Holyroodhouse and Falkland Palace mentioned above. If this was not feasible there was nothing for it but to clean the pits periodically by hand, often dismantling and rebuilding part of the enclosing wall in the process.

Latrines of this type survive in many of the royal castles and palaces, including Doune, Ravenscraig, Dundonald and Linlithgow, where a pit and discharge shaft which formerly served the early royal lodging in the south quarter can be seen at the foot of the external face of the south wall. Payments for cleaning and maintenance operations occur from time to time in the accounts. In 1513, for example, payment of 8s was made to two workmen 'for the clenging of closettis' at Linlithgow (*TA*, iv, 525), while in 1535–36 a waller (an inferior category of stone mason) at Holyroodhouse was employed in 'biging and casting of ane gret cobyll for the closet of the toure and pending of the samyn' (*MW*, i, 191), perhaps roughly translatable as 'repairing and cleaning out a large cess pit for the tower latrine and re-covering the same'; the reference may be to the south tower of the palace rather than to the great tower.

Even when cleaned at regular intervals and kept fresh with sweet-smelling herbs, such latrines must have been disagreeable to use, and by about the beginning of the sixteenth century a more comfortable type of convenience, the stool of ease (in England a close-stool, in France a *chaise percée*), had been introduced for the use of the king and selected members of the household. This was simply a large wooden box having an upholstered seat with a hole in it, beneath which there was placed a bowl or basin that could be emptied by a servant after use. The box was still usually kept within a mural cubicle designed for that purpose, but the absence of an external drainage shaft allowed the closet — as it was sometimes called — to be kept warm and free from draughts, while the use of a portable basin reduced unpleasant smells.

Exactly when stools of ease became fashionable is hard to say for similar contraptions had no doubt been employed for emergency use and in sickrooms (as they are today) from an early date. They were certainly in use in James IV's day for in 1501 8d was spent 'for ane stule of es bocht to the King', together with another 3s 1½d for the purchase of three quarters of white cloth to cover it (*TA*, ii, 25). A stool of ease installed in one of James V's ships was covered with tan velvet, while basins were purchased for two other stools in 1533 at a cost of 25s (*TA*, vi, 182; vii, 310).

Turning to the physical evidence provided by the royal residences it may be noted that the royal lodgings at Linlithgow, probably completed during the 1490s, were equipped with shafted latrines, as was the contemporary lodging in the King's Old building at Stirling Castle (Fawcett 1990b, 177). There is no obvious sign of shafts in the mural closets that served the royal chambers in James V's great tower of 1528–32 at Holyroodhouse, however, and it would seem that these, like the similar cubicles in the palace of Stirling (*c.*1538–42) were intended to accommodate stools of ease. At Falkland the galleries of the royal lodging in the east range (*c.*1530) have shafted latrines, while the gate-house, erected some ten years later, seems to have been constructed without shafts. All this suggests that by about the end of James V's reign the king and higher ranks of the household had effectively abandoned the traditional shafted latrine in favour of the stool of ease, a development that was to have a discernible effect upon the design of future royal residences, as also upon that of the castles and houses of the nobility and gentry who sought to emulate them.

While improvements of this kind were in line with current developments abroad,[4] no corresponding advance seems to have been made in bathing practices at the Scottish court. In particular there is no evidence of the existence in Scotland during the first half of the sixteenth century of sophisticated bathrooms with hot-water systems such as were installed by Henry VIII and Francis I (Thurley 1993, 170–177; Mesqui 1991–93, ii, 186). So far as we know, bathing was still usually carried out in a wooden tub placed in one of the inner chambers of the royal suite (p. 136). The tub itself, known as a bath fat (vat), seems to have been no more than a large kitchen cask adapted for the purpose. Thus, in 1504 3s was paid to James IV's master cook 'for ane pipe (cask) to be ane bathing fat, sawing and grathing (dressing) of it' (*TA*, ii, 112, 439). No doubt the kitchens also supplied the hot water to fill the tub, which was lined with cloth and draped with a canopy to keep the bather warm. In 1473, for example, eight ells of broad cloth were purchased to cover a bath for the use of Queen Margaret of Denmark, together with three ells of the same material 'for a schete to put about the Quene in the bath fat' (*TA*, i, 30, 35).

COURTIERS' AND OFFICIALS' LODGINGS

In addition to meeting the residential needs of the king and his family, space in or near the royal houses had to be found for those having regular business at court, as well as for visiting delegates and other guests. Little is known in detail, however, of the accommodation arrangements made for these purposes during the period now under consideration and, although certain chambers in some castles and palaces can be identified as lodgings, specific information as to the way in which they were allocated is seldom forthcoming.

In most cases household officials and servants probably lived in or near the departments in which they worked, as seems to have been the case in England and France (Thurley 1993, 128; Chatenet 1988, 27–28). For the lower ranks this would have meant sleeping, and in some cases eating, in the workplace or in shared accommodation nearby. Thus, the king's chamber servants were accustomed to sleep in the outer rooms of the royal suite (p. 135), while the minstrels and choristers might occupy chambers adjacent to the hall and chapel (pp. 115, 125). Officers of state, senior officials and leading courtiers, however, invariably had their own chambers, some of which are referred to in the documents.

At Holyroodhouse mention is made towards the end of James IV's reign of the Secretary's chamber and of others occupied by Lords Elphinstone (one of the king's favourites), Galloway and Gordon (a son-in-law of the king) (*TA*, iv, 529). During the following reign we hear of chambers occupied by the Regent Albany, the Chancellor, the Treasurer, the Abbot of Jedburgh and the Earl of Rothes, among others (*TA*, v, 11–12, 114; *MW*, i, 7, 103, 166). No doubt the master of works also had his own accommodation at the palace, as he certainly did during the seventeenth century (*MW*, ii, 205; *Bannatyne Misc.*, i, +185). Where these chambers were we do not know, although it is suggested in Chapter 2 that some of them may have been situated in the east range of the inner courtyard, which seems to have been used for this purpose during the late sixteenth and sveneteenth centuries (*MW*, i, 308).[5] Others may have been in lodgings and houses standing elsewhere within the palace precincts.

One of the few identifiable locations at Holyroodhouse that has come down to us is that of the residence of Thomas Peebles, the king's glazier, who occupied the upper floors of the forecourt gatehouse during part of the mid 1530s (p. 235). Subsequently this accommodation was made available to the king's tapestry maker (p. 178), while during the early seventeenth century the rooms over the outer gate were occupied by the Chancellor and were known as the chancellor's lodging (*RPC*, x, 517). Another of James V's leading craftsmen, the royal armourer, had what seems to have been a combined lodging and workshop within the palace precincts, although its exact position is uncertain. The 'kingis armynhous', to which a new loft was added in 1531–32, incorporated chambers and beds for the armourer and his staff; there was also a horse-mill to provide power for machinery (*MW*, i, 96–97, 101–102, 288, 290).

There are fewer references to lodgings at the other castles and palaces, but several royal houses contain chambers that can probably be identified as such.

At Linlithgow there is little record of lodgings prior to the seventeenth century, but the late fifteenth-century south-west tower contains a stack of chambers, four in all, each having a fireplace, together with a latrine placed either *en suite* or in an adjacent corridor. These have all the appearance of being individual lodgings and it is clear that each was provided with separate access via the newel stair at the adjacent corner of the courtyard. There are other similarly equipped chambers on the upper floors of the remaining corner-towers, while the medieval north quarter may likewise have incorporated a number of lodgings, as its seventeenth-century successor is known to have done (Ferguson 1910, 331–332).

At Falkland mention is made in 1538–39 of the wester lodging, while a year or so later, when the royal suite in the east quarter was being remodelled, the king was temporarily accommodated in 'the inner lying chalmer on the cloce syd of the nether north luging' (*MW* i, 217, 260). Neither of these can now be identified, but the south range of the palace contains what were evidently the living quarters of the keeper, or captain, together with a series of individual lodgings. The keeper's lodging occupied the first and second floors of the gatehouse, each of which contains what can best be interpreted as a two-room suite (outer and inner chamber) with a closet, this last being contained within the south-west turret. Access is obtained via the spiral stair in the south-east turret, which opens into the outermost room of each suite. The floor plans are very similar to those found in James V's slightly earlier lodging in the great tower at Holyroodhouse and this suggests that the first floor was occupied by the keeper and the second floor by his wife. Mention is made in the building accounts of the great chamber of the fore-entry and of the captain's forechamber (*MW*, i, 218, 280), possibly alternative names for the outermost chamber of the first-floor suite. The third floor of the gatehouse contained a similar lodging presumably intended for the use of another member of the keeper's family or an important guest.

Immediately to the east of the gatehouse, and occupying the first floor of the main body of the south quarter, is a series of chambers served by a corridor on the north. The west one was evidently the kitchen of the keeper's lodging (*MW*, i, 280), but the remainder appear to have been single-room lodgings. Each was equipped with a fireplace, but unlike the chambers in the keeper's lodging, there were no *en suite* latrines; presumably the occupants had to make do with a stool of ease placed in the corridor outside. The east chamber, which is larger than the others, may have been allocated to the chaplain, for it had direct access to the chapel vestry above by means of a private stair. Above the chapel and vestry is another series of chambers opening off a corridor. These, too, are likely to have been lodgings, although the original planning arrangements are not clear.

1.12

C.9

1.12

At Stirling Castle we hear in the early 1530s of chambers occupied by Lord Fleming (whose wife was a step-sister of the king), the Comptroller, the Treasurer and the master of the household (the Earl of Argyll), whose lodging evidently had both outer and inner chambers (*MW*, i, 106, 108–110). The Treasurer's chamber, where in March 1532 there took place a preliminary audit of certain accounts relating to repairs at the castle, may have formed part of the 'compt hous' (counting house) mentioned in the previous year (*MW*, i, 56; *TA*, vi, 49). Here household expenditure would have been monitored on a daily basis, while it was presumably also within the counting house that audits of the royal revenues by the court of the exchequer were held from time to time (Bateson 1904, 41–42). Mention is also made of a counting house at Falkland Palace *c.* 1460 (*ER*, vi, 565, *domus compotorum*; vii, 79, *camera ex parte occidentali vocata le counthouse*) and of another at Holyroodhouse *c.*1540 (*MW*, i, 290).

So far as surviving buildings at Stirling Castle are concerned, it seems likely that James IV's lodging in the King's Old Building was turned over to courtiers and guests once the new palace was completed *c.*1542, but we have no proof of this.[6] Within the palace itself the extensive space directly above the royal suite was probably utilised as lodgings from the beginning, although evidence of such use becomes available only in the seventeenth century (*MW* ii, 256–257). The existing room divisions date from the turn of the seventeenth and eighteenth centuries. The west quarter of the palace, which was demolished sometime during the seventeenth century, may also have contained a number of lodgings. Adjoining the south quarter of the palace was the west tower of the forework, known as the Prince's Tower. As noted in Chapter 5, the name probably derives from its occupation by Prince Henry, who was born in the castle in 1594, but when not required for royal use the tower may well have been utilised as a guest suite. The corresponding tower at the east end of the forework probably takes its name from Alexander Elphinstone, who was appointed keeper of the castle in 1508, just about the time that the forework was approaching completion (*RSS*, i, No. 1590). It may therefore have been designed as the keeper's lodging and it is interesting to find that, like the keeper's lodging at Falkland, it was equipped with its own kitchen; the dwelling accommodation would have been on the upper floors, which have now disappeared.

Another example of a keeper's lodging can possibly be identified within the frontal block of Doune Castle, although its exact location is uncertain (p. 149). Doune also has an interesting series of lodgings contained in a tower opening off the lower end of the great hall. The two lower floors of this tower are occupied by cellars and kitchens, but above there are a number of chambers, including one with a fine, moulded fireplace and two mural closets heated by the kitchen flue. These were presumably designed for members of the Duke of Albany's family and household, and of those of his son, Earl Murdoch, as also for the

2.5

3.5

use of guests. The accommodation was probably allocated on a flexible system, some rooms functioning as individual lodgings and others as two-room suites. Finally, mention may be made of the chamber tower at Ravenscraig Castle which, like that at Linlithgow Palace, contained a stack of well-equipped chambers — probably three or more in the original conception — each provided with its own access.

Although every effort was made to provide lodgings within the royal residence for those who had some claim to them, it would be a mistake to imagine that this could always be achieved. Little direct evidence of contemporary practice is available, but we have already seen that a separate house was rented for the use of the wardrobe on some occasions (p. 177) and various other references suggest that it was by no means uncommon for guests and officials to be accommodated in private lodgings. Thus, when the French knight Sir Anthony D'Arcy came to Scotland in 1506 to participate in a number of tournaments, the king paid for his lodging expenses with a certain James Aikman, presumably in either Edinburgh or the Canongate (*TA*, iii, 366). Following the arrival of Queen Madeleine at Holyroodhouse in 1537 some of her servants were accommodated in lodgings in the Canongate and when Sir James Hamilton of Finnart, principal master of works, was superintending building operations at Stirling Castle a year or so later he took lodgings in the burgh (*TA*,, vii, 482; viii, 59). During the latter part of the sixteenth century, by which time court life had become centred in Edinburgh and Stirling, many of the leading courtier families acquired lodgings of their own in these towns. When James VI brought his newly married bride to Dunfermline Palace in 1590, however, there was a general shortage of accommodation, so that money had to be spent on hiring and furnishing chambers within the burgh (*Marriage Papers*, Appendix ii, 20).

RECREATIONAL BUILDINGS

The favourite recreational pursuits of the kings of Scots were hunting and hawking, which normally required little in the way of purpose-built accommodation other than that already available within the stables of the royal houses. As we have seen, this might include separate quarters for different kinds of horses, dog-kennels and cages both for hawks and game birds.

When field sports took the king away from the immediate environs of the royal residences he sometimes chose to live under canvas with a minimum of equipment, as James V did in 1531 during a hunting expedition to Meggetland, which lay about a day's journey from Newark Castle (*TA*, v, 422–423, 436). In some favoured localities, however, hunting seats were erected for seasonal occupation. In 1458–59, for example, James II built, or more probably rebuilt, a lodge comprising a hall, chamber, kitchen and four office houses at Loch Freuchie, in the forest of Strathbraan, some 40km north of Doune Castle, together with a smaller establishment, described in James IV's time as a 'Hwnt Hall', at Glenfinglas, about a day's journey to the west (*ER*, vi, 579; *TA*, i, 93, 198, 200. 274; Gilbert 1979, 80–82).

We have no idea what these hunting lodges looked like, but they were almost certainly a good deal less elaborate than the 'fair palace' that the Earl of Atholl erected for James V when he entertained the king and his party to three days of sport in the Forest of Atholl in 1531. According to Lindsay of Pitscottie, this was a three-storeyed building of timber designed as a miniature castle, complete with corner-towers, gatehouse, drawbridge and moat; the chambers within were decorated with fine tapestries and silk hangings and the windows were of glass. As soon as the festivities were over the pavilion was ostentatiously burnt down in front of the royal party (Pitscottie 1899–1911, i, 335–338). Although Lindsay's account may exaggerate, this was clearly a remarkable building, whose lavish appearance hints at the transient and now largely undiscoverable splendours of contemporary court pageantry.

Another popular pastime of the court circle was tilting, or jousting, of which displays were held regularly at the major royal residences. Like archery, this had the great benefit of promoting military skills as well as providing exercise and recreation. In England Henry VIII constructed elaborate tiltyards with permanent viewing galleries and towers at some of the principal palaces (Thurley, 1993, 181–182), but most Scottish tournament fields seem to have been fairly simple affairs, with any standing buildings being of a temporary or, at best, semi-permanent character. The main desideratum was for a sizeable area of enclosed, level ground, known as a barras, or barrace (from the Old French *barres*, barriers). When this was used for jousting a low fence was erected down the middle, on either side of which two mounted and armoured knights charged each other with couched lances and thereafter (if there were a thereafter) engaged in hand to hand combat with other weapons. The barras was also used for duels and trials by combat, as well as for hunting wild animals imported for that purpose. Overlooking the central area were timber stands, known as lists, for spectators, while the combatants were sometimes provided with pavilions equipped with changing rooms and, perhaps, medical facilities.

At Edinburgh the barras was situated beneath the south side of the castle rock a little to the west of the king's stables (Harris 1996, 82). It was probably in existence by the time of Robert I and was reinstated in the mid 1330s, when a stone wall of enclosure was built (RCAHMS 1951, 2–3; *Cal. Docs. Scot.*, iii, 359). This, or its successor, may be the wall upon which the 'masons of the barres' were set to work in April 1507 in preparation for a celebrated tournament held there later that year (*TA*, iii, 384). For this event, in which James IV himself took part, the barras was decorated with arms and banners and five pavilions of silk and canvas were erected, including a large one of silk adorned with five standards. Within the lists there stood a 'tree of esperance'— perhaps a real tree decorated with artificial leaves, fruits and flowers, upon which were hung the shields of the competitors (*TA*, iii, pp.xlv–lii, 393–398).[7]

It was probably also in preparation for this tournament, or for the similar one held in the following year, that a chapel, known as the chapel of the barras, or the chapel of conscience, was constructed nearby. Here, presumably, the chaplain would hear the contestants' confessions before combat and afterwards minister to the dead and wounded (*ER*, xiii, 96; xiv, p.clii; *TA*, iv, 22–23, 41; Harris 1996, 381–382). At the tournament of 1508 certain animals, including a tame hart, were brought to the barras and hunted for sport (*TA*, iv, 128, 140).

As the tournaments of 1507–08 demonstrate, the tilting ground beneath the walls of Edinburgh Castle continued in use after the kings of Scots made Holyroodhouse their principal residence at the capital. Thus, in 1508 the tournament at the barras was followed by revels within the great hall of the palace (p. 109). But there were also occasions when tournaments were held at Holyroodhouse itself. During the royal wedding celebrations of 1503 jousts and combats on foot took place in the palace forecourt. Describing these events the English herald, John Young, explains that 'the Place was without Barreres, and only the Tyllt', perhaps indicating that there were no purpose-built enclosure rails or stands for spectators, but only a central dividing fence (Leland 1770, 298). In fact, as described in Chapter 2, the royal party watched proceedings from within the palace, some of them possibly making use of a timber gallery that had recently been erected.

In 1527 John Drummond, the king's wright, was paid £30 to buy timber to make lists in the abbey (i.e. at Holyroodhouse) and two years later payment was made for refurbishing the lists and laying sand (*TA*, v, 326; *MW*, i, 36). Further work on what may have been the same lists was carried out in connection with the festivities accompanying Mary of Guise's coronation in the abbey church in February 1540, when wet weather made it necessary to put down 200 loads of gravel brought from Salisbury Craig 'for drying of the saidis lists' (*MW*, i, 288). Eight years later timber from the lists was re-used to make a temporary kitchen on the occasion of the marriage of one of Regent Arran's daughters (*TA*, ix, 271–272). The whereabouts of the lists are not stated, but it seems likely that they were situated within the palace gardens. In 1532, however, a combat between Sir James Douglas of Drumlanrig and John Charteris of Amisfield was fought within the inner close of the palace, the stone setts of the courtyard being taken up and replaced by sand for the occasion (*MW*, i, p.lix, 102–103).

There was a barras of some kind at Stirling by 1401, when £6 13s 4d was spent upon railing off a space for judicial combat (*pro barreris factis pro duello apud Strivelin ER*, iii, 596). This may have been the scene of the famous contest

2.12

between Scottish and Burgundian knights 'focht in the barres at Strivling' in February 1448. From a contemporary account of this event it would appear that the combatants fought both on horse and on foot. Pavilions, in the form of tents, were erected, as well as a judge's throne for James II, who eventually brought the hard-fought contest to a close by throwing down a baton (Brown 1891, 30–38). There are also records of jousting at Stirling during the following century, for example in 1507, as a sort of side-show of the Edinburgh tournament, as also 1529 and 1534, when payment was made for extending the lists 'under the castell of Striveling' (*TA*, iii, 364, 395, 410; v, 381, 411–412; vi, 225). It would appear from this last entry and from another of *c.*1540 concerning repairs to the park gate 'bewest the listis in Striveling' (*MW*, i, 289) that in James V's reign, at least, the barras lay beneath the south side of the castle in the vicinity of the royal gardens and the king's stables.

The most detailed surviving accounts for the erection of lists relate to the preparations made for the reception and entertainment of Mary of Guise at St Andrews upon her arrival from France in the early summer of 1538. Responsibility for the organisation of this event was entrusted to George Elphinstone, one of James V's familiars, and large sums were spent on the making of new jousting gear for the king's own use. Mr John Scrymgeour, master of works, arranged for the carriage of timber from Leith and for the transport of various craftsmen, with their work looms, from Edinburgh, including Richard Stewart, a leading master-wright. Construction costs amounted to about £86, including carriage of 'ane gret copper mell (mallet) for dryving of the gret standartis (poles) of the listis'. Mention is made in the accounts of the construction both of lists and 'compter listis', presumably referring to stands for spectators facing each other across a central display area (*TA*, vi, 402, 412–413; *MW*, i, 221–222).

Other royal sports included shooting and golf, neither of which needed elaborate architectural settings. Shooting with the crossbow and longbow was practised at butts erected in the royal gardens — two pairs of great butts with associated benches constructed in the outer and little gardens of Holyroodhouse in 1537–38 cost just under £20, including the transport of turf from Liberton (*TA*, ii, pp. cvi–cvii, 368, 448; *MW*, i, 222). By James IV's time handguns, known as culverins, were also available and the king used these weapons both for shooting matches with his cronies and for hunting. When the weather allowed shooting matches generally took place out of doors, but on winter days and after dusk they were held in some suitable building within the royal residence. During the winter of 1507–08, for example, James IV, having recently been presented with a new culverin, took part in several shooting contests, including two in the great hall at Holyroodhouse and one in the great hall at Stirling Castle (*TA*, iv, 97–98, 103, 105–06). Golf was presumably played in the outskirts of the royal gardens.

James IV was also fond of bowls and the Treasurers' accounts contain a number of references to his expenses — usually betting losses — both at 'lang bowlis' and 'row bowlis'. Row bowls seems to have been the equivalent of the modern game of bowls, while long bowls involved the use of skittles, as did a third game, known as kyles, which the king also played (*TA*, i, pp. ccliv–cclv, 275, 332; ii, 112; iii, 134). Precisely how these games were organised and what they required in the way of pitches and equipment is uncertain, although it seems likely that some varieties of the game were played in the open air. In a glazing estimate of 1654 for the palace of Dunfermline, however, mention is made of an instruction to dismantle 23 windows on the west side of a 'wark callit the kylspell' (i.e. skittle play) (SRO GD 28/1705). Presumably this building, which was evidently of considerable length, was an enclosed bowling alley of the type found in English Tudor palaces (Thurley 1993, 188–190). Neither its location nor its date of erection is known, but since the kylespell appears to have been derelict in 1654 it seems likely to have been constructed in Anne of Denmark's time, if not before.

One game that certainly benefited from the erection of a purpose-built structure of considerable size and elaboration was tennis and it is a measure of the popularity of this sport at the Scottish court that nearly all the major royal residences were equipped with tennis courts. The game has a long history and may well have been played in Scotland as early as the thirteenth century, but the earliest known reference to it comes in an account of the assassination of James I within his lodging at Perth in 1437. According to a near-contemporary source, the king's attempts to escape his murderers by crawling through a sewer beneath his chamber were thwarted because the outlet had been blocked up to prevent the loss of royal tennis balls (Brown 1994, 187 quoting *The Dethe of the Kynge of Scotis*). While this story probably gives a misleading impression of the efficiency of contemporary sanitary arrangements, it certainly indicates that tennis was not infrequently played in the immediate vicinity of the king's lodging.

Some clues as to the nature of the facilities available to the royal sportsmen in Perth, and perhaps also to the form of tennis played in fifteenth-century Scotland generally, are provided by an account for repairs made to the king's lodging in Aberdeen, probably in connection with a proposed visit by James II in 1460. The work done included repairs costing £1 10s to the penthouse within the said lodging for playing hand ball (*pro reparacione unius loci dicti penteyse in dicto hospicio pro ludo ad palmam*) (*ER*, vi, 364, 407, 508, 600; vii, 160, 304).[8] The reference is evidently to what was known in France as *jeu de paume* (game of the palm of the hand), the forerunner of today's real, or royal, tennis, which was played initially with the bare hand, then with a glove and eventually with a racket. In its developed form the game was played within an oblong court having a penthouse, or pentice (i.e. a corridor with a lean-to roof) on one or more sides and a net stretched across the middle; the ball was served on to the penthouse roof and returned across the net. In late fifteenth- and sixteenth-century Scotland tennis was usually known as cache and a tennis court as a cachepell (i.e. tennis play), terms evidently derived from their Dutch and, perhaps more distantly, medieval French equivalents. The game seems to have been played both by hand and with a racket and it is likely that different sizes and types of court were in use, as was also the case in England and the Continent (Thurley 1993, 182–188; Butler and Wordie 1989).

Since facilities for tennis were provided at comparatively minor residences, such as the king's lodging at Aberdeen, it is likely that the game was also played at the major castles and palaces, but it is only when the Treasurers' accounts become available towards the end of the fifteenth century that we have firm evidence of this. James IV was something of an enthusiast for the game, which he seems to have played chiefly at Stirling (*TA*, i, 275, 277, 360, 386, 389; ii, 150, 152–153; iv, 111, 132–133). It is not certain that there was a tennis court within the precincts of the castle during the first half of the sixteenth century, however, for James V appears to have played on a court belonging to local notability, William Bell, to whom in 1539 he gave £20 'to help him to big ane kechpule in Striveling', perhaps at Bell's lodging in the burgh (*TA*, vii, 168, 296, 371). It is likely, however, that some kind of royal tennis court was in existence in Stirling by 1576, when the 10-year old James VI was beginning to take up the game, for in that year payment of £7 was made by the Treasurer for the carriage of timber to Stirling and for workmanship in making a 'catchep-uill' there. This may be the one referred to as the king's cachepell three years later and, to judge from the materials used, it is possible that it was of timber-framed construction with boarded walls. (*TA*, xiii, 131, 307).

In Edinburgh, too, James V seems to have played on private cachepells, of which there were evidently several in the burgh by the second quarter of the sixteenth century (*TA*, v, 256–257, 275, 277; vi, 29). Subsequently, however, and certainly by 1623, a tennis court was built at Holyroodhouse (*MW*, ii, p. lxxxvii, n.8; SRO GD 90/2/58). The court erected at that time, which cost at least £75 sterling (£900 Scots), is probably the one depicted on Gordon's bird's eye view of Edinburgh of 1647 as a large, oblong building standing immediately to the north west of the king's privy garden, overlooking the foot of Abbeyhill. Slezer's north prospect of Edinburgh (Slezer 1693)[9] shows that the building was roofed at two levels and lit by a series of high-level windows facing Abbeyhill, while a sketch plan of *c.*1670 suggests that it was laid out as a *court quarré*, having penthouses running along one long side and across the end wall opposite to the server (Mylne 1893, opp.169; Butler and Wordie 1989, 38–43).

The palace of Linlithgow also contained a tennis court, which first comes on record in 1563, when it was described as 'the Queen's Kaichpeel'; Lord Darnley, father of James VI, is known to have played there (*Prot. Bk. Johnsoun*, No. 678; *TA*, xii, 383). Like the one at Holyroodhouse, this seems to have been a covered court, for in 1626–27 payment was made for supplying 11,000 slates for 'the great caitchpule at the pallace' (*MW*, ii, 204). The court is said to have stood on the site of the later palace lodge (*Prot. Bk. Johnsoun*, No. 678), i.e. within the outer court,[10] but there are no traces of it in Slezer's late seventeenth-centry views of Linlithgow. There was also a cachepell at Dunfermline, where, according to Macky, the monastic cloister was turned into a tennis court after the Reformation (1723, 175).

The only surviving tennis court of the period in Scotland, however, is the one at Falkland Palace, constructed in 1539–41. The building accounts survive, showing that this was erected in conjunction with the main programme of work undertaken at the palace at that time (p. 30), using some of the same craftsmen, including John Brownhill, master-mason. Mention is made of the construction of hazards (perhaps the four small openings in the back wall) and toofalls (pent-

6.4 Falkland Palace. Interior of tennis-court of 1539–41. Refurbished in 1617 and 1629 and restored in 1892–96 and during the 1950s. The ball was served onto the penthouse roof and returned across the net (not shown). The apertures in the end wall may be hazards or lunes, into which the player attempts to hit the ball.

houses), as well as of the harling of the whole 'caichpule' externally and the pargeoning of it internally. The internal walls seem to have been painted black. It is not possible to calculate the total costs of the work, but the contract for the masonry of the outer walls, together with some or all of the paved floor, amounted to £83 (*MW*, i, 244–286; ii, 76). The court was carefully restored by Lord Bute in 1892–96 and again by the National Trust for Scotland during the 1950s and there is no reason to doubt that its present appearance closely matches that of the original (Butler and Wordie 1989, 26–35).

1.14

6.4

Unlike those at Holyroodhouse and Linlithgow, the Falkland cachepell was open (i.e. unroofed), the internal dimensions being about 32.3 x 13.1m (106 x 43ft) inclusive of the penthouses along one side and one end. It was thus a good deal bigger than the Holyroodhouse court (perhaps 27.4 x 9.1m or 90 x 30ft) and the largest of the several courts, both closed and open, erected by Henry VIII at Whitehall and Hampton Court during the early 1530s (about 25.3 x 7.9m or 83 x 26ft). These last had a third penthouse at the service end and were probably intended for playing major, or *dedans*, tennis rather than the minor, or *quarré* game that was played at Falkland. In France, the largest courts, like the one at the Louvre in Paris, could measure up to 34.7 x 11.6m or 114 x 38ft (Thurley 1993, 182–188; Butler and Wordie 1989, 13). Nevertheless, James V's new cachepell at Falkland, begun only a few months after his second French marriage, must have made a very favourable impression upon Mary of Guise's household and the court circle in general.

An unusual feature of the court is the attached and roofed building on the west side, which seems to have been added some time during the latter part of the sixteenth century. As suggested above, this may at one time have been used as a stable, but it seems more likely that it was originally designed to provide additional recreational facilities, such as bowls and billiards (Butler and Wordie 1989, 39–40). It is worth noting that one of the Hampton Court tennis courts had a bowling alley alongside it (Thurley 1993, 188) and that James VI owned a billiard table in 1578 (*TA*, xiii, 223). It has to be said, however, that the existing fenestration seems unsuitable for recreational use of this kind.

This is not the place to attempt a description of the gardens of the royal castles and palaces, but any account of recreational buildings must include a brief mention of the king's menagerie. Almost every European court of the period had a collection of exotic beasts, and animals of this kind were frequently exchanged as presents between monarchs or received by them as gifts from distinguished visitors. In Scotland the practice goes back at least to the time of Robert I, who had a pet lion which sometimes travelled with him. In 1330 and 1331 payments were made for hiring a house for the lion in Perth and the beast was also provided with a cage at a cost of 23s (*ER*, i, 277, 288, 307, 372). The choice of species was, of course, particularly appropriate because the lion rampant was adopted as the royal arms of Scotland in or before the thirteenth century (Innes 1956, 213).

James II kept a lioness, while in 1506 James IV, too, was presented with a lion, which was transported from Leith to Holyroodhouse in a cage (*ER*, v, 590, 615; *TA*, iii, 200). At about the same time we also hear of gifts of a Portuguese horse, a 'must cat' (civet cat) and two bears (*TA*, ii, 465, 468; iii, 148, 191). No doubt the horse was used for riding, but the other animals seem to have been kept mainly within the gardens of Holyroodhouse (Jamieson 1994), where a stone-built lion house was erected in 1512 (*TA*, iv, 275–276, 372, 377). The menagerie at Holyroodhouse was maintained throughout the sixteenth century and beyond and in 1595 there is record of payment to the keeper of the palace garden of £244 for the annual maintenance of a lion and lynx 'and the rest of the pettis and beistis' (*ER*, xxiii, 46). Partridges were also kept within the gardens, apparently in an aviary (not to be confused with an avery house) approached by a stair (*MW*, i, 98). At Stirling Castle the central court of James V's palace has for long been known as the Lions' Den, a name which suggests that it was sometimes used to house the royal menagerie. A young lion, which had been purchased in Flanders, was presented to the king in 1539, whilst the palace was in course of construction, although there is no record of it actually being kept there (*Cal. State Papers*, i, 39).

NOTES

1 In 1511 William Quhet (White), a potter, was employed to make vessels for the royal kitchens and the mint-house (*TA*, iv, 272).

2 For general considerations governing the provision of water see Ruckley 1990.

3 The word *aqueductus* is also used to describe the lade of the nearby mill of Thomastown (*ER*, xv, 36).

4 Cf. the blocking up of latrines and their replacement by *chaises percée*, at the château of St. Germain in the mid sixteenth century (Chatenet 1988, 29).

5 A number of these chambers are shown on Mylne's plan of 1663 (Mylne 1893, opp. 148).

6 It is possible that the hall, great chamber and chamber occupied by Sir William Alexander *c.*1628, described in the accounts as being 'upon the gairdein syde', were located within the King's Old Building (*MW*, ii, 257).

7 A similar tree is depicted in a painting of *c.*1545 of the Field of the Cloth of Gold (Thurley 1993, 184).

8 I am grateful to Dr. Athol Murray for pointing out to me that the exchequer rolls for 1460–69 contain a number of payments going back to the previous reign and that all the references cited may, in fact, refer to a single proposed visit by James II in 1460.

9 This view appears in the editions of 1797 and 1814, but not in that of 1693.

10 The distance between the cachepell and the woman house in the palace (wherever that was) seems to have been about 49m (*MW*, ii, 204).

Chapter 7

THE ORGANISATION OF
BUILDING OPERATIONS

FINANCE

The construction and maintenance of the royal castles and palaces were normally financed from the king's ordinary revenues, mainly comprising the rents of crown lands and royal burghs, customs dues, feudal casualties and the proceeds of judicial fines and forfeitures (*ER*, i, pp.xxxiv–xxxv). Occasionally, however, extraordinary revenues gathered in from other sources were allocated to the royal works. Thus, James I's building operations at Linlithgow Palace were partly funded from the large sums that had been raised to ransom him from captivity in England, while much of the expenditure incurred by James V on the remodelling of Falkland Palace during the late 1530s and early 1540s was met from the proceeds of taxation (*ER*, iv, 554–556; v, 10–11; Grant 1984, 162–166; *MW*, i, p.xiv). A number of major building projects were also undertaken in Scotland by the English crown during periods of occupation and these works, mainly affecting castles and fortifications in the southern part of the country, are documented in the records of the English exchequer (Colvin, 1963–73, i, 409–422; ii, 818–821; iv, pt. ii, 607–726). These for the most part fall outside the scope of the present study.

The ordinary royal revenues were collected locally and initially they were also spent locally. So far as the royal houses were concerned this meant that the officials who collected the revenues, such as the chamberlains of the crown lands (*ballivi ad extra*) and the custumars, also paid the bulk of the costs of building operations at the castles and palaces situated in their localities. Not infrequently these officials also acted as masters of the fabric and in that capacity maintained detailed records of expenditure, in the form of fabric books (*ER*, iv, 513, 530), for audit in the exchequer, usually at yearly intervals. The auditors, appointed by the king on an *ad hoc* basis, normally comprised the Chamberlain, who prior to the 1420s was the principal financial officer of the crown, half a dozen or so magnates, both lay and ecclesiastical, and some royal clerks. The audited accounts were afterwards written up in Latin on parchment rolls in summary form to constitute what are known as the exchequer rolls (*ER*, i, pp.xxxv–xxxvi; Nicholson 1974, 22–23).

The reign of James III brought a number of changes in the administration of the royal revenues, including a clarification of the roles of the Comptroller and Treasurer, two offices which had been created by James I as part of a package of reforms designed, among other aims, to reduce the powers of the Chamberlain. These changes, which became fully effective *c.*1470, gave the Comptroller responsibility for administering those revenues drawn from the crown lands, burghs and customs and the Treasurer a corresponding responsibility for revenues drawn from feudal casualties and the profits of justice. Thereafter, in theory if not always in practice, the Comptroller's receipts (known as the 'property') were used to meet the expenses of the royal household, while the Treasurer's receipts (known as the 'casualty') were used to defray all other expenses, including those of the king's works, together with shipbuilding and artillery. The Treasurer's transactions were subject to audit in the exchequer at intervals of up to three years, the audited accounts of these proceedings, written in book form and mainly in Scots, comprising what are known as the Treasurer's accounts (*TA*, xii, pp.xii–xlix; Murray 1970).

For the historian of the royal works, then, the exchequer rolls constitute the main source of information up to about 1470, while for building operations undertaken after that date reference must be made to the Treasurer's accounts and to the closely related, but separate, series of masters of works' accounts. None of these sources, however, provides anything like a complete picture of building activity.

So far as the exchequer rolls are concerned, there are numerous gaps in the surviving record. It has been estimated, for example, that between 1425 and 1472 approximately one third of the original rolls are lost. In particular, there is a lack of accounts relating to money not coming directly from the crown lands and customs, including sums handled for or on behalf of the king himself. In the few cases where fabric accounts survive, for example at Linlithgow Palace in 1434 and 1469 (*ER*, iv, 554–556; vii, 656–657), we can assume that these disclose the full costs of current building activity. Likewise, during the period 1425–60, when nearly all recorded expenditure on the royal works was funded from customs revenues, we can be fairly confident that the sums allowed in the custom accounts represent the bulk of the expenditure in those cases where the custumar was also acting as master of the fabric. In all other cases, however, references in the exchequer rolls provide only a general indication that work was in progress at the time in question. This is particularly true of Edinburgh Castle, where operations were evidently funded from sources not covered by the surviving exchequer rolls. By the late 1460s nearly all funding was coming from such sources, mainly but not exclusively the Treasurer. After about 1470 expenditure recorded in the exchequer rolls relates mainly to payment of salaries of individual craftsmen, which were funded from the rents of specific crown lands, and to routine maintenance operations on the royal houses undertaken by the chamberlains or receivers of crown lands.[1]

Apart from an incomplete account for 1438 contained in the exchequer rolls (*ER*, v, 38–39) and an account for 1473–74 (*TA*, i, 1–75), the surviving series of Treasurer's accounts commences only in 1488 and between then and the end of James V's reign there are several gaps in the record. The form and content of the earlier accounts also vary a good deal and those between 1488 and 1498, all of which are defective in one way or another, are particularly difficult to interpret. After 1501–02 the accounts became more uniform and from then until 1538 the discharge contained separate accounts of different branches of expenditure, including that incurred on the royal works. Some of these were presented chronologically and others under individual headings for the main castles and palaces (*TA*, ii, 81–89, 269–281). Like the earlier entries in the exchequer rolls, these were summary accounts compiled from more detailed records kept by the masters of works, a few of which themselves survive for the last year of James IV's reign (*TA*, iv, 523–530). In addition to the consolidated entries contained in the fabric sections of the Treasurer's accounts, a considerable number of miscellaneous payments, including sums paid to masters of works and to individual craftsmen, appear in the accounts as payments *ad extra*, up to 1501, or *bursa regis* (the king's purse), from 1502 onwards.

During the latter part of James V's reign further changes took place in the form of the Treasurer's accounts. The consolidated accounts of expenditure on the royal works were discontinued or abbreviated and after 1530 miscellaneous expenditure previously included among *bursa regis* entries was split up, part being taken over by the king's pursemaster and part defrayed by the Treasurer under other heads. There was another change in 1538, after which the discharge of the account was presented on a monthly basis covering each branch of expenditure. Additional sources of revenue were also tapped and during the last few years of James V's reign a considerable proportion of the funds allocated to the masters of works was drawn not from the Treasurer but from the proceeds of four separate taxes imposed upon the clergy, the last of these supposedly being intended to pay the expenses of the king's marriage negotiations in France (*TA*, xii, pp. xxxvii–xxxviii; *MW*, i, pp. xiv–xv).

Little architectural activity is recorded during James V's minority, but between about 1528 and 1542 major building campaigns were undertaken at most of the principal castles and palaces. For this period several volumes of a separate series of masters of works' accounts survive to supplement the entries in the Treasurer's accounts. This material is very much more detailed in scope than that contained in the exchequer rolls and in the main series of the Treasurer's accounts and where the masters of works' accounts survive they often enable us to obtain a fairly complete picture of the progress of building operations. The series is, however, incomplete. It is clear, for example, that two volumes relating to work at Holyroodhouse (and perhaps elsewhere) in 1528–29 and 1530–31 are missing, as also a volume dealing with operations at Linlithgow Palace in 1534–35 and probably one relating to work at Falkland Palace in 1537 (*MW*, i, pp. ix–x, 218, 234; *TA*, vi, 349). Nor do any detailed exchequer records survive for the construction of James V's palace of Stirling *c.*1538–42, since this work seems to have been largely funded on a personal basis by Sir James Hamilton of Finnart.

COSTS OF THE PRINCIPAL BUILDING CAMPAIGNS

As explained above, the source material now available for the period under review does not provide anything approaching a comprehensive record of the activities of the royal works. Even for those building campaigns for which detailed accounts survive there are almost invariably gaps in the record or other inadequacies which make it impossible to arrive at an accurate computation of costs. The following table should be read with these deficiencies in mind. It lists the main building campaigns that can be identified at the principal residences dealt with in this book so far as these relate to the erection of new works and to major schemes of alteration and improvement; it does not include routine maintenance operations and minor repairs. The table gives the approximate recorded costs of each campaign, as set out more fully in Chapters 1 to 3, and also offers estimates of total expenditure for those campaigns for which it seems feasible to do so. The table takes no account of royal building projects that lie outside the scope of this study, such as the construction of Trinity College Church, Edinburgh, and the figures cited cannot be used to produce records or estimates of overall expenditure by the royal works at any given period.

		Approximate Recorded Expenditure (£ Scots)	Estimated Total Expenditure (£ Scots)
Doune Castle	Late 14th–early 15th century	—	—
Dunfermline Palace	Late 15th–early 16th century	—	—
	Mid 16th century	—	—
Edinburgh Castle	*c.*1368–79	700	—
	*c.*1433–37	800	—
	Late 1490s	50	—
	*c.*1510–12	1520	—
Falkland Palace	*c.*1501–13	3900	6000+
	1537–41	11,700	14,000

Holyroodhouse	1501–05	3800	4000+	
	1528–32	5450	7000	
	1535–36	5600	5600	
Linlithgow Palace	c. 1426–37	5260	7000	
	Mid 1460s–c. 1500	1670	—	
	1534–42	4860	—	
Newark Castle	c. 1465–90	310	—	
Ravenscraig Castle	1461–63	630	—	
Stirling Castle	1496–1512	12,710	17,500	
	1538–42	2240	10,000+	

Incomplete as they are, these figures certainly demonstrate James IV's and James V's lavish expenditure on the royal houses. Leaving aside James IV's important building projects at Linlithgow Palace and Edinburgh Castle, for which the recorded expenditure must represent only a small part of the total costs, the king evidently spent at least £20,400, and probably more than £27,500, on new works at Falkland Palace, Holyroodhouse and Stirling Castle between 1496 and 1513. Such expenditure seems modest, however, when compared with that on the royal navy, upon which the king's average annual outlay (including victualling) rose from some £600 in 1501–04 to £5000 in 1505–07 and to more than £8710 in 1511–13 (Macdougall 1989, 228).

During the last 15 years or so of his reign, when wages and prices were somewhat higher — masons' wages, for example, were about 14s – 16s a week as against 6s – 10s a week in the 1500s (p. 238; Gemmill and Mayhew 1995, 21–22), James V spent at least £29,800 and probably more than £41,500 on new works and major alterations at his palaces of Falkland, Holyroodhouse, Linlithgow and Stirling. As noted above, some of this expenditure was funded, not from the king's ordinary revenues, which rose to about £46,000 per annum during the late 1530s (Donaldson 1965, 56), but from taxation. These figures can be compared with Francis I's expenditure on the French royal houses which, at a conservative estimate, amounted to about 25,000 *écus* a year (about £27,500 Scots) during the 1530s (Knecht 1994, 418–419). Henry VIII spent about £46,000 (about £207,000 Scots) on Hampton Court alone between 1529 and 1538 and more than £70,000 (about £315,000 Scots) on the palaces of Whitehall, Nonsuch and Oatlands during the closing years of his reign (Colvin 1963–73, 129, 189, 206, 313; Thurley 1993, 58).

OFFICIALS AND TRADESMEN

Masters of Works

The master of works was primarily a financial and administrative official, responsible for engaging and paying tradesmen, supervising the progress of building operations and rendering accounts for audit in the exchequer. The office took some time to acquire a separate identity, however, and initially the responsibilities and title of the office-holder varied. Prior to the reign of James III post-holders were normally described as masters of the fabric, although the term master of work was also used. From the late fifteenth century onwards post-holders were generally entitled masters of work (*TA*, i, 74) or masters of works (not always with any clear distinction between these variants), although the term master of the fabric was occasionally used well into the following century (*RSS*, v, No. 1060).

The earliest known mention of the title comes in the account for the custumars of Edinburgh for 1375–76. Among the items for which they accounted was substantial expenditure on the construction of the Constable's Tower at Edinburgh Castle, including the (unquantified) fee of the master of work (*magister operis*). The official is not named and it is not clear whether his duties were administrative or technical or both (*ER*, ii, 475–476). He may, in fact, have been an executant tradesman, like his contemporary, Nicholas, the mason, at Stirling Castle, who had duties of both kinds (p. 224). William Dishington, who acted as master of the fabric (*magister fabrice*) for the building of St Monan's Church by David II during the 1360s, was also steward of the king's household. His duties, which appear to have been primarily financial, included the hiring of ships to bring timber to the work (*ER*, ii, p. cvii, 243, 307).

Not infrequently the custumars themselves acted as masters of the fabric, although not always accounting as such. During the construction of James I's palace of Linlithgow, for example, John Waltoun, a local merchant and one of the custumars of the burgh, initially acted as master of the fabric, being succeded in 1434 by Robert Wedale, a monk (shortly afterwards abbot of Culross) and Robert Livingstone, another custumar of Linlithgow (*ER*, iv, pp. cxxxvi–cxxxix). Much of Waltoun's expenditure on the fabric was allowed to him in the audit of the custumars' accounts, but some payments were the subject of separate fabric accounts. In 1430 and 1431 Waltoun's expenditure was allowed in the custumars' accounts following the examination of his fabric books, while in 1434 he accounted as master of the fabric for the balance of his account as custumar. The account for 1431 included a payment of 40s to William Kers, writer, as comptroller of the fabric (*computorum rotulator* i.e. enroller of the accounts); no doubt his principal task was the maintenance of the fabric books (*ER*, iv, 512–513, 528–530, 579–580). At Stirling Castle, during the same period, Alexander Guild, one of the custumars of the burgh, was master of the fabric. Although Guild drew sums from the customs, he accounted for expenditure as master of the fabric and it would appear that there was a separate series of fabric accounts (not necessarily enrolled) which has not survived (*ER*, iv, 402–403, 434–435, 467–468, 501–502, 527–528, 564–565, 604–606).[2]

The duties of the masters of the fabric at Linlithgow and Stirling seem to have been primarily financial, but the title might also embrace technical responsibilities. For many years payments were made from the royal revenues towards the maintenance of the Bridge of Tay in Perth. From about the early 1440s to the mid 1460s these payments were received by John of Peebles, mason, who was described by the royal clerks as master of the fabric of the Bridge of Tay (*ER*, v–vii *passim*). During the first three decades of the sixteenth century similar payments were received by Thomas Fothringham, who was initially described as a mason working on the Bridge of Tay, then as mason and master of the fabric, then as principal mason (*ER*, xi–xv *passim*).[3] Their role seems to have been similar to that of Nicholas, the mason, at Stirling Castle in 1362 in that they were master craftsmen engaged on the fabric whilst also exercising some financial and administrative responsibility (p. 224).

The title of master of work, like that of master of the fabric, covered a broad range of activities. Two municipal masters of work were appointed in Aberdeen in 1441 with responsibility for collecting all the burgh's rents and spending the proceeds as directed by the alderman and common council. A principal master of work appointed for the building of the choir of St Nicholas Church in 1477 also seems to have been a financial official, but a subsequent master of work at St Nicholas, Master John Gray, mason, was evidently an executant tradesman. Appointed in 1484 Gray was required 'to do al car concerning the said wark that accordis til a master of wark, baith in labouring of his awyin persoun, devysing, be seyng and ourseyng of vtheris masons and warkmen that sal be vnder him'; he received an annual fee of £23 6s 8d (*Abdn Counc.*, i, 7, 35–36, 41; Knoop and Jones 1939, 22–23).

It would seem, then, that during the late fourteenth and fifteenth centuries financial and technical responsibility for building operations was in some cases exercised separately and in others in combination, with no clear distinction being drawn between the roles of administrator and tradesman. Nor did the actual title of the office-holder usually give any clear indication as to the duties of the post. In these respects, however, Scotland was no different from medieval England and France (Mortet and Deschamps 1911–29, i, 496, *s.v. magister*; Knoop and Jones 1933, 18–27; 1939, 23; Salzman 1967, 6–13).

Rather more information about the royal masters of works is available for the reigns of James IV and V and a brief account of some of the principal office-holders may help to illuminate their responsibilities. Although few seem to have been local custumars (since building expenditure was no longer financed mainly from customs revenues), a number of them were royal officials, such as chamberlains of crown lands and constables of royal castles.

Andrew Aytoun, who administered building operations at Stirling Castle between about 1497 and 1508, was chamberlain of crown lands in Stirlingshire and deputy chamberlain for Strathearn. For the latter part of this period he was also keeper of Stirling Castle and custumar of Moray, Ross and Caithness (*ER*, xi, 312, 343; xii, *passim*; xiii, 21, 91; *RSS*, i, No. 629). Aytoun is described as 'entering to the work of Stirling' and he received numerous payments for that work from the Treasurer and others, but the surviving accounts do not actually designate him master of works. He received annual fees for his chamberlainships and keepership, as also a livery payment, but there is no specific mention of a fee or pension with respect to his building activities (*TA*, i, 372; ii, 52, 81–85, 269–281; *ER*, xi, 315, 347; xiii, pp. xcii, 25).

Thomas Kincaid was described in 1512 as 'maister of the werk in the Castele of Edinburgh'; he was also constable of the castle. He received moneys from which to pay the wages of masons, wrights and other tradesmen, as also to purchase materials, and his responsibilities evidently included artillery works as well as building operations (*TA*, iv, 278–279, 399, 445–446). Curiously, the contract for slating the roof of the great hall at the castle was made not with Kincaid, but with Robert Calendar, who had succeeded Andrew Aytoun as master of works and keeper of Stirling Castle. Possibly this is to be explained by the fact that the slater, who was named Kelso, resided in Stirling (*TA*, iv, 279; v, 115; *ER*, xiii, p. xcii).

Many, perhaps most, masters of works at this period, however, were clerics and all of them seem to have combined their duties with other responsibilities, either clerical or secular. Andrew Cavers, abbot of the Benedictine monastery of Lindores, entered to 'the Kingis werk in Strivelin' in January 1497, just when James IV's new lodging at the castle was approaching completion. Cavers received considerable sums of money for disbursement on building operations at Stirling Castle, but his connection was short-lived and in November 1497 he entered to the work at Linlithgow, being appointed keeper of the palace a year later (*TA*, i, pp. cclxvi, 311, 322, 339, 355, 364, 368, 384). Again, however, he moved on quickly, being succeeded at Linlithgow by Henry Forest before 1501, when he is found occupying a similar position with respect to building operations at Falkland Palace, his duties there evidently including the payment of workmen's wages. Cavers remained at Falkland for only two years and resigned as abbot of Lindores in 1502 (*TA*, ii, 86–88, 271; *Lindores Chartulary*, 310).

Another cleric whose name crops up in connection with operations at more than one residence is John Sharp, chaplain of the chapel royal within the palace of Holyroodhouse. Sharp was evidently highly valued for his horticultural skills and during the latter part of James IV's reign was paid for various garden works at Holyroodhouse, including the making of a new garden there and the draining of a loch on the south side of the palace. By 1511 he was drawing an annual fee of £6 13s 4d as keeper of the king's garden at the palace (*TA*, ii, 329; iii, 299, 407; iv, 44, 268; *ER*, xii, 593). In 1505 Sharp spent several months making a garden at Stirling, for which he seems to have been paid a weekly or monthly wage, but neither there nor at Holyroodhouse is the exact nature of his duties stated (*TA*, iii, 132, 137, 140, 146). By 1511, however, if not before, Sharp appears to have been acting as master of works at Holyroodhouse and the fabric account of 1511–13 records payments made to him for expenditure on tradesmen's wages and the purchase of materials for works undertaken both in the garden — including the building of a lion house — and elsewhere in the palace (*TA*, iv, 275–276, 372–373, 377, 445, 528–529). Similar payments were made during the early years of the following reign, although nowhere is Sharp specifically described as master of works. His annual fee as chaplain and keeper of the palace and garden of Holyroodhouse continued to be paid into the 1530s; Sharp also received livery payments (*TA*, v, 13–15, 71, 94–95, 115, 199, 259–260, 311, 438; *ER*, xiv, 269; xv, *passim*; xvi, 374).

James Inglis, too, had a long career as a royal chaplain, serving James IV as clerk of the closet and chaplain to the young Prince James (*TA*, iv, 268, 441), and James V as chancellor of the chapel royal (*RSS*, i, No. 2573; TA, v, 82, 126, 199, 310). Although Sharp was paid for some minor building work carried out at Holyroodhouse in 1525 (*TA*, v, 259), it was Inglis who supervised the more extensive operations of 1527, being specifically described in the Treasurer's accounts as 'maister of werk'; his expenditure was detailed in his account book which was countersigned by the king. Although operations were centred on Holyroodhouse, Inglis was also responsible for minor works carried out contemporaneously at Falkland Palace, for which the expenditure seems to have been recorded in the same account book (*TA*, v, 325–327).

As the career of Mr Leonard Logy demonstrates, this was not the first occasion on which a master of works can be shown to have exercised responsibility for two or more undertakings being carried on simultaneously at separate royal houses. Logy first comes on record *c*.1500 as a minor official of the royal household and in the following year was steward to James IV's mistress, Janet Kennedy (*ER*, xi, 263, 267; *TA*, ii, 40). He was also a prebendary of the chapel royal of St Mary on the Rock, St Andrews and vicar of Kilconquhar, Fife (*Prot. Bk. Young*, No. 1450). From 1501 to 1504 he administered the building of James IV's new palace of Holyroodhouse and, although not described as master of works in the surviving accounts, was in the latter year granted an annual pension of £40 for his services to the king in respect of the construction of the palace (p. 57).[4] Logy seems also to have had major responsibilities for the building of the New Haven on the River Forth, as also for shipbuilding operations there. He was also involved, but to a lesser extent, in building operations at the palaces of Linlithgow and Falkland and in artillery works (*TA*, ii, 274, 276–279, 425–426, 432; iii, 82–85).

When Logy died in or before 1506 (*TA*, iii, 89) his position seems to have been filled by another cleric, Walter Ramsay, although the loss of the Treasurer's accounts for 1508–11 makes it difficult to be sure of this. Ramsay, of whose background little is known, was described in 1511 as 'Maister of werk of the schippis' and in the following year as 'Maister of the Kingis werkis', titles which suggest that he exercised some degree of general supervision in these spheres; he received a livery payment but there is no record of a fee (*TA*, iv, 250, 444). His responsibilities would appear to have related mainly to shipbuilding, although this may simply reflect the king's current priorities, and his duties included payment of tradesmen's wages, purchase of materials and provisioning of ships. So far as building operations at the royal castles and palaces are concerned, he received moneys in 1512 for disbursement at Linlithgow Palace and the castles of Stirling and Edinburgh. Other payments for work (possibly artillery operations) at Edinburgh were made by the Treasurer directly to Thomas Kincaid, master of work at the castle, and for task work at Stirling Castle directly to John Lockhart, the principal mason there (p. 226). Likewise John Sharp received moneys for contemporary works at Holyroodhouse directly from the Treasurer (*TA*, iv, 285–295, 305–306, 444–446, 488–489).

The careers of the masters of works who administered the building campaigns of James V between 1528 and 1542 have been outlined by Mylne (1895–96) and Paton (*MW*, i, pp. xxiii–xxvi). The most important of them was Mr John Scrymgeour, who was principal master of works to the crown from about 1528 to the early 1560s. Scrymgeour was the son of a minor landowner in Fife, from whom *c.*1530 he inherited the lands of Myres, near Auchtermuchty, together with the offices of king's macer and sergeant-at-arms. He rendered all the surviving masters of works' accounts for the latter part of James V's reign, with the exception of that for Linlithgow Palace in 1535–36, which was rendered by Sir James Hamilton of Finnart. At Stirling Castle he was assisted by a deputy or overseer, but he evidently took personal charge of the work at Holyroodhouse[5] and Falkland Palace, his services to the king being marked in 1542 by a confirmation charter of the lands of Myres for his labours concerning the building and repair of the palaces and castles of Holyroodhouse and Falkland and other royal works in Scotland (*RMS*, iii, No. 2568). He was described variously as 'principale maister of werk', master of (the king's) work (*magister sui operis*), master of (the king's) works and buildings (*magister operum sive edificiorum*) and, in 1562, as master of (the king's) fabric (*magister nostre fabrice*) (*TA*, vi, 213; *RMS*, iii, Nos. 992, 1609; *RSS*, v, No. 1060). Scrymgeour was paid an annual fee of £20, rising in the late 1530s to £40; he also had an annual livery of £20 (*TA*, vi, 213; vii, 200, 335).

Sir James Hamilton of Finnart (McKean 1991 and 1995) was an illegitimate son of the 1st Earl of Arran and a second cousin of James V, whose personal favour he would seem to have enjoyed on more than one occasion. Hamilton's turbulent political career does not concern us here, except insofar as it impinged upon his activities as master of works. He was a considerable builder in his own right (p. 237) and it may have been a genuine interest in architecture, coupled with a desire to maintain his standing with the king, that led to Hamilton's direct engagement in the activities of the royal works.

Hamilton amassed numerous royal appointments from the mid 1520s onwards and his involvement with the royal works evidently commenced some time before 1535, when he is found in charge of building operations at Linlithgow Palace (p. 19), of which he had been appointed keeper some years previously. Although apparently not holding a formal appointment as master of works at that time, Hamilton accounted for work done at the palace in 1535–36 'at the command of our soverane Lord the kingis grace', the designated master of works, Thomas Johnson, acting as his overseer or assistant. Hamilton and Johnson also rendered an account for the previous year, but this does not survive (*MW*, i, 115, 130–131). Hamilton's involvement in building operations at Linlithgow continued during the late 1530s, although the main programme of work may have been complete by that time; he was also responsible for contemporary works at Blackness Castle (*TA*, vi, 304, 448; vii, 60, 91, 195, 302).

Hamilton's principal undertaking during the late 1530s, however, was the commencement of the palace block at Stirling Castle, where work probably began in spring 1538 (p. 50). The financial arrangements for this enterprise were distinctly unusual, for it would seem that, in return for various royal favours sought or received, including extensive grants of land, Hamilton himself undertook both the personal direction and also the greater part of the funding of this work (MacIvor 1991; MacKean 1991, 13–14). At least £4000 is known to have passed through his hands or been credited to him and a charter grant of September 1539 specifically acknowledged his service to the king in the completion of the palaces of Linlithgow and Stirling (*RMS*, iii, No. 2021; *TA*, vii, 256; SRO, E 21/37 fol. 3ᵛ; *RSS*, ii, No. 3199).[6]

A few days before this charter was issued Hamilton was appointed principal master of work to the king of all works then building or to be built within the realm, with power to nominate three or four deputies to answer to him and to his overall direction; he was to receive an annual fee of £200, half to be paid by the Treasurer and half by the Comptroller (*RSS*, ii, No. 3144). Precisely how Hamilton's powers of universal jurisdiction would have worked out in practice, bearing in mind that similar powers were already being exercised by Scrymgeour (the terms of whose appointment are not known) is far from certain. As it happened, the issue was never put to the test, for Hamilton was in post for less than a year, falling victim to political intrigue in July 1540 and suffering execution and forfeiture a month later.

Hamilton's assistant at Linlithgow, Thomas Johnson, has already been mentioned. He was a chaplain and public notary who for a time acted as town clerk and sheriff clerk of Linlithgow. Johnson is described in the accounts both as master of work at Linlithgow and as overseer under Sir James Hamilton, for which duties he received 14s a week, or £36 8s 0d per annum (*MW*, i, 130–131). He continued to act as master of works at Linlithgow for a year or so after Hamilton's death, also holding office as keeper of the palace (*TA*, vii, 339, 401, 480).

Another chaplain, James Nicholson, was appointed master of work within the castle of Stirling in 1530 at an annual fee of 20 merks (£13 6s 8d) until he obtained a benefice worth £20 (*RSS*, ii, No. 487; *TA*, v, 438). He was evidently subordinate to Scrymgeour, for his account for work done in 1531–32 was included within Scrymgeour's own account for that year (*MW*, i, 103–111). In 1538 Nicholson's accounts were examined by Scrymgeour and payment made to him prior to Sir James Hamilton's entry to the work (*MW*, i, 228). The following year Nicholson was presented to the vicarage of the church within the castle; he also held office as a custumar of Stirling (*MW*, i, p. xxiv; *ER*, xvii, 180). Following Hamilton's death, Nicholson resumed his duties as master of works until August 1541, when he was succeeded by Robert Robertson, who had been employed as a wright and carver in James V's building operations at Holyroodhouse and Falkland Palace (*MW*, i, 58–70, 214). Robertson was appointed 'principale ourseare and maister of all werkis concernyng his craft and utheris within the castell of Striveling', but his weekly wage, probably in the region of 14s, was not increased; we do not know whether or not he continued to work as a carver (*RSS*, ii, No. 4191; *MW*, i, 60). It was probably Robertson who supervised the completion of the palace block at Stirling.

Summing up the situation that prevailed during the reigns of James IV and James V, it would appear that administrative and technical oversight of building operations were usually managed separately, the master of works acting primarily as a financial controller and the master tradesman, as will be shown below, primarily as a technical director. Only exceptionally, as in the case of Robert Robertson, do we find an executant craftsman exercising financial and administrative control of operations. As we shall see below, some masters of works, such as John Sharp and Sir James Hamilton, may also have had a role in planning and design. During the reign of James IV the Treasurer sometimes played a direct role in building operations, entering into contracts with leading tradesmen and settling their accounts, as well as himself paying the costs of materials and carriage (p. 225). Towards the close of the reign, however, the masters of works assumed greater responsibility for the purchase of materials, while during the latter years of James V's reign they accounted for virtually the entire costs of building apart from the fees and pensions of individual tradesmen.

At the same time they relinquished some of their responsibilities for the provision and maintenance of artillery (*TA*, xii, pp. xxxvii–xxxviii).

Although some masters of works were drawn from the ranks of local officials, such as collectors of crown revenues and constables of royal castles, most office-holders were now clerics, a number of them being members of the royal household. Scrymgeour, however, was a laird and Hamilton a bastard nobleman; only Robertson appears to have been a tradesman. Nearly all of them held other offices or benefices and, except in the case of Sir James Hamilton, their emoluments as masters of works, in the few cases where these can be quantified, were modest. As in the previous period, most masters of works were locally based, although some, like Cavers, might be engaged successively at different houses. But there is now evidence of the emergence of an official having a more general oversight of the king's works, although his relationship with local masters of works is not always clearly defined.

Masons

The master mason was a chief technical officer, responsible to his employer for the masonwork of a building project and often also for its overall design and execution. A craftsman by training he would often work on site with his own hands, cutting some of the architectural details himself and preparing templates of mouldings for his assistants. At a lower level of responsibility the term was also applied to a master tradesman working with his servants and apprentices either by task or as a wage-earning employee (Knoop and Jones 1939, 15–20; 1933, 33–34; Coldstream 1991, 8–18).

As noted above, there was at first no clear distinction between the duties of a master mason and a master of works, technical and financial responsibility for a project being exercised by the same individual. The most senior appointment of this kind within the royal works was that of master mason to the king, of which the first known incumbent was Master Nicholas of Hane.[7] To judge from the scanty evidence that is available, Master Nicholas's career spanned the years between the late 1370s and the early 1400s (*ER*, ii, 553; iii, 562). During the last part of this period he was described as king's macer (a royal officer of arms) and mason or, more simply, as king's mason (*simentarius domini regis*), drawing a yearly fee of £10 from the Dundee customs for the two posts (*ER*, iii, 458, 483, 536, 562). The only work that can certainly be ascribed to him is the erection of Robert II's tomb at Scone Abbey, for which he had contracted during the king's lifetime at a price of £120 (*ER*, ii, 585, 622; iii, 348), but it is possible that he was also involved in other royal or semi-royal building projects of the period, such as the erection of the castles of Dundonald and Doune.

Apart from the fact that Master Nicholas's responsibilities might include the carriage of materials (*ER*, iii, 348), we know nothing of his duties, but some idea of what these may have been can perhaps be deduced from an account rendered by another master mason in the royal service, Master Richard, a century or so earlier. Master Richard, who is known to have been employed at the royal castles of Edinburgh and Stirling (and perhaps also that of Aberdeen) during the latter part of the thirteenth century may well have occupied a similar position to that of Master Nicholas of Hane, although he is described simply as a mason (*cementarius*) (*ER*, i, 12, 40, 42, 48). The account that he presented for audit in 1289 covered expenditure on works at Stirling Castle amounting to some £103, including the hiring of masons, quarriers, smiths and other workmen, the maintenance of horses carrying stone, and the provision of lime (*ER*, i, 40). Presumably Master Richard also provided professional oversight of the building programme.

Like their counterpart, the king's master carpenter, whose duties are discussed below, Master Richard and Master Nicholas no doubt had to be prepared to work wherever the king wished, travelling from one house or castle to another as necessary. Some masons, however, were attached to particular castles or palaces, receiving an annual fee as a retainer for their services. The role of Nicholas (not to be confused with Nicholas of Hane), a mason employed at Stirling Castle, has already been mentioned (p. 216). In 1362 the custumars of Stirling paid him £5 from which he was to pay the other masons then engaged upon the repair of the castle. Nicholas had himself acted as one of the custumars of the burgh of Stirling two years earlier and in 1361 rendered the account of the bailies of Stirling (*ER*, ii, 14, 28, 60–61, 69, 85–86, 116). For his post as principal mason at the castle he received an annual fee of 10 merks (£6 13s 4d) (*ER*, ii, 28). His successors in what seems to have been the same post received an annual fee of £13 6s 8d during the last two decades of the fourteenth century, and there is record of a similar post at Dumbarton Castle at the same time (*ER*, iii, 400, 676, 702).

It is unlikely that the post of king's mason was left vacant following the death of Master Nicholas of Hane sometime after 1402 (*ER*, iii, 562), but we cannot identify any of his possible successors with any degree of confidence until the reign of James IV, when more detailed information about the activities of the royal works becomes available in the Treasurer's accounts. Walter Merlioun played a prominent part in James IV's building programme between about 1496 and 1505, working at Stirling Castle (p. 41), Dunbar Castle (*TA*, i and ii, *passim*) and Holyroodhouse (p. 57); he was still active in the royal service in 1512, but was dead by 1521 (*TA*, iv, 340; *Prot. Bk. Foular*, iii, No. 186). Although Merlioun is described in the accounts simply as a mason, he received an annual fee of £40 from the Treasurer from 1496 onwards (*TA*, i, 280, 323, 342; ii, 94; iii, 118, 121, 125, 327) and the fact that he was paid such a substantial sum on a long term basis suggests that he may indeed have held the post of king's master mason, although no record of his appointment has survived. In

1499 the king granted Merlioun an annual pension of £40 for life, to be drawn from the customs revenues of Edinburgh (*RSS*, i, No. 399). This provision may have been intended to replace, rather than augment, the annual payment from the Treasurer, but there appears to be no record of the pension actually being paid.

Merlioun's involvement in the royal building programme seems usually to have been by way of contracts under which he undertook specific tasks for fixed sums of money, a system which is known to have been in operation in the royal works as early as the reign of Robert I (*ER*, i, 53). Thus, at Dunbar Castle he was paid £200 in June 1497 'for his task of Dunbar, that is the pending of the hall, bigging of Hannis toure, and the bigging within the place as his endenture beris' (*TA*, i, 342). He had previously undertaken the construction of the forework of the castle under a separate agreement, which apparently included provision for the wages of the masons and barrowmen who assisted him (*TA*, i, 328, 331, 334, 338, 351, 364). The contracts themselves have not survived and it is uncertain whether they were drawn up with the Treasurer himself or with the master of works, Andrew Wood, who was also keeper of the castle (*TA*, i, 350). Merlioun accounted directly with the Treasurer, maintaining his own account books (*TA*, i, 364), but the costs of materials and carriage were for the most part met directly by the Treasurer (*TA*, i, 331, 334–335, 338; ii, 82, 115), who also paid for the preliminary quarrying operations and site clearance (*TA*, i, 328). Subsequent quarrying costs, however, were defrayed mainly by the master of works, who also purchased local materials, such as sand and lime (*TA*, i, 323, 338, 342). So far at least as Hans' Tower was concerned, it would seem that Merlioun's contract was for masonwork only, for the Treasurer defrayed the costs of wrightwork and slatework, the former by daily wages and the latter by contract (*TA*, i, 353, 358).

At Stirling Castle Merlioun undertook the building of the king's house (p. 41) in accordance with what was probably a similar agreement, receiving 6s 8d as earnest money in June 1496 after the terms of the contract had been agreed (*TA*, i, 277); in this case payment was made by instalments (*TA*, i, 278, 284, 286, 302–303, 310). Associated with him in the project was John Merlioun, perhaps a son or brother, who appears to have received an annual fee for his service at Darnaway Castle in 1502 (*TA*, i, 286, 310, 367; ii, 48). Similar arrangements prevailed at Holyroodhouse, where Walter Merlioun contracted to build the forework and new chapel in October 1502 (*TA*, ii, 344), receiving some £360 by instalments for the work. Other tasks in the same building campaign were contracted out to other tradesmen, including the master mason William Turnbull, some of the payments for taskwork being made directly by the Treasurer and others through Leonard Logy, the master of works (p. 219; *TA*, ii, 269–281; SRO, E 21/6 fols. 54–63).

When Walter Merlioun left Stirling in 1497 to take up employment at Dunbar Castle, his place as principal mason at Stirling Castle may have been taken by John Lockhart, who certainly filled that position between 1501 and 1512. Lockhart may have had a hand in the building of the great hall there and certainly featured prominently in the construction of the Stirling forework (p. 43). In 1508 James IV, in letters which described Lockhart as the king's beloved servant and mason and took note of his past and future good service in his practice and art (*in suis practica et arte*), granted him an annual pension of £20 from the customs revenues of the burgh of Ayr for life. By the terms of this grant Lockhart was forbidden to work for any other employer without royal licence and was to receive, alongside his pension, appropriate remuneration as agreed between the king's master of works and himself (*ER*, xiii, 360–361; *RSS*, i, No. 1770). Two years later Lockhart, who seems to have had Ayrshire connections, was granted a charter of certain lands in that county in lieu of £100 owed to him by the king for work undertaken at Stirling Castle (*RMS*, ii, No. 3461), while in 1511 he received a livery payment of £5 10s (*TA*, iv, 258). If the royal grant of 1508 did, indeed, signal Lockhart's appointment as king's master mason, as seems likely, the post may have overlapped with that already held by Walter Merlioun, but such a situation was to recur more than once during the following reign.

Like Merlioun, Lockhart undertook successive contracts, or indentures, for specific items in the building programme. Between 1502 and 1506 he erected the forework gatehouse at a cost of some £1067 (*TA*, iii, 88). He moved on to work on the east section of the forework and then, in or about the spring of 1509, took on a third contract relating to the north-east tower, or Mint, and probably also to the east curtain wall. Finally, in 1512, Lockhart undertook a fairly small contract for the remodelling of the wall-walk of the great hall. The following year he and his servants were drafted into the ill-fated military expedition to England, after which his name disappears from the records. The indentures of 1509 and 1512 are specifically stated to have been drawn up between Lockhart and the Treasurer who, in most cases, himself paid the sums due, by instalments, directly to Lockhart (*TA*, ii, 269–270; iii, 84, 88–89, 296–297; iv, 281, 372, 520).

The next known holder of the post was John Ayton, who was appointed 'maister mason to the Kingis grace' in or before 1526. He received an annual pension of £20 from the Treasurer from life, together with regular livery payments (*TA*, v, 268, 328, 384, 431). Ayton was principal mason during the first phase of James V's building programme at Holyroodhouse, including the erection of the great tower (p. 64). His name appears in the earliest surviving master of works' account for that undertaking, covering the period from August 1529 to August 1530 (*MW*, i, 1–55). During that time Ayton worked for 14 weeks at a weekly wage of 18s (on one occasion 38s for two weeks) and for up to 24 weeks on taskwork 'for the masonry of this new werk in Halirudehous', for which he received £338 0s 11d for that portion completed within the period of the account (*MW*, i, 55). John Scrymgeour, the master of works, paid the entire cost of the operation, including wages, materials and carriage, from moneys provided to him by the Treasurer for that purpose (*TA*, v, 389). The terms of Ayton's contract for taskwork are not known, but the figures suggest that the payments made to him by the master of works included the wage and other costs of his own band of masons, as also of the materials used.

Ayton died in or before January 1532, when John Brownhill (Burnhill) was appointed king's master mason for life with the same fees, liveries and duties (none of which are stated) as his predecessor (*RSS*, ii, No. 1119). Brownhill certainly did receive an annual fee of £20, the last recorded payment being in 1542; he also received a livery payment in 1540, but apparently not in previous years (*TA*, vii, 415; viii, 104, 148). During 1535–36 Brownhill played a leading role in the second phase of the king's building programme at Holyroodhouse (p. 65), receiving a weekly wage of 18s; his two servitors were paid 12s each (*MW*, i, 153–165). He then moved to Falkland Palace where, in addition to practising his craft, he helped the master of works, John Scrymgeour, to gather in the tax revenues that had been allocated to the project (*MW*, i, 197, 200, 236–237). As a leading master mason at Falkland, Brownhill worked both for weekly wages, probably again at the rate of 18s, and by contract. Initially his immediate assistants comprised three servitors, and latterly two servitors and an apprentice, their overall weekly wage varying between 43s and 50s according to the composition of the team and the season of the year. Payment was made directly by the master of works, who also defrayed the costs of tools and scaffolding (*MW*, i, 207–211, 252–255, 277–278). The contract, drawn up between Brownhill and another mason, Henry Bawte, on the one hand and the master of works on the other, was for the completion of the palace gatehouse (p. 32). As in the case of Ayton's contract at Holyroodhouse in 1530, the total sum paid, £400, probably covered the costs of materials and carriage, as well as wages (*MW*, i, 279).

During the latter part of James V's reign a number of additional appointments were made to the post of king's mason. In 1535 Thomas French, then working at Linlithgow Palace (p. 21), was appointed master mason to the king for life at an annual fee of £40, payable by the Treasurer (*RSS*, ii, No. 1643). In addition to his salary (of which, however, there is no record of payment in the surviving Treasurer's accounts), he received a bounty of £20 in recognition of his work at the palace, for which he was also paid a weekly wage of 20s; four of his assistant masons were paid 16s weekly and six 12s weekly (*MW*, i, 121–122). From Linlithgow French moved to Holyroodhouse, where in 1535–36 he received a weekly wage of 18s (*MW*, i, 154–162), and thence to Falkland Palace. At Falkland, where he operated with a group of up to five assistants, most of whom had previously been with him at Holyroodhouse, he worked both for weekly wages and by task, being paid an additional bounty of £10 for taskwork on the south quarter of the palace (p. 33), undertaken jointly with another master mason, James Black (*MW*, i, 209–211, 254–256).

Moyse (Mogin) Martin, a Frenchman, was master mason of Dunbar Castle. He appears to have accompanied James V on his visit to France in 1536–37 and while the royal party was at Orléans, in December 1536, the king appointed him royal master mason during pleasure at a salary of £5 a month (£60 for a full year), to be paid by the Comptroller out of the Edinburgh customs revenues; in addition Martin was to receive a weekly fee from the master of works 'as utheris masounis gettis' when employed on the royal works (*TA*, vi, 464; *RSS*, ii, No. 2199; Dunbar 1991, 5). Martin probably played a major part in the remodelling of Falkland Palace (p. 36), where he worked from December 1537 to March 1538, when he died suddenly. He may also have been employed there during the preceding months, for which the accounts are missing (*MW*, i, 206, 208; *RMS*, iii, No. 1763). His weekly wage is not specifically stated, but was probably 20s.[8]

The last recorded appointment of this kind during James V's reign was that of another Frenchman, Nicholas Roy, one of a group of six French masons sent to Scotland by the king's parents-in-law, the Duke and Duchess of Guise. Two days after his arrival in Scotland in April 1539 Roy was appointed king's master mason during the king's pleasure at a monthly salary of £6 13s 4d (£80 for a full year), half to be paid by the Treasurer from the king's casualties and half by the Comptroller from the Edinburgh customs dues. In addition Roy was to receive a weekly fee from the master of works when employed by the crown (*Balcarres Papers*, i, 20, 33; *TA*, vii, 48, 184; *RSS*, ii, No. 3002). Like Martin, Roy played an important role at Falkland Palace, where he worked from July 1539 until the summer of 1541 at a weekly wage of 21s, the same rate as that of his assistants (*MW*, i, 254–255, 277–278). Payment of Roy's monthly salary continued until August 1541, while two years later he is found working for Mary of Guise at Stirling Castle (*TA*, vii, 472; *ER*, xvii, 291; p. 52).

Among other masons whose careers are of particular interest in themselves or which throw light on contemporary conditions of employment mention may be made of three connected with Linlithgow Palace. Robert Jackson was master mason there in 1469. His terms of employment are not known, but his weekly remuneration was evidently paid partly in victuals (*ER*, vii, 657). This was not unusual, especially outside the larger towns. At Dingwall Castle in 1506 the annual remuneration of Thomas Mason, mason, comprised £3 in cash together with one chalder of flour and eight bolls of barley (*ER*, xii, 514), while in 1581 the master mason at Doune Castle completed a contract payable partly in cash and partly in malt and oatmeal (Mylne 1893, 60). Nicholas (Nichol) Jackson, perhaps a son or nephew of Robert, was employed at Linlithgow in the early 1500s. He was paid directly by the Treasurer for various items of taskwork, for the purchase of materials and for the expense of bringing his 'werklumys' from Kirk of Steill (Ladykirk), Berwickshire, where he acted as master mason during the main phase of construction (*TA*, ii, 347, 359, 362, 366, 391, 440). At Kirk of Steill, too, he was paid for taskwork by the Treasurer, also receiving certain sums for disbursement on the fabric on behalf of the master of works (*TA*, iii, 86–88, 295–299).

During the final years of James IV's reign the leading mason at Linlithgow Palace was Stephen Balty (Bawty). There were no major building operations in progress at that time, but Balty seems to have exercised fairly wide responsibilities for minor works and maintenance, purchasing materials, arranging carriage, hiring other tradesman and paying their wages. He kept his own accounts ('the said Stevinnis compt buke'), sometimes accounting directly with the Treasurer and sometimes with the master of works, Walter Ramsay. On at least two occasions he received moneys from the Treasurer on behalf of Ramsay. Balty and his apprentice normally worked at a weekly wage of 14s (perhaps comprising 10s for Balty and 4s for the apprentice), while his two assistant masons received 7s each (*TA*, iv, 279, 374, 379, 445–446, 520, 523–525). During the early years of the following reign Balty's duties were organised on a more formal basis, in accordance with which he received an annual fee of £20 for life, payable from the customs revenues of Linlithgow, for maintaining the palace and upholding its roof; his assistant received a fee of £10. Presumably Balty, who died in or before 1516, also received weekly wages when working as a mason (*ER*, xiv, 3, 48, 94, 195).

One other name that deserves mention is that of Cressent, the Italian mason who may have been involved in the erection of James IV's great hall at Edinburgh Castle (p. 79). The terms of Cressent's employment were unusual in that his monthly remuneration of £7 (£84 for a full year) included wages, expenses and fees (*TA*, iv, 271, 439). Possibly his period of service in the royal works was not long enough to warrant the more customary arrangement under which an annual salary was paid separately from weekly wages.

Looking at the composition of the royal mason force as a whole it can be seen that the same names crop up time and time again and this is an indication of the important role played by certain leading families. The Jacksons and Martins have already been mentioned, but the two most prominent families in this respect were undoubtedly those of Merlioun (Merlzion) and French (Franche). The provenance of the Merlioun family is uncertain and their genealogy as yet unresolved (Black 1946, 597), but the name is suggestive of an early connection with hawking and falconry. The first individual of this name known to have been employed in the royal works was Henry Merlioun, who appears to have been master mason at Ravenscraig Castle during the first phase of construction in the early 1460s (p. 103). Merlioun received certain moneys allocated to the fabric on behalf of the master of works, David Boys, and his responsibilities included the hiring of one or more additional masons (*ER*, vii, 197). Outside the royal works a mason named John Merlioun was employed by the abbey of Lindores during the early 1480s (*ADA*, *137), while the accounts for the construction of a bridge at Dunkeld *c*. 1510–16 contain the names of John, Andrew and Robert Merlioun, the last named being a master mason (*Dunkeld Rentale*, 279–301). It seems likely that these masons were related to one another and that there were also family links between them and the Walter and John Merlioun whose careers in the royal works at about the same time have been mentioned above. In the next generation John Merlioun, mason, was active at Holyroodhouse and Falkland Palace during the mid and late 1530s (*MW*, i, 136–139, 223, 256–257). It was probably he who contracted with the Clerk Register (the official responsible for the state records), Mr James Foulis, to build a new register house at Edinburgh Castle (p. 83), receiving £300 from the Treasurer for his work, which included 'laubouris, warkmanschip and furnesing', in 1541 (*TA*, vii, 337, 474).

The earliest recorded mason of the family of French — an appellation probably indicative of their national origin — was John, who was buried at St Michael's Church, Linlithgow in 1489 (Mylne 1893, 36). As already suggested (p. 17), he may well have worked not only on the church but also on the adjacent palace. John's son, Thomas, was employed in Aberdeen as master mason of the bridge of Dee and of the south transept of the cathedral during the second and third decades of the sixteenth century (Mylne 1893, 39; Fawcett 1994, 74, 201; Macfarlane 1995, 268–269, 328). He then resumed the family's connection with Linlithgow, contracting in 1530 and 1532 for the finishing stages of the church, in which he was assisted by two of his sons, one probably called Patrick (Waldie 1879, 62).[9] Thomas also found time, in 1533, to act as master mason of the Bridge of Tay, Perth (*ER*, xvi, 234), while between about 1534 and 1540 he was employed almost continuously in the royal works, as described above. At Holyroodhouse he was assisted by George French, perhaps a son, and at Falkland Palace by George and Robert French, perhaps another son (*MW*, i, 154–162, 211, 254). In the Falkand building accounts he and his team are lumped together with Nicholas Roy and his assistants under the heading of 'French masons' (*MW*, i, 254; SRO, E 36/6, fol. 20), which suggests that the family's links with that country had been preserved at least into a second generation. French's subsequent career included appointment as master of the masons during the construction of New College (St Mary's College), St Andrews, where in 1543–44 his assistants included at least one mason who had previously worked with him at Holyroodhouse and Falkland Palace (*St Andrews Rentale*, 198). He afterwards worked for the Earl of Bothwell at Hailes Castle, but was dead in or before 1551 (Mylne, 1893, 44).

Carpenters and Wrights

Like the master mason, the master carpenter, or master wright, was a leading technical official whose duties within the royal works might include the design and implementation of a building project, as well as responsibility for the work of his own trade. The scope of this work was wide ranging, embracing not only wright work required in building construction and roofing, but also ship-building, the construction of war machines and, as time went on, the operation and maintenance of artillery.

The post of king's master carpenter probably goes back at least to the thirteenth century, but early holders of the post are not clearly identifiable as such in the surviving records (Mylne 1899–1900). Likely candidates include John, the carpenter, a Dominican friar, who seems to have held a royal appointment of this kind in the early 1340s (*ER*, i, 510), Adam, the carpenter, who worked at Edinburgh Castle and St Monan's Church, Fife, during the 1360s (*ER*, i, 608; ii, 3, 177, 333–334) and the unnamed carpenter who was said in 1381 to have an agreement with the king under which he was to practise his trade in various royal castles (*ER*, iii, 46).

Some castles had their own leading carpenters attached to them on a long term basis. These received an annual fee for their services, in addition to which they were probably paid weekly or daily wages when working. In 1375 the carpenter at Stirling Castle received an annual fee of £10, as against the £13 6s 8d paid to his counterpart in the mason trade (p. 224), but in the mid 1380s the carpenter's fee, too, was raised to £13 6s 8d (*ER*, ii, 477; iii, 372, 683, 687). At about the turn of the fifteenth and sixteenth centuries, when the post was occupied by David Borg, the annual fee was again £10 (*ER*, xi, 223, 370). At Edinburgh Castle during the late fourteenth century there seems to have been a resident carpenter named Duncan, who received an annual fee of £10, together with a military engineer, Dederic (Theoderic), the carpenter, who specialised in the construction of war machines and received an annual fee of up to £24. In 1384 Dederic was paid £20 for making a great machine capable of hurling projectiles in three different ways (*per tres vices*) in accordance with a contract made between Adam Forrester, keeper of the castle, and himself. At about the same time a horse was hired to carry Dederic from Edinburgh to the Isle of Bute, where he probably had business at Rothesay Castle (*ER*, iii, 53, 82, 98, 117–118, 129, 133, 170, 187, 660, 665).

The earliest named holder of the post of king's carpenter appears to have been Andrew Lesouris (Lisouris), a lay brother of the Cistercian abbey of Coupar Angus, who was described as such (*carpentarius regis*) in 1453. He may, however, have succeeded a relative, John Lesouris, who was still in post in the following year. Andrew Lesouris, known also as Brother Andrew Wright, received a annual fee of £10 in 1454, although the amount of his annual remuneration seems to have varied (*ER*, v, 535–536, 622, 689; vi, 80, 566; vii, 544). Much of Lesouris's time was spent in servicing the royal artillery and in 1455 he was responsible for transporting a great bombard from Linlithgow to the siege of Threave Castle, including the replacement of a carriage wheel which broke on the return journey (*ER*, vi, 116, 161, 200, 204). Lesouris was also directly involved in most of the major royal building projects of the 1460s. At Falkland Palace he and his assistants worked for 80 days in 1461–62 on the construction and fitting out of a new chamber for Mary of Gueldres (p. 23), while at about the same time he was busy buying timber for use in the construction of Ravenscraig Castle (*ER*, vii, 75, 138). During the late 1460s Lesouris undertook what must have been a major reconstruction of the chapel roof at Stirling Castle (p. 40), for which he received payment of some £180 (*ER*, vii, 449, 544). His final appearance in the documents comes in the fabric account of 1467–69 for Linlithgow Palace, where there is record of payments to Lesouris for the purchase of timber (*ER*, vii, 657).

Lesouris was probably succeeded in or before 1476 by Robert Lowry (Lourison), described in 1478 as king's carpenter (*carpentarius domini regis*). He drew an annual fee of £10, payable from the customs revenues of the burgh of Haddington, until 1480 (*ER*, viii, 386, 542, 623; ix, 75–76). In the absence of surviving Treasurer's accounts for this period nothing is known of Lowry's activities in the royal works, but he seems to have been alive in 1490 (*RMS*, ii, No. 1923).

Two holders of the post are on record during the reign of James IV, although their dates of appointment are not known. Thomas Gourlay was described in 1516 as carpenter to the late king (James IV), from whom he held certain lands within the lordship of Fife in feu ferm (*ER*, ix–xiii, *passim*; xiv, 175). He is known to have been employed as a shipwright in the royal works in 1506–07 and again in 1512–13, being described in the accounts both as wright and turner. When working at New Haven in 1512–13 Gourlay was paid 20s weekly, including the wages of a son who assisted him; he appears to have died early in 1523 (*TA*, iii, 196, 384; iv, 451, 454, 513, 520; *ER*, xv, 45).

The most distinguished holder of the post during the first half of the sixteenth century, however, was John Drummond, who gave some 45 years of service to the royal works, during which he contributed to many of the principal building undertakings of James IV and James V. His name first appears in the Treasurer's accounts in 1505, when he is found working as a wright at

Lochmaben Castle. Possibly he was a son or nephew of the Thomas Drummond, wright, who was employed there the previous year (*TA*, ii, 279–280; iii, 130, 173, 194). Promotion was rapid for by 1506 Drummond was receiving a livery payment and in December of the following year he was granted an annual fee of £10 from the customs dues of Edinburgh in recognition of his great service to the king (*TA*, iii, 114; *ER*, xiii, 96–97; *RSS*, i, No. 1574). In 1512 Drummond, described simply as a carpenter, was granted the £10 lands of Ballincreiff, in the constabulary of Haddington, while two years later he is specifically referred to as the king's carpenter (*ER*, xiv, 39; *RMS*, ii, No. 3760).

Further grants followed, including those of the lands and mill of Mylnab, Perthshire, in 1524–25 in exchange for his £10 fee from the Edinburgh customs (*RSS*, i, Nos. 3300, 3329; *ER*, xv, 141). Despite this Drummond was shortly afterwards granted an even larger fee of £40 from the Edinburgh customs (*ER*, xv, 365, 439). In 1532 Drummond, described as king's principal wright and military engineer (*principalis carpentarius et rerum nostrarum bellicarum machinator*), renounced this gift in exchange for another grant of Ballincreiff (the earlier one apparently having lapsed) which, with Mylnab, eventually came into the hereditary possession of the family (*ER*, xvi, 223–24; xvii, 520–522; *RMS*, iii, Nos. 453, 1603, 2338; iv, Nos. 122, 808). Drummond continued to be paid as a wright and gunner until the end of 1550, but his name does not appear in the wage list for February 1551. He may have died at about that time and was certainly dead by 1553 (*TA*, ix, 459, 475; *RMS*, iv, No. 808).

During the closing years of James IV's reign Drummond seems to have been involved mainly in shipbuilding and artillery operations. In the spring of 1513 he and his team of four wrights were busy fitting out the *Margaret*, one of the leading ships in the king's fleet, while later in the same year he was drafted into the Flodden expedition (*TA*, iv, 350, 479, 520). Some time during 1512 or the first half of 1513 he also found time to select and prepare timber for the roofs of the great hall at Falkland Palace and of the new chapel at Edinburgh Castle. Indeed, as already suggested, he may well have been involved in the design of these roofs, as also of that of the great hall at Edinburgh Castle. While working at Edinburgh Castle (probably on artillery) in 1513 Drummond was paid 14s a week, each of his assistants receiving 9s a week, but by 1515 his weekly wage had risen to 18s and that of an assistant to 10s. An account for artillery work presented at that time shows Drummond dealing directly with the Treasurer and receiving payments for transport and hire charges, as well as the wage costs of his team (*TA*, iv, 508; v, 17–18).

To judge from entries in the Treasurer's accounts, the operation and maintenance of the royal artillery continued to occupy the greater part of Drummond's time throughout his remaining years in the royal works. Clearly, however, he was a versatile, as well as a highly skilled, craftsman — in 1531, for example, he made two *lit-de-camp* beds for the king at a cost of £10 (*TA*, v, 421) — and he also played a prominent part in James V's building operations. At Edinburgh Castle he was employed in the remodelling of David's Tower in 1517, while at Holyroodhouse he was principal wright both during the construction of the great tower in 1528–32 and during the alterations of 1535; he also made an organ loft for the chapel there (p. 126). Drummond worked in a similar capacity at Falkland Palace in 1538, his employment there being interrupted by a short visit to France during the spring of that year (*MW*, i, 213–214). He may also have had a hand in the fitting out of James V's palace at Stirling Castle (p. 52).

At Holyroodhouse and Falkland Drummond received a weekly wage of 20s, higher than that of most master masons, while his assistant (at Holyroodhouse) received 12s a week (*MW*, i, 74, 170–175, 214). His final appearance in the Treasurer's accounts, however, shows him receiving no less than £8 6s 8d monthly as a wright and gunner at Edinburgh Castle in the late 1540s; possibly this sum included expenses and other wage costs (*TA*, ix, 33, 41, 459).

Another wright who seems to have had the status of a king's carpenter, although not described as such in the surviving records, was John Maware. In 1488 James IV granted him lands in Morayshire to the annual value of 20 merks (£13 6s 8d) for life in recognition of his past services to the late king, as also his future service to himself (*ER*, x, 85; *RMS*, ii, No. 1744). Maware received an additional grant in 1497 and was also in receipt of a livery; he died in 1502 or 1503 (*RSS*, i, No. 105; *TA*, i, 232; *ER*, xii, 223). We can only speculate as to the nature of his services to James III, but Maware was certainly employed, together with his son of the same name, on James IV's building projects at Edinburgh Castle during the late 1490s (p. 79), as also on certain artillery works. His weekly wage in 1496 was 13s 4d, while other wrights received 9s 4d each (*TA*, i, 255, 281, 319–320).

Other Trades

Among the other craftsmen and operatives employed by the royal works were carvers (sometimes described as masons or wrights), painters, plasterers, glaziers, plumbers, slaters, smiths, quarriers and carters, but it is not possible, within the scope of this study, to do more than mention a few individual tradesmen whose careers throw light on the nature and conditions of their work.

Painters were expected to carry out many different kinds of painting — portraiture, manuscript illumination and heraldic blazonry — as well as the internal and external decoration of ships and buildings (Apted and Hannabuss 1978, 1–12). As in other crafts, leading practitioners often received specific royal recognition and the post of king's painter is on record as early as the reign of James I, when both Matthew (*pictor regis*), who worked at Linlithgow Palace, and Master John (*pinctor regis*) evidently held that position (*ER*, iv, 579, 617).

Another who may have occupied a similar post was David Pratt, who helped to decorate the chapel royal at Stirling Castle during the 1490s (p. 126) and afterwards worked on the tomb of James III at Cambuskenneth Abbey (Apted and Hannabuss 1978, 75–77). Pratt received an annual fee of £10 from the Treasurer and, from 1498 onwards, a life tenancy of certain crown lands in Fife; he also received livery payments (*TA*, i, 323; ii, 50, 54; *ER*, xi, 298–299; *RSS*, i, No. 256). Pratt's commission at Cambuskenneth seems to have been undertaken by contract, payable by instalments, with some at least of the materials being supplied separately (*TA*, ii, 150, 289–290, 351, 360). When Andrew Laing, painter, was employed at Falkland Palace in 1512 he was paid monthly wages in advance, while Piers, a French painter brought to Scotland in 1505, received a monthly wage of £2 16s from the Treasurer (afterwards £3 10s), as well as a livery and a rent free house (*TA*, iii, pp. xci, 121–122, 350; iv, 58, 138, 380; Apted and Hannabuss 1978, 70–72). At Linlithgow in 1535–36 John Ross, painter, was paid by the master of works for what seem to have been two separate contracts, one relating to stone sculpture and the ironwork of windows and the other to the timber loft and ceiling of the chapel (*MW*, i, 128).

During the latter part of James IV's reign and for almost the whole of the following reign Thomas Peebles, a glazier, received an annual fee — initially £13 6s 8d and subsequently £20 — for maintaining the palaces of Holyroodhouse, Falkland and Linlithgow, together with the castle of Stirling, in glass; at times he also received a livery (*ER*, xii, 216; xiii, 403, xvii 326; *TA*, iv, 259; v, 313; *RSS*, i, No. 2116). For some years Peebles also occupied the upper part of the gatehouse of Holyroodhouse rent free by virtue of an agreement with the abbey under which he maintained the church and other principal abbey buildings in glass (*ER*, xvii, 283; *RSS*, ii, Nos. 1535 and 2360; *MW*, i, 166)). He worked both by contract, as when re-glazing the great hall at Linlithgow in 1512, and by the piece, piecework rates varying in accordance with the type of glass — plain or coloured — and its condition — new, or old set in new lead (*TA*, iv, 280; *MW*, i, 93–95, 128, 189–190, 260, 285).

Robert Murray's responsibilities were similar to those of Peebles, but related to the plumbing trade. Indeed, each probably held a position in his trade broadly equivalent to that of king's master mason and king's master wright. In 1538 he was granted an annual pension of £20 for life for maintaining the roofs of the palaces of Holyroodhouse and Linlithgow in lead (*TA*, vii, 199; viii, 148; *RSS*, ii, No. 2690) and after 1542 he received £3 monthly as a plumber and gunner (*RSS*, ii, No. 4814; *TA*, viii, 225). Like Peebles, Murray seems to have worked both by contract and by the piece, piecework in his case being measured by weight rather than by area; during certain operations, however, he was paid daily wages (*TA*, viii, 47; *MW*, i, 73–74, 99, 189, 261).

2.8

Evidence from England and other Western European countries indicates that medieval building design was normally a co-operative process between the patron, or his representative, and the master mason, or other master tradesman, the latter invariably assuming full responsibility for all technical aspects of construction (Salzman 1967, 1–29; Harvey 1972, 69–86; Coldstream 1991, 24–39). Such information as we have for the period under review — there is rather more for the later sixteenth and seventeenth centuries (Dunbar and Davies 1990) — suggests that the position was no different in Scotland, although it has to be said that the evidence is meagre.

So far as patrons are concerned, James I's proficiency in drawing and the mechanical arts has already been mentioned (p. 7). James III's reputation as a benefactor of the arts stands less high — a different picture might emerge if the Treasurer's accounts were more complete — but he certainly initiated important architectural works at Linlithgow Palace and Stirling Castle, as also at several major churches (Fawcett 1994, 303–304).

Both James IV and James V were prodigal builders with wide-ranging interests in art and architecture. It is noticeable that the Treasurer's accounts for James IV's reign record large numbers of payments of drinksilver to masons and other craftsmen employed not only on the king's own works but also on other contemporary building operations. Thus, in 1501–02 alone the king seems to have visited building projects as far apart as Aberdeen (King's college), Perth (Charterhouse), Paisley and Whithorn as well as his own undertakings at Falkland Palace, Holyroodhouse, Stirling Castle and Cambuskenneth Abbey (*TA*, ii, 97, 99, 103–104, 109, 118, 124, 137, 140, 145–146, 149, 153, 156–157, 159). A building contract of 1512 for alterations to the wall-walk of the great hall at Stirling Castle embodied 'certane appunctuamentis (appointments) maid be the Kingis devis' (*TA*, iv, 372) perhaps relating to the design or specification of the work, while in the same year a payment of drinksilver was made to the mason, John Cowper, 'to big in Rose (Rothesay) efter the Kingis devise' (*TA*, iv, 335). James V took one of his leading master masons to France with him in 1536 (p. 32) and the king and his second wife, Mary of Guise, subsequently requested the queen's parents to recruit French masons for the royal building programme at Falkland Palace and Stirling Castle. While none of this evidence quite matches that pointing to Henry VIII's abilities as a designer (Thurley 1993, 39–40), it suggests at the very least that both James IV and James V had a close personal involvement in the works that they commissioned.

In some cases important officials such as the Treasurer and the master of works may have had a say in the design of those buildings for whose construction they had some financial or administrative responsibility. As well as being keeper of Falkland Palace and chamberlain of Fife from about 1505 onwards James Beaton held office as Treasurer from 1505–09 (*ER*, xiii, pp. clviii–clix; *TA*, ii, 271). As archbishop of Glasgow from 1508–22 he enclosed the bishop's castle there with a strong curtain wall, while as archbishop of St Andrews from 1522–39 he is credited with the building of fourteen bridges in and around Fife, as well as the castle of Monimail and large parts of the castle of St Andrews (Macfarlane 1900–08, i, 6; *TA*, iii, p. xiv). Given Beaton's reputation as a builder and his close association with Falkland Palace during James IV's programme of works at the palace it would be surprising if the archbishop had not exercised some influence on these, but there is no actual evidence of this.

The same is true of the activities of two masters of works, John Sharp and Sir James Hamilton of Finnart. Sharp appears to have been a recognised garden designer and is likely to have brought similar skills to his building activities at Holyroodhouse during the second and third decades of the sixteenth century (p. 218). For example, it is more than likely that he had some input into the design of the lion house that was erected in the palace gardens under his direction, but information of this kind is seldom to be found in building accounts.

Hamilton was first described as an 'architector' by a late seventeenth-century family historian and the case for seeing him as an influential architect and designer both within the royal works and in his private building activities has recently been strongly argued by Charles McKean (1991; 1995, 1086–1087). Certainly the range and volume of Hamilton's activities is impressive, embracing as it does notable works at the palaces of Linlithgow and Stirling on the one hand and major artillery fortifications at the castles of Craignethan and Cadzow on the other. But no evidence is as yet forthcoming to suggest that Hamilton's role, either as a private builder or as master of works to James V, was any different in kind from that of other patrons and leading officials of the day, although his wide experience and forceful personality no doubt ensured that the master masons with whom he collaborated were stretched to the limit of their abilities.

The documents now available to us have very little to say about the design role of the Scottish master mason at this period, but if we can transpose the evidence of English and Continental sources we may assume that this would normally include the preparation of the necessary plans and drawings, the making of templates of mouldings for the use of other masons and the specification of the principal materials and methods of construction, all, of course, in close consultation with the patron and his master of works (Coldstream 1991, 24–55). The crucial role of the master mason in design is, however, clearly demonstrated at Falkland, where the marked differences in style seen in those parts of the palace erected during the campaign of 1537–41 can be linked to the work of different masons. Likewise the similarity between the Falkland gatehouse and the great tower at Holyroodhouse is probably to be explained by the transfer of a particular master mason from one residence to another (p. 36).

We have already seen that the duties of the master mason appointed to St Nicholas Church, Aberdeen in 1484 included 'devysing' (p. 217) and that in 1497 the master mason of Linlithgow rode to Stirling 'to gif his devis to the werk' (p. 44). While the first of these references suggests an overall design role, the second could as well relate to a specific issue or problem of design or construction about which advice was being sought. This was also probably the case in 1539 when payment of £5 10s was made to French masons travelling to St Andrews (almost certainly from Falkland) to give advice about the building of St Mary's College, then newly begun or about to be begun (*St Andrews Rentale*, 68), although it is interesting to find that one of the Falkland masons subsequently became master mason there (p. 230). So far as templates are concerned, there is a reference in the Holyroodhouse building accounts for 1529–30 to the sawing of timber boards as moulds for the master mason, John Ayton, for founding of 'durris and eismentis' (doorways and openings) on the first floor of the great tower (*MW*, i, 4). The 'patrown' (pattern) of a double staircase mentioned in the Holyroodhouse accounts of 1535–36 (*MW*, i, 191) was probably a design drawing, but we know nothing of its authorship (p. 71).

WORKING CONDITIONS

Something has already been said about the pay and conditions of service of individual master tradesmen and others mentioned in previous sections of this chapter. Information is scrappy prior to the middle decades of the sixteenth century and much of the available evidence has been analysed by Knoop and Jones (1939, 9–15, 26–60) and Paton (*MW*, i, pp. xliii–li). While additional research would undoubtedly produce a more comprehensive picture, this has not been attempted here and the following remarks do no more than summarise the available information in those areas most relevant to the present study.

Operatives were paid both by time rates and by task. In the first half of the sixteenth century, at any rate, time rates usually took the form of weekly wages, but sometimes wages were paid at a daily or monthly rate. Sometimes payment was made partly in kind. During the 1500s masons' weekly wages usually ranged from 6s to 10s and during the years 1529–41 from 14s to 16s (Knoop and Jones 1939, 36; *MW*, i, p. xliii). Wage rates for wrights employed in the royal works during the latter part of James IV's reign ranged from 8s to 12s a week (*TA*, ii, 278; iv, 276, 523; v, 11), while by the latter part of James V's reign the average weekly wage of a wright had risen to 14s or 15s (*MW*, i, p. xliii). In most cases a six day week was worked, payment being made on a Saturday.

A lot of work was done by task, either by the allocation of a specific item to an individual tradesman for a fixed sum — a method sometimes described as by 'contract of task' (*MW*, i, 282) — or by paying piecework rates, for example during mid winter when the days were short (*MW*, i, 245–246). Additional payments were often made at the signing of a contract, as a reward for completing a particular task or stage in the work, or to celebrate a visit from the king or other dignitary. Many leading master craftsmen in the royal works received an annual salary, usually described as a fee or pension, in addition to remuneration at the appropriate rate when actually working at their trade.

Hours of work varied according to the season of the year, ranging from up to 14 hours a day in summer to eight hours a day in winter, when certain operations were normally suspended. Likewise there were three breaks for meals during the summer but only one in winter. A six day week was usually worked and there were up to 45 holidays (saints' days and festivals) a year, including Christmas and Easter. Because of pressure of work, however, holidays were not infrequently curtailed or suspended.

Covered working space was required to enable tradesmen to carry out preliminary construction tasks, such as stone dressing and the prefabrication of roof frames, and any suitable building that happened to be available was liable to be requisitioned for this purpose. In 1513–14 timber for the great hall of Falkland Palace was placed in the new chapel there (*ER*, xiii, 504–505; xiv, 11), while a few years later the great hall at Holyroodhouse was used as a wrights' workshop (*MW*, i, 69, 72). At the commencement of James IV's building campaign at Falkland ground was purchased close to the palace gate for the erection of a masons' lodge (*ER*, xii, 205), while two purpose-built lodges were in use at Holyroodhouse during the 1530s, as well as a 'litill hous' for the masons' tools and equipment (*MW*, i, 17–22, 24, 49). It is possible that lodges of this kind also contained living accommodation for tradesmen recruited from outlying parts.

NOTES

1 This paragraph leans heavily upon notes kindly provided by Dr A. L. Murray.

2 I am grateful to Dr A. L. Murray for elucidating the details of these transactions.

3 Fothringham is described in the English abstract of the 1529 account as 'chief engineer' of the bridge, but in the original as *lathomus principalis* (*ER*, xv, 524 and SRO, E 38/384).

4 A similar pension seems to have been paid in previous years (*TA*, ii, 335).

5 At Holyroodhouse there was an overseer of the quarry on Salisbury Craig, who received 9s a week (*MW*, i, pp. xxvi, 147). The post-holder was William McDowell, a cleric, who subsequently became principal master of works to the crown.

6 I am grateful to Dr A. L. Murray for elucidating these transactions.

7 The name is suggestive of a French or Flemish origin. There is a village of Haisnes, near Lens, in northern France, while the River Aisne flows through the present department of the same name in north east France.

8 Martin and his servitor were paid 30s weekly. The servitor is likely to have been Martin's son of the same name, also a mason, who was paid 10s a week after his father's death (*MW*, i, 206, 208, 253).

9 Another son, Thomas, died in Aberdeen in 1530 (Mylne 1893, 39).

BIBLIOGRAPHY

List of Commonly Used Abbreviations

DOST	*A Dictionary of the Older Scottish Tongue,* Craigie, W A (ed.), 1931–
MSS	Manuscripts
NGS	The National Galleries of Scotland
NLS	The National Library of Scotland
NMRS	The National Monuments Record of Scotland
NTS	The National Trust for Scotland
pers. comm.	personal communication
PSAS	*The Proceedings of the Society of Antiquaries of Scotland*
RCAHMS	The Royal Commission on the Ancient and Historical Monuments of Scotland
SRO	The Scottish Record Office, Edinburgh

Bibliography

Abdn. Counc. Extracts from the Council Register of the Burgh of Aberdeen, Spalding Club, 1844–48

ADA The Acts of the Lords Auditors of Causes and Complaints AD MCCCCLXVI–AD MCCCCXCIV, Thomson, T (ed.), 1839

Angels, Nobles and Unicorns Exhibition Catalogue, National Museum of Scotland, 1982

APS The Acts of the Parliaments of Scotland, Thomson, T and Innes, C (edd.), 1814–75

Apted, Michael, 1966 *The Painted Ceilings of Scotland 1550–1650*

—— and Hannabuss, Susan 1978 *Painters in Scotland 1301–1700 A Biographical Dictionary,* Scottish Record Society

Babelon, Jean-Pierre, 1986 *Le Château en France,* Paris

—— (ed.), 1989 *Châteaux de France au Siècle de la Renaissance,* Paris

Baillie, Hugh Murray, 1967 Etiquette and the Planning of the State Apartments in Baroque Palaces, in *Archaeologia,* 101, 169–99

Balcarres Papers Foreign Correspondence with Marie de Lorraine Queen of Scotland, from the Originals in the Balcarres Papers, Wood, M (ed.) Scottish History Society, 1923–25

Balfour, James, 1824–4 *The Historical Works of Sir James Balfour*

Bannatyne Misc. The Bannatyne Miscellany, Bannatyne Club, 1827–55

Bateson, Mary, 1904 The Scottish King's Household and Other Fragments, in *Miscellany*, ii, 5–43, Scottish History Society

Bentley-Cranch, D 1986 An Early Sixteenth-Century French Architectural Source for the Palace of Falkland, in *Review of Scottish Culture*, 2, 85–96

Black, George F 1946 *The Surnames of Scotland*, New York

Boece, 1938–41 *The Chronicles of Scotland compiled by Hector Boece*, translated into Scots by John Bellenden 1531, Chambers, R W *et al.* (edd.), Scottish Text Society

Boudon, F and Chatenet, M, 1994 Les logis du roi de France au XVIᵉ Siècle, in Guillaume, J (ed.), *Architecture et Vie Sociale*, (Université de Tours), 65–82

Bower, Walter, 1987–98 *Scotichronicon*, Watt, D E R *et al.* (edd.)

Brown, Michael, 1994 *James I*

Brown, P Hume, 1891 *Early Travellers in Scotland*

Brown, W and Jamieson, J, 1830 *Select Views of the Royal Palaces of Scotland*

Butler, L St. J and Wordie, P J, 1989 *The Royal Game*, Falkland Palace Real Tennis Club

Cal. Docs. Scot. Calendar of Documents relating to Scotland, Bain, J *et al.* (edd.), 1881–

Cal. State Papers Calendar of the State papers relating to Scotland 1509–1603, Thorpe, M J (ed.), 1858

Caldwell, David M, 1981 Royal Patronage of Arms and Armour Making in Fifteenth and Sixteenth Century Scotland, in Caldwell, David M (ed.), *Scottish Weapons and Fortifications 1100–1800*, 73–93

—— 1994 The Beaton Panels — Scottish Carvings of the 1520s or 1530s, in Higgit, John (ed.), *Medieval Art and Architecture in the Diocese of St Andrews*, British Archaeological Association, 174–184

and Lewis, John, 1996 Linlithgow Palace: an excavation in the west range and a note on finds from the palace, in *PSAS*, 126, 823–870

Cameron, J S, 1996 French Holiday of James V 1536 to 1537, in McNeill, Peter, G B and MacQueen, Hector L (edd.), in *Atlas of Scottish History to 1707*, 122

Campbell, Ian, 1994 Linlithgow's 'Princely Palace' and its Influence in Europe, in *Architectural Heritage* V, 1–20

—— 1995 A Romanesque Revival and the Early Renaissance in Scotland *c.*1380–1513, in *Journal of the Society of Architectural Historians*, 54.3 (September 1995), 302–325

Campbell, Tom, 1996 Cardinal Wolsey's Tapestry Collection, in *The Antiquaries Journal*, 76, 73–138

Campbell, William, (ed.), 1873–7 *Materials for a History of the Reign of Henry VII* (Rolls Series)

Chalmers, Peter, 1844–59 *Historical and Statistical Account of Dunfermline*

Chatenet, Monique, 1988 Une demeure royale au milieu du XVIᵉ siècle; la distribution des espaces au château de Saint-Germain-en-Laye, in *Revue de l'Art*, 81, 20–30

Cherry, John, 1991 Pottery and Tile, in Blair, John and Ramsay, Nigel (edd.), *English*

Clifford, Arthur, 1809 *The State Papers and Letters of Sir Ralph Sadler*

Coldstream, Nicola, 1991 *Masons and Sculptors*

Colvin, H M (ed.), 1963–73 *The History of the King's Works*

Cowan, Ian B, 1967 *The Parishes of Medieval Scotland*, Scottish Record Society

Cross, Moraig, 1994 *Bibliography of Monuments in the Care of the Secretary of State of Scotland*

CSP Calendar of the State Papers relating to Scotland and Mary, Queen of Scots 1547–1603, Bain, J *et al.* (edd.), Edinburgh, 1898–

Diurnal of Occurrents. A Diurnal of Remarkable Occurrents that have passed within the country of Scotland since the death of King James the Fourth till the year 1575, Bannatyne and Maitland Clubs, 1833

Dixon, Philip, 1992 From Hall to Tower: The Change in Seigneurial Houses on the Anglo-Scottish Border after *c.*1250, in Coss, P R and Lloyd, S D (edd.), *Thirteenth Century England*, IV, 87–95

—— 1993 *Mota, Aula et Turris*: The Manor-houses of the Anglo-Scottish Border, in Meirion-Jones, Gwyn and Jones, Michael, *Manorial Domestic Buildings in England and Northern France*, 22–48 (Society of Antiquaries of London)

Donaldson, Gordon, 1965 *Scotland James V – James VII* (The Edinburgh History of Scotland)

Douglas-Irvine, H, 1911 *Royal Palaces of Scotland*

Drummond, The Hon. William, 1831 *The Genealogy of the Most Noble and Ancient House of Drummond*

Dunbar, A H 1906 *Scottish Kings A revised Chronology of Scottish History 1005–1625*

Dunbar, John G, 1964 The Palace of Holyroodhouse during the First Half of the Sixteenth Century, in *The Archaeological Journal*, cxx, 242–54

—— 1975 *The Stirling Heads*

—— 1984 Some aspects of the planning of Scottish royal palaces in the sixteenth century, in *Architectural History*, 27, 15–24

—— 1991 Some Sixteenth-Century French Parallels for the Palace of Falkland, in *Review of Scottish Culture* 7, 3–8

—— and Davies, K, 1990 Some Late Seventeenth-Century Building Contracts, in *Miscellany*, xi, 269–327, Scottish History Society

Duncan, A A M, 1974 Perth: the first century of the burgh, in *Transactions of the Perthshire Society of Natural Science* Special Issue for 25th Anniversary of Archaeological and Historical Section 1973, 30–50.

Dunkeld Rentale Rentale Dunkeldense, Scottish History Society, 1915

Elphinstone MSS Historical Manuscripts Commission, 9th Report, pt. ii (2nd Appendix), 182–229, *Lord Elphinstone's MSS*, 1883–4

Emery, Anthony, 1985 Ralph, Lord Cromwell's Manor at Wingfield (1439–*c.*1450): its Construction, Design and Influence, in *The Archaeological Journal*, 142, 276–339

—— 1996–, *Greater Medieval Houses of England and Wales 1300–1500*

ER The Exchequer Rolls of Scotland, Stuart J *et al.* (edd.), Edinburgh, 1878–1908

Evans, Joan, 1952 *Art in Medieval France 987–1498*

Everson, P, 1996 Bodiam Castle, East Sussex; Castle and Designed Landscape, in *Château Gaillard*, xvii, 79–84

Ewart, Graham, 1994 Dundonald Castle – Recent Work, in *Château Gaillard*, xvi, 167–178

Faulkner, P A 1963 Castle Planning in the Fourteenth Century, in *The Archaeological Journal*, cxx, 215–235

—— 1970 Some Medieval Archiepiscopal Palaces, in *The Archaeological Journal*, cxxvii, 130–146

Fawcett, Richard, 1986 *Edinburgh Castle* (Official Guide)

—— 1988 *The Palace of Holyroodhouse* (Official Guide)

—— 1990a *The Abbey and Palace of Dunfermline* (Official Guide)

—— 1990b Stirling Castle: the King's Old Building and the late medieval royal planning, in *Château Gaillard*, xiv, 175–95

—— 1994 *Scottish Architecture from the Accession of the Stewarts to the Reformation 1371–1560*

—— 1995 *Stirling Castle*

—— 1997 *Glasgow Cathedral* (Official Guide)

Ferguson, The Rev. John, 1910 *Linlithgow Palace. Its History and Traditions*

Fleming, David H, 1910 *The Reformation in Scotland*

—— 1924 *Handbook to St Andrews*

Fleming, J S, 1898 *Old Nooks of Stirling*

Fraser, Alexander, of Philorth 1879 *The Frasers of Philorth*

Fraser, Sir William, 1858 *The Stirlings of Keir*

—— 1881 *The Red Book of Menteith*

Gemmill, E and Mayhew, N 1995 *Changing Values in Medieval Scotland*

Gibson, A and Smout, T C, 1988 Food and Hierarchy in Scotland 1550–1650, in Leneman, Leah (ed.), *Perspectives in Scottish Social History*, 33–52

Gifford, John, 1988 *Fife* (The Buildings of Scotland)

Gifford, John, McWilliam, Colin and Walker, David M 1984 *Edinburgh* (The Buildings of Scotland)

Gilbert, John, 1979 *Hunting and Hunting Reserves in Medieval Scotland*

Gloag, John and Bridgewater, Derek, 1948 *A History of Cast Iron in Architecture*

Gordon, J F S, 1868 *Monasticon. An Account (based on Spottiswood's) of all the Abbeys, Priories —— in Scotland*

Gow, Ian, 1995 *The Palace of Holyroodhouse* (Official Guide)

Grant, Alexander, 1984 *Independence and Nationhood Scotland 1306–1469*

Graves, C Pamela, 1994 Medieval Stained and Painted Window Glass in the Diocese of St Andrews, in Higgit, John (ed.), *Medieval Art and Architecture in the Diocese of St Andrews*, British Archaeological Association, 124–136

Grose, Francis, 1797 *The Antiquities of Scotland*

Guillaume, Jean (ed.), 1985 *L'Escalier dans L'Architecture de la Renaissance*, Actes du Colloque tenu à Tours du 22 au 26 mai 1979 (Université de Tours)

Hare, J N 1988 Bishop's Waltham Palace, Hampshire: William of Wykeham, Henry Beaufort and the Transformation of a Medieval Episcopal Palace, in *The Archaeological Journal*, 145, 222–254

Harris, Stuart, 1996 *The Place Names of Edinburgh. Their Origins and History*

Harrison, John, 1919 *The History of the Monastery of the Holy-Rude and of the Palace of Holyroodhouse*

Harvey, John, 1972 *The Mediaeval Architect*

Henderson, Ebenezer, 1879 *The Annals of Dunfermline*

Hewison, J K, 1893–95 *The Isle of Bute in the Olden Time*

Hill, Oliver, 1953 *Scottish Castles of the Sixteenth and Seventeenth Centuries*

Howard, Deborah, 1995 *Scottish Architecture from the Reformation to the Restoration 1560–1660*

Innes, Sir Thomas, 1956 *Scots Heraldry A Practical Handbook* ——

James, T B, 1990 *The Palaces of Medieval England c.1050–1550*

Jamieson, Fiona, 1994 The Royal Gardens of the Palace of Holyroodhouse 1500–1603, in *Journal of the Garden History Society*, 22:1, 18–36

Kemp, Martin and Farrow, Clare, 1990 Humanism and the Visual Arts, *circa* 1530–1630, in MacQueen, John (ed.), *Humanism in Renaissance Scotland*, 32–47

Kerr, Andrew, 1880–81 Notes of Ancient Tile Paving in Linlithgow Palace, in *PSAS*, xv, 194–198

Knecht, R J, 1994 *Renaissance Warrior and Patron The Reign of Francis I*

Knoop, Douglas and Jones, G P, 1933 *The Mediaeval Mason*

—— 1939 *The Scottish Mason and The Mason Word*

Laing, Henry, 1866–68 Remarks on the Carved Ceiling and Heraldic Shields of the Apartments in Holyroodhouse, commonly known as 'Queen Mary's Audience Chamber', in *PSAS*, vii, 381–384

Laing, Lloyd R, 1968–69 Medieval and other Material in Linlithgow Palace Museum, in *PSAS*, 101, 134–145

Leland, John, 1770, *De rebus Britannicis collectanea* – - -, Hearne, T (ed.), iv, 290–300

Lesley, John, 1830 *The History of Scotland from the Death of King James I in the Year 1436 to the Year 1561*, Bannatyne Club

Lindores Chartulary: Chartulary of the Abbey of Lindores, Scottish History Society, 1903

Loveday, John, 1890 *Diary of a Tour in 1732* (Roxburghe Club)

Macadam, Ivison, 1886–87 Notes on the Ancient Iron Industry of Scotland, in *PSAS*, xxi, 89–131

Macdougall, Norman, 1989 *James IV*

Macfarlane, Leslie J, 1960 The Book of Hours of James IV and Margaret Tudor, in

Innes Review, II, 3–21

—— 1995 *William Elphinstone and the Kingdom of Scotland 1431–1514*, (Quincentenary edition)

Macfarlane, Walter, 1900–08 *Genealogical Collections*, Scottish History Society

MacGibbon, D and Ross, T, 1887–92 *The Castellated and Domestic Architecture of Scotland*

McGladdery, Christine, 1990 *James II*

MacIvor, Iain, 1991 Hamilton of Finnart: Stirling (unpublished paper)

—— 1993 *Edinburgh Castle*

McKean, Charles, 1991 Finnart's Platt, in *Architectural Heritage*, II, 3–17

—— 1995 Craignethan: the castle of the Bastard of Arran, in *PSAS*, 125, 1069–1090

MacKechnie, Aonghus, 1991 Stirling's Triumphal Arch, in *Welcome: News for Friends of Historic Scotland* (September 1991)

Mackenzie, W Mackay (ed.), 1932 *The Poems of William Dunbar*

Mackie, R L (ed.), 1953 *The Letters of James the Fourth, 1503–1513* Scottish History Society

[Macky, John], 1723 *A Journey through Scotland – – – being the Third Volume which compleats Great Britain*

MacPhail, I M M, 1979 *Dumbarton Castle*

MacWilliam, Colin, 1978 *Lothian* (The Buildings of Scotland)

Mar & Kellie MSS Historical Manuscripts Commission, lxviii, *Manuscripts of the Earl of Mar and Kellie*, 1904

Marks, Richard, 1991 Window Glass, in Blair, John and Ramsay, Nigel (edd.), *English Medieval Industries*, 265–94

Marriage Papers Papers relative to the marriage of King James the Sixth of Scotland, with the Princess Anna of Denmark; A.D. MDLXXXIX ——, Bannatyne Club, 1828

Marshall, Rosalind, 1993 The Queen's Table, in Cheape, Hugh (ed.), *Tools and Traditions*, 138–143

Maxwell-Irving, Alastair, 1996 The dating of the tower-houses at Comlongon and Elphinstone, in *PSAS*, 126, 871–880

Meirion-Jones, Gwyn, Jones, Michael and Pilcher, Jon R, 1993 The Seigneurial Domestic Buildings of Brittany, 1000–1700, in Meirion-Jones, Gwyn and Jones, Michael, *Manorial Domestic Buildings in England and Northern France*, (Society of Antiquaries of London), 158–191.

Melville, Sir James of Halhill, 1827 *Memoirs of his own life MDXLIX–MDXCIII*, Bannatyne Club

Mesqui, Jean, 1991–93 *Châteaux et Enceintes de la France Médiévale*, Paris

—— 1996 Les Ensembles Palatiaux et Princiers en France aux XIVe et XVe Siècles, in Renoux, Annie (ed.), *Palais Royaux et Princiers au Moyen Age*, Université du Maine, 51–70

Millar, A H, 1895 *Fife: Pictorial and Historical*

Mortet, V and Deschamps, P, 1911–29 *Recueil de textes relatif à l'histoire de l'architecture et à la condition des architectes en France au Moyen Âge* (reprinted, Paris 1995)

Moysie, David, 1830 *Memoirs of the Affairs of Scotland 1577–1603*, Bannatyne Club

Murray, A L, 1965 Accounts of the King's Pursemaster 1539–1540, in *Miscellany X*, 13–51, Scottish History Society

—— 1973 The Comptroller 1425–1488, in *The Scottish Historical Review*, LII, 1–29

—— 1975 Crown Lands 1424–1542, in McNeill, P and Nicholson, R (edd.), *An Historical Atlas of Scotland*, 72–73.

—— 1996 Place-dates: Robert II (1371–90) and Place-dates: duke of Albany, governor (1420–24), in McNeill, Peter G B and MacQueen, Hector L (edd.), *Atlas of Scottish History to 1707*, 173, 176

MW Accounts of the Masters of Works for Building and Repairing Royal Castles and Palaces, Paton, H M, Imrie J and Dunbar, J G (edd.), Edinburgh, 1957–

Mylne, R S, 1893 *The Master Masons to the Crown of Scotland*

—— 1895–96 The Masters of Work to the Crown of Scotland, with the Writs of Appointment, from 1529 to 1768, in *PSAS*, xxx, 49–68

—— 1899–1900 Notices of the King's Master Wrights of Scotland, with Writs of their Appointments, in *PSAS*, xxxiv, 288–296

National Art Survey: National Art Survey of Scotland; Examples of Scottish Architecture from the 12th to the 17th century, Anderson, R R *et al.* (edd.), 1921–33

Neilson, George, 1900–01 Sir Hew of Eglintoun – – – , in *Proceedings of the Philosophical Society of Glasgow*, xxxii, 111–150

Nicholson, Ranald, 1974 *Scotland The Later Middle Ages* (The Edinburgh History of Scotland)

Norton, Christopher, 1994 Medieval Floor Tiles in Scotland, in Higgit, John (ed.), *Medieval Art and Architecture in the Diocese of St Andrews*, British Archaeological Association, 137–173

Oldrieve, W T 1913–14, Account of the Recent Discovery of the Remains of David's Tower at Edinburgh Castle, in *PSAS*, xlviii, 230–270

Pevsner, N, 1953 *County Durham* (The Buildings of England)

Pitscottie, R Lindesay of, 1899–1911 *The Historie and Cronicles of Scotland*, Scottish Text Society

Pringle, Denys, 1987 *Doune Castle* (Official Guide)

—— 1989 *Linlithgow Palace* (Official Guide)

—— 1995 *Rothesay Castle and St. Mary's Church* (Official Guide)

Prinz, Wolfram and Kecks, Ronald G, 1985 *Das französische Schloss der Renaissance* (Berlin)

Prot. Bk. Foular Protocal Book of John Foular 1501–28, Macleod, W and Wood, M (edd.), Scottish Record Society, 1930–53

Prot. Bk. Johnsoun Protocol Books of Dominus Thomas Johnsoun 1528–78, Beveridge, J and Russell, J. (edd.), Scottish Record Society, 1920

Prot. Bk. Young Protocol Book of James Young 1485–1515, Donaldson, G (ed.), Scottish Record Society, 1952

Pugin, A and A W, 1831–38 *Examples of Gothic Architecture*

Puttfarken, T, Hartley, C and Robson, E 1989 *Falkland: Palace and Royal Burgh* (Official Guide)

RCAHMS 1929 *Inventory of Midlothian and West Lothian*

—— 1933 *Inventory of Fife, Kinross and Clackmannan*

—— 1951 *Inventory of the City of Edinburgh*

—— 1957 *Inventory of Selkirkshire*

—— 1963 *Inventory of Stirlingshire*

—— 1994 *South East Perth: an archaeological landscape*

Renaissance Arts Renaissance Decorative Arts in Scotland 1480–1650, Exhibition Catalogue, National Museum of Antiquities of Scotland, 1959

Richardson, James S, 1925–26 Unrecorded Scottish Wood Carvings, in *PSAS*, lx, 384–408

RMS Registrum Magni Sigilii Regum Scotorum, Thomson, J M *et al.*, (edd.), Edinburgh, 1882–1914

Rogers, Charles, 1882 *History of the Chapel Royal in Scotland,* Grampian Club

Roxburghe MSS Historical Manuscripts Commission, xxxix, 14th Report, *Duke of Roxburghe's MSS*, Appendix 3, 1–55, 1894

RPC The Register of the Privy Council of Scotland, Burton, J H *et al.*, (edd.), Edinburgh 1877–

RSS Registrum Secreti Sigilii Regum Scotorum, Livingstone M *et al.* (edd.), Edinburgh 1908–

Ruckley, R A, 1990 Water Supply of Medieval Castles in the United Kingdom, in *Fortress*, 7, 14–26

St Andrews Rentale: Rentale Sancti Andree, Scottish History Society, 1913

Salter, Mike, 1994 *The Castles of the Heartland of Scotland*

Salzman, L F, 1967 *Building in England down to 1540*

Saunders, Andrew, 1989 *Fortress Britain*

Scots Peerage: The Scots Peerage, Balfour Paul, James (ed.), 1904–14

Seton, George, 1886–87 Notices of Four Stained-Glass Shields of Arms and a Monumental Slab in St. Magdalene's Chapel, Cowgate, in *PSAS*, xxi, 266–274

Shire, Helena M, 1996a The King in his House: Three Architectural Artefacts belonging to the Reign of James V, in Williams, Janet Hadley (ed.), *Stewart Style 1513–1542 Essays on the Court of James V*, 62–96

—— 1996b Music for 'Goddis Glore and the Kingis', in Williams, Janet Hadley (ed.), *Stewart Style 1513–1542 Essays on the Court of James V*, 118–141

Simpson, A T and Stevenson, S, 1982 *Historic Perth: the archaeological implications of development*, Scottish Burgh Survey

Simpson, W D, 1922–23 The Royal Castle of Kindrochit in Mar, in *PSAS*, lvii, 75–97

—— 1928 The Excavation of Kindrochit Castle, Aberdeenshire, in *The Antiquaries Journal*, viii, 69–75

—— 1929–30 Urquhart Castle, in *Transactions of the Gaelic Society of Inverness,* xxxiii, 214–39.

—— 1937–40 The Architectural History of Rothesay Castle, in *Transactions of the Glasgow Archaeological Society*, ix, 152–183

—— 1938a Doune Castle, in *PSAS*, lxxii (1937–38), 73–83.

—— 1938b *Ravenscraig Castle*

—— 1947–49 Dundonald Castle, in *Ayrshire Archaeological and Natural History Collections*, Second Series, i, 42–51

—— 1949 *The Earldom of Mar*

—— 1982 *Doune Castle* (Official Guide)

Sinclair, John, 1904–05 Notes on the Holyrood 'foir-yet' of James IV, in *PSAS*, xxxix, 352–362

Slezer, John, 1693 and later editions *Theatrum Scotiae*

Small, J W, 1878 *Scottish Woodwork of the Sixteenth and Seventeenth Centuries*

Smith, H Clifford, 1924 *The Panelled Rooms VI, The Waltham Abbey Room,* Victoria and Albert Museum

Starkey, David, 1987 Intimacy and innovation: the rise of the Privy Chamber, 1485–1547, in Starkey, David (ed.), *The English Court from the Wars of the Roses to the Civil War,* 71–118

Stat. Acct. The Statistical Account of Scotland, Edinburgh, 1791–1799

Stell, Geoffrey 1981 Late Medieval Defences in Scotland, in Caldwell, David H (ed.), *Scottish Weapons and Fortifications 1100–1800,* 21–54

—— and Baillie, Michael, 1993 The Great Hall and Roof of Darnaway Castle, in Sellar, W D H (ed.), *Moray: Province and People,* Scottish Society for Northern Studies, 163–186

TA Accounts of the Lord High Treasurer of Scotland, Dickson, T and Balfour Paul, J (edd.), Edinburgh, 1877–

Tabraham, C and Stewart, F, 1994 *Urquhart Castle* (Official Guide)

Thomas, Andrea, 1995 Tailors, Trumpeters and Turnspits: Class and Hierarchy in the Household of King James V 1528–1542 (Unpublished paper)

Thompson, Michael, 1995 *The Medieval Hall: The Basis of Secular Domestic Life, 600–1600 AD*

[Thomson, Thomas (ed.)], 1815 *A Collection of Inventories and other Records of the Royal Wardrobe – – – in some of the Royal Castles*

Thurley, Simon, 1988 Henry VIII and the building of Hampton Court: A Reconstruction of the Tudor Palace, in *Journal of the Society of Architectural Historians of Great Britain,* 31, 1–58

—— 1993 *The Royal Palaces of Tudor England*

Waldie, George, 1829 *A History of the Town and Palace of Linlithgow* (3rd edition)

Warrack, John, 1920 *Domestic Life in Scotland 1488–1688*

Watt, Donald, 1969 *Fasti Ecclesiae Scoticanae Medii Aevi*

Whitely, Mary, 1996 Public and Private Space in Royal and Princely Châteaux in Late Medieval France, in Renoux, Annie (ed.), *Palais Royaux et Princiers au Moyen Age,*

Université du Maine, 71–76

Williams, Neville, 1971 *Henry VIII and his Court*

Wood, Margaret, 1965 *The English Medieval House*

Zeune, Joachim 1992 *The Last Scottish Castles*, International Archaeology, vol. 12, Buch am Erlbach

INDEX

(Italicised page numbers indicate principal entries)